Kanishka Jayasuriya
STATECRAFT, WELFARE AND THE POLITICS OF INCLUSION

Dominic Kelly and Wyn Grant (*editors*)
THE POLITICS OF INTERNATIONAL TRADE IN THE 21ST CENTURY
Actors, Issues and Regional Dynamics

Mathias Koenig-Archibugi and Michael Zürn (*editors*)
NEW MODES OF GOVERNANCE IN THE GLOBAL SYSTEM
Exploring Publicness, Delegation and Inclusiveness

Craig N. Murphy (*editor*)
EGALITARIAN POLITICS IN THE AGE OF GLOBALIZATION

George Myconos
THE GLOBALIZATION OF ORGANIZED LABOUR
1945–2004

John Nauright and Kimberly S. Schimmel (*editors*)
THE POLITICAL ECONOMY OF SPORT

Morten Ougaard
THE GLOBALIZATION OF POLITICS
Power, Social Forces and Governance

Richard Robison (*editor*)
THE NEO-LIBERAL REVOLUTION
Forging the Market State

Timothy J. Sinclair and Kenneth P. Thomas (*editors*)
STRUCTURE AND AGENCY IN INTERNATIONAL CAPITAL MOBILITY

Fredrik Söderbaum and Timothy M. Shaw (*editors*)
THEORIES OF NEW REGIONALISM

Susanne Soederberg, Georg Menz and Phillip G. Cerny (*editors*)
INTERNALIZING GLOBALIZATION
The Rise of Neoliberalism and the Decline of National Varieties of Capitalism

International Political Economy Series
Series Standing Order ISBN 0–333–71708–2 hardcover
Series Standing Order ISBN 0–333–71116–6 paperback
(*outside North America only*)

You can receive future titles in this series as they are published by placing a standing order. Please contact your bookseller or, in case of difficulty, write to us at the address below with your name and address, the title of the series and one of the ISBNs quoted above.

Customer Services Department, Macmillan Distribution Ltd, Houndmills, Basingstoke, Hampshire RG21 6XS, England

Global Restructuring, State, Capital and Labour

Contesting Neo-Gramscian Perspectives

Andreas Bieler
School of Politics and International Relations, University of Nottingham

Werner Bonefeld
Department of Politics, University of York

Peter Burnham
Department of Politics and International Studies, University of Warwick

Adam David Morton
School of Politics and International Relations, University of Nottingham

palgrave
macmillan

First published in 2006 by
PALGRAVE MACMILLAN
Houndmills, Basingstoke, Hampshire RG21 6XS and
175 Fifth Avenue, New York, N.Y. 10010
Companies and representatives throughout the world.

PALGRAVE MACMILLAN is the global academic imprint of the Palgrave Macmillan division of St. Martin's Press, LLC and of Palgrave Macmillan Ltd. Macmillan® is a registered trademark in the United States, United Kingdom and other countries. Palgrave is a registered trademark in the European Union and other countries.

ISBN-13: 978–1–4039–9232–1 hardback
ISBN-10: 1–4039–9232–0 hardback

This book is printed on paper suitable for recycling and made from fully managed and sustained forests sources. Logging, and pulping and manufacting processes are expected to conform to the environmental regulations of the country of origin.

A catalogue record for this book is available from the British Library.

Library of Congress Cataloging-in-Publication Data

Global restructuring, state, capital and labour : contesting neo-Gramscian perspectives / by Andreas Bieler ... [et al.].
    p. cm.—(International political economy series)
    Includes bibliographical references and index.
    Contents: Global restructuring and theoretical
perspectives – State, capital and labour – Global restructuring:
contesting neo-Gramscian perspectives.
    ISBN 1–4039–9232–0 (cloth)
    1. Globalization. 2. International relations. 3. Historical materialism.
    I. Bieler, Andreas, 1967–. II. Series.

JZ1318.G55842 2006
303.48'2—dc22   2005046628

Printed and bound in Great Britain by
CPI Antony Rowe, Chippenham and Eastbourne

Contents

Part III Global Restructuring: Contesting Neo-Gramscian Perspectives

List of Illustrations

vii

List of Abbreviations

AmCham	American Chamber of Commerce
ATTAC	Aid of Citizens
BIP	Border Industrialisation Programme
CANACINTRA	National Chamber of Manufacturing Industries
CCE	Business Coordinating Council
CCF	Congress for Cultural Freedom
CEE	Central and Eastern Europe
CMHN	Mexican Businessmen's Council
CNTE	National Co-ordinating Committee of Educational Workers
COPARMEX	Employers' Confederation of the Republic of Mexico
CONCAMIN	Confederation of Chambers of Industry
CONCANACO	Confederation of National Chambers of Commerce, Services and Tourism
CSE	Conference of Socialist Economists
ECB	European Central Bank
EMU	Economic and Monetary Union
EP	European Parliament
ERT	European Round Table of Industrialists
ESF	European Social Form
EU	European Union
EZLN	Ejército Zapatista de Liberación Nacional
GATS	General Agreement on Trade in Services
GATT	General Agreement on Tariffs and Trade
GDP	gross domestic product
GMB	General, Municipal and Boilermakers' Union (UK)
GPE	Global Political Economy
FESEBES	Federation of Goods and Services Unions
FDI	foreign direct investment
ILO	International Labour Organisation
IMF	International Monetary Fund
IPE	International Political Economy
IR	International Relations
ISI	Import Substitution Industrialisation
LOPPE	Law on Political Organisation and Electoral Processes
NAFTA	North American Free Trade Agreement

NED	National Endowment for Democracy
NIEO	New International Economic Order
NGOs	non-governmental organisations
OECD	Organisation for Economic Co-operation and Development
PAN	Partido Acción Nacional
PCM	Mexican Communist Party
PRI	Institutional Revolutionary Party
PRONASOL	National Solidarity Programme
PSE	Economic Solidarity Pact
PSUM	Unified Socialist Party of Mexico
SNTE	National Education Workers' Union
SEA	Single European Act
SECOFI	Sectretariat of Commerce and Industrial Development (Mexico)
SEDESOL	Ministry of Social Development (Mexico)
SHCP	Ministry of the Treasury and Public Credit (Mexico)
SPP	Ministry of Programming and Budget (Mexico)
STRM	Mexican Telephone Workers' Union (Mexico)
SUD	Solidaries, Unitaires ed Démocratique (France)
TELMEX	Mexican Telephone Company
TNCs	Transnational Corporations
UN	United Nations
UNCTAD	United Nations Conference on Trade and Development
UNDP	United Nations Development Programme
UNISON	Public Service Union (UK)
USAID	US Agency for International Development
VÖI	Federation of Austrian Industrialists
WHO	World Health Organisation
WTO	World Trade Organisation

Acknowledgements

This book began as an idea for a collection that would bring together in one place a set of writings exploring global restructuring with an explicit focus on the centrality of state, capital and labour. Whilst some of the essays have been published previously, all of the chapters have been revised, updated, and given new critical edge. This process of revision was enabled through a series of workshops collectively organized by the authors, which resulted in greater coherence within and between chapters. The dialogue that follows reveals an extensive coverage of themes linked to political economy, philosophy, historical sociology, state theory, European politics, uneven development, neoliberal globalization and resistance. Definition is given to these themes through the focus on state, capital and labour; elements so often absent from mainstream International Relations (IR) and International Political Economy (IPE).

We are grateful to Jennifer Nelson and Alison Howson at Palgrave for supporting the book as well as two anonymous referees that provided constructive criticisms in order to improve structure and content. Interest and comments on the subject of the book have been gratefully received from Paul Cammack, Greig Charnock, Bob Jessop and Iain Pirie. Fulya Memisoglu helped in the preparation of the manuscript at the closing stages of the project. We also acknowledge:

Gerry Strange and *Capital & Class* for permission to revise parts of Chapter 2 taken from Andreas Bieler and Adam David Morton, 'A Critical Theory Route to Hegemony, World Order and Historical Change: neo-Gramscian Perspectives in International Relations', *Capital & Class*, 82 (2004): 85–113; as well as for permission to revise Chapter 3 taken from Peter Burnham, 'Neo-Gramscian Hegemony and the International Order', *Capital & Class*, 45 (1991): 73–93; and for permission to revise Chapter 11 taken from Peter Burnham, 'Marx, international political economy and globalisation', *Capital & Class*, 75 (2001): 103–112.

Palgrave/Macmillan for permission to revise parts of Chapter 4 taken from Werner Bonefeld, 'The Spectre of Globalisation', in W. Bonefeld and K. Psychopedis (eds) (2001) *The Politics of Change* (London: Palgrave).

Tony Payne and Routledge, an imprint of Taylor & Francis Group, for permission to reprint Chapter 6 taken from Peter Burnham, 'The Politics of Economic Management in the 1990s', *New Political Economy*, 4:1 (1999): 37–54.

Shahid Qadir and Carfax Publishing for permission to revise parts of Chapter 7 taken from Adam David Morton, 'Structural Change and Neoliberalism in Mexico: "passive revolution" in the global political economy', *Third World Quarterly*, 24:4 (2003): 631–53.

The journal *Theomai: Journal of Society, Nature and Development* for permission to revise parts of Chapter 8 taken from Werner Bonefeld, 'Human Progress and Development', *Theomai: Journal of Society, Nature and Development*, 8 (2003); http://revista-theomai.unq.edu.ar/numero8/artBonefeld8.htm, accessed 26 October 2005.

David Marsh and Blackwell Publishing for permission to revise parts of Chapter 9 taken from Andreas Bieler and Adam David Morton, 'Globalisation, the State and Class Struggle: A "Critical Economy" Engagement with Open Marxism', *British Journal of Politics and International Relations*, 5:4 (2003): 467–99.

Christopher Pierson and Blackwell Publishing for permission to edit and reprint in revised form Chapter 10 taken from Werner Bonefeld, ' "Critical Economy" and Social Constitution', *British Journal of Politics and International Relations*, 6:2 (2004): 231–7.

List of Contributors

Andreas Bieler is a Senior Lecturer in the School of Politics and International Relations, University of Nottingham, UK. His publications include *Globalisation and Enlargement of the European Union* (Routledge, 2000) and *The Struggle for a Social Europe: Trade Unions and EMU in Times of Global Restructuring* (Manchester University Press, 2006).

Werner Bonefeld teaches at the Department of Politics, University of York, and is an Associate Fellow at the Centre for Comparative Labour Studies, University of Warwick. His most recent publications include *Human Dignity: Social Autonomy and the Critique of Capitalism* (with Kosmos Psychopedis) and *Revolutionary Writing*.

Peter Burnham teaches in the Department of Politics and International Studies at the University of Warwick. His publications include *The Political Economy of Postwar Reconstruction* (Macmillan, 1990) and *Remaking the Postwar World Economy* (Palgrave Macmillan, 2003).

Adam David Morton is a Senior Lecturer in the School of Politics and International Relations at the University of Nottingham. He is author of *Unravelling Gramsci: Hegemony and Passive Revolution in the Global Political Economy* (Pluto Press, 2007 Forthcoming) and co-editor (with Andreas Bieler) of *Images of Gramsci: Connections and Contentions in Political Theory and International Relations* (Routledge, 2006).

1
Globalization, the State and Class Struggle
An Introduction

Andreas Bieler, Werner Bonefeld, Peter Burnham and
Adam David Morton

This book publishes an exchange between neo-Gramscian and Open Marxism approaches to contemporary capitalism, ranging from theoretical debate on, for example, the meaning of the state and its relationship to the economy, to the analysis of the meaning and significance of class struggle. Our theoretical disagreements are significant and their practical or political consequences formidable. However, and here we agree strongly, our disagreements are too important to be left undebated and unexplored. The Marxist critique of ideology has been pivotal in enabling critical theories of society to make their mark on the study of world politics. Yet, there has been a notable silence within critical international theory on the contributions of Open Marxism and neo-Gramscian perspectives.

This book responds to this silence through a detailed engagement between neo-Gramscian and Open Marxist approaches, drawing out similarities as well as differences at the theoretical and empirical level. In more detail, the book explores the complex relationship between labour, capital and the state in the so-called era of globalization. The aim is not to present a detailed analysis of the workings of any one political economy but rather to reflect on neo-Gramscian attempts to understand the dynamics of modern capitalism. In this way, the book contributes to debates within critical international theory and to wider analysis of how Marxist approaches can be employed to understand contemporary developments in the area of International Relations and International Political Economy. It should be stressed at the outset that the objective of the book is not to reconcile neo-Gramscian approaches with more orthodox Marxist analysis. Our aim is not to offer a synthesis or establish the 'superiority' of any one approach. Rather, we show how the fundamental concepts of Marxist analysis can be used in subtly different ways depending on particular readings of Marx and Gramsci. Indeed, we hope that our distinct approaches, and the debate between them, will illuminate the discussion on the meaning and significance of contemporary processes of restructuring, labour struggles, and the creation of alternatives to neo-liberal globalization and the world market society of capital.

One of the key themes to emerge from the book is how apparently similar starting points can lead to radically different conclusions concerning the nature of contemporary capitalism. The neo-Gramscian approach grants priority to a focus on the social relations of production whilst drawing attention to class struggle and the 'transnationalization' of capitalism (thereby theorizing periodizations within capitalism). The 'Open Marxist' approach wishes to reinstate a focus on Marx's analysis of the social relations of production, which it is argued are neither national nor global' whilst offering a critique of capitalism in theoretical terms (thereby denying the need for so-called updated concepts or the positing of periodizations within capitalism). From different perspectives, the book thus debates the significance and meaning of globalization, neo-liberalism, the changing relationship between state and economy, the importance of labour as a force of resistance, and the global restructuring of capitalism. The debate develops through more general theoretical chapters that set out our respective frameworks to develop critical assessments. The dialogue continues by means of contrasting interpretations of contemporary developments and it concludes with a direct exchange between the two theoretical perspectives.

The first part of the book introduces the key aspects of the neo-Gramscian and Open Marxist perspectives. In Chapter 2, Bieler and Morton provide an outline of the conceptual framework developed by Robert Cox that has been seminal to neo-Gramscian theorizing of capitalist world order. Cox's approach is situated in relation to the world economic crisis of the 1970s and more recent debates on the nature of structural power. The chapter also engages with the various forms of criticism and critique of neo-Gramscian perspectives. This provides the perfect context for Chapter 3 in which Burnham offers a critique of early forms of neo-Gramscian 'hegemony'. Burnham's principal argument is not that global capitalism needs to be theorized as a system of 'national capitalisms' but rather that neo-Gramscian approaches in their headlong dash to offer something new fail to fully conceptualize Marx's account of the capital relation and its applicability to contemporary capitalism. Bonefeld, in Chapter 4, continues this theme through an analysis of Marx's approach to the world market, crisis and the state. Contrary to neo-Gramscian perspectives that posit a new form of class struggle based on the creation of a world market ushered in by globalization, Bonefeld notes that for Marx the world market is both the precondition and the result of capitalist production. The state cannot be understood in abstraction from the world-market society of capital nor can its class character be defined in national terms. Rather, its class character is entailed in its form-determined purpose to protect the capitalist law of property and contract and therewith secure labour's continued divorce from the means of production. This powerful critique draws attention, Bonefeld and Burnham would argue, to the fetishism implicit in neo-Gramscian analysis.

Part two of the book provides some indication of how these critical Marxist approaches understand contemporary developments. In Chapter 5, Bieler takes the subject of European integration and argues that a neo-Gramscian methodology can overcome the principal problems encountered in the mainstream and Open Marxist literature. Rather than being the outcome of inter-state co-operation and conflict, it is concluded that the deepening and widening of European integration has been part and parcel of the intensified neo-liberal restructuring of the European social relations of production driven by transnational class fractions. Utilizing a judicious mix of primary and secondary archival material, Burnham, in the following chapter (chapter 6), shows how Open Marxist principles can be employed to understand the politics of economic management. Drawing extensively on the British experience, this chapter analyses how state managers responded to crisis expressed in terms of labour militancy and inflation by switching from politicized to rules-based, depoliticized modes of economic management. Depoliticization is not in this context to be understood as a new mode of regulation corresponding to a new accumulation regime but rather as an 'old' mode of governing drawing on principles articulated clearly in the return to the Gold Standard in 1925. For Burnham, depoliticizing strategies are an enduring feature of capitalism. It is argued that this approach contrasts sharply with the neo-Gramscian contention that this form of management can be characterized as the emergence of a new constitutionalism of disciplinary neo-liberalism.

Subsequently in Chapter 7, Morton builds on the analytical distinction between an accumulation strategy and a hegemonic project to present a view of structural change in Mexico. The movement from Import

Substitution Industrialization to neo-liberalism was, he notes, constituted or authored by particular social class forces in Mexico. In short, structural change is explained in terms of an unfolding process of class struggle brought about by the expansion of capital and the *internalization* of class interests between various fractions of classes within state–civil society relations. It is clear that one of the central themes of this book is the contested relationship between the national state and the global character of accumulation. According to neo-Gramscian writers this relationship has undergone a fundamental structural change, necessitating the development of categories of analysis that understand current transformations in terms of a transition within capitalism. Bonefeld in Chapter 8 subjects this view to a rigorous critique. Crisis does not, he argues, entail the transition from one epoch of capitalism to another. Rather, crisis is an expression of the contradictory form of capitalist accumulation. Bonefeld develops this approach looking at the relationship between monetary and productive accumulation.

The final part of the book pulls together some of the main themes explored in Parts I and II. As noted above, the aim of the book is not to reconcile but to highlight some of the principal differences in approach and explore the implications of divergent views both in terms of method and analysis. In Chapter 9, Bieler and Morton start the section with a critical appreciation of Open Marxism, arguing that a neo-Gramscian development of critical economic analysis overcomes what they identify as the economism of Open Marxism. Developing insights from Nicos Poulantzas and Antonio Gramsci, their 'critical economy' conception of the state is shown to analyse capitalist processes of neo-liberal globalization without falling into the trap of economic determinism. Instead, class forces within the state are seen to contribute to the process of internationalization, shaping the form the state actually takes as well as being affected by it. In the subsequent consecutive chapters (Chapters 10 and 11), Bonefeld and Burnham contend that a central weakness of the neo-Gramscian approach lies in its conception of the relationship between the political and the economic. As Bonefeld summarizes in Chapter 10, the relationship is deemed to be indeterminate: at one moment the economy is run by the state, at another the state is run by the economy; and since globalization is said to be an epoch in which capital has attained hegemony one is led to believe that prior to globalization, the national state was in charge of capitalism and governing in favour of non-capitalist interests. In his wide-ranging critique Bonefeld reiterates that Marx's critique of political economy amounted to a theory of the social constitution of 'economic' categories. This is the starting point, in Chapter 11, of Burnham's articulation of the concepts of Open Marxism in terms of emphasizing the centrality of the circuit of capital. Anticipating Bieler and Morton's final chapter, Burnham contends that much of their critique is misplaced once states are seen as political nodes in the global flow of capital. Bieler and Morton's final contribution in Chapter 12 responds to the above criticism whilst stressing the value of the neo-Gramscian approach in empirical research. Their chapter highlights processes of class formation in the context of resistance to capitalist processes of neo-liberal globalization. They thus show how social class forces within state apparatuses internalize the interests of transnational capital and how this process also generates new collective actors that challenge neo-liberal restructuring.

Theorizing the character of labour, capital and state relations is central to all radical political economy and to critical theory accounts of international politics. This volume will have achieved its purpose if it brings these debates to a wider audience and contributes to understanding the character of contemporary capitalism and the possibilities for its transcendence.

Part I

Global Restructuring and Theoretical Perspectives

2
A Critical Theory Route to Hegemony, World Order and Historical Change

Neo-Gramscian Perspectives in International Relations

Andreas Bieler and Adam David Morton

Introduction

Situated within a historical materialist problematic of social transformation and deploying many insights from the Italian Marxist Antonio Gramsci, a crucial break with mainstream International Relations (IR) approaches emerged by the 1980s in the work of Robert Cox. In contrast to mainstream routes to hegemony in IR, which develop a static theory of politics, an abstract ahistorical conception of the state and an appeal to universal validity (e.g. Keohane, 1984, 1989; Waltz, 1979), debate shifted towards a critical theory of hegemony, world order and historical change (for the classic critique, see Ashley, 1984). Rather than a problem-solving preoccupation with the maintenance of social power relationships, a critical theory of hegemony directs attention to questioning the prevailing order of the world. It 'does not take institutions and social and power relations for granted but calls them into question by concerning itself with their origins and whether they might be in the process of changing' (Cox, 1981, p. 129). Thus, it is specifically critical in the sense of asking how existing social or world orders have come into being, how norms, institutions or practices therefore emerge, and what forces may have the emancipatory potential to change or transform the prevailing order. As such, a critical theory develops a dialectical theory of history concerned not just with the past but with a continual process of historical change and with exploring the potential for alternative forms of

9

development (Cox, 1981, pp. 129, 133–4). Cox's critical theory of hegemony thus focuses on interaction between particular processes, notably
springing from the dialectical possibilities of change within the sphere
of production and the exploitative character of social relations, not as
unchanging ahistorical essences but as a continuing creation of new
forms (Cox, 1981, p. 132). In order to focus on aspects of global restructuring, state, capital and labour in relation to neo-Gramscian hegemony
this chapter provides an outline of the conceptual framework developed
by Robert Cox. This overview is essential before discussion in subsequent chapters can move to a critical engagement with aspects of the
historical materialist basis of the framework. Within the parameters of
this chapter, Cox's approach will also be situated in relation to the world
economic crisis of the 1970s, more recent debates about globalization,
and how this period of 'structural change' has been conceptualized.
Attention will then turn to what has been recognized (see Morton, 2001)
as similar, but diverse, neo-Gramscian perspectives in International
Relations (IR) that build on Cox's work and constitute a distinct critical theory route to considering hegemony, world order and historical
change. Finally, the conclusion will trace various controversies sur-
rounding the neo-Gramscian perspectives some of which are then taken
up more directly within the ensuing chapters.

A critical theory route to hegemony, world order and historical change

Unlike conventional IR theory, which reduces hegemony to a single
dimension of dominance based on the economic and military capabilities of states, a neo-Gramscian perspective developed by Cox broadens
the domain of hegemony. It appears as an expression of broadly based
consent, manifested in the acceptance of ideas and supported by material resources and institutions, which is initially established by social
forces occupying a leading role within a state, but is then projected out-
wards on a world scale. Within a world order a situation of hegemony
may prevail 'based on a coherent conjunction or fit between a configuration of material power, the prevalent collective image of world order
(including certain norms) and a set of institutions which administer the
order with a certain semblance of universality' (Cox, 1981, p. 139).
Hegemony is therefore a form of dominance, but it refers more to a consensual order so that 'dominance by a powerful state may be a necessary
but not a sufficient condition of hegemony' (Cox, 1981, p. 139). If hegemony is understood as an 'opinion-moulding activity', rather than brute

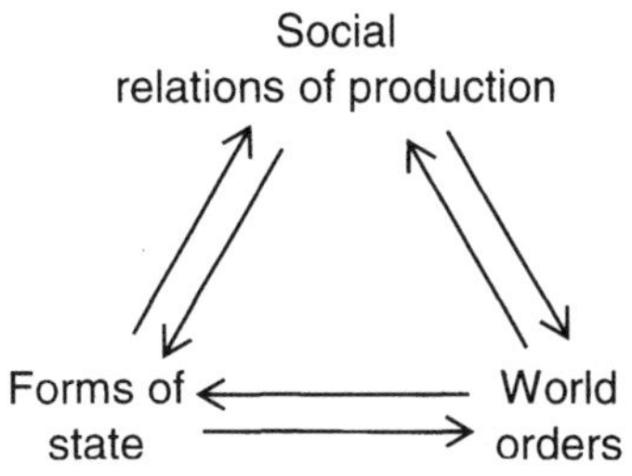

Social
relations of production

Forms of ←————— World
state   —————→ orders

Figure 2.1   The dialectical relation of forces

force or dominance, then consideration has to turn to how a hegemonic social or world order is based on values and understandings that permeate the nature of that order (Cox, 1992/1996, p. 151). Hence it has to be considered how intersubjective meanings – shared notions about social relations – shape reality. ' "Reality" is not only the physical environment of human action but also the institutional, moral and ideological context that shapes thoughts and actions' (Cox, 1997, p. 252). The crucial point to make, then, is that hegemony filters through structures of society, economy, culture, gender, ethnicity, class and ideology.

Hegemony within a historical structure is constituted on three spheres of activity: *the social relations of production*, encompassing the totality of social relations in material, institutional and discursive forms that engender particular social forces; *forms of state*, consisting of historically contingent state–civil society complexes; and *world orders*, which not only represent phases of stability and conflict but also permit scope for thinking about how alternative forms of world order might emerge (Cox, 1981, pp. 135–8). These are represented schematically in Figure 2.1 (Cox, 1981, p. 138).

If considered dialectically, in relation to each other, then it becomes possible to represent the historical process through the particular configuration of historical structures. Social forces, as the main collective actors engendered by the social relations of production, operate within and across all spheres of activity. Through the rise of contending social forces, linked to changes in production, there may occur mutually reinforcing transformations in forms of state and world order. There is no unilinear relationship between the spheres of activity and the point of departure to explain the historical process may equally be that of forms of state or world order (Cox, 1981, p. 153n.26). Within each of the three main spheres it is argued that three further elements reciprocally combine to constitute a historical structure: *ideas*, understood as intersubjective

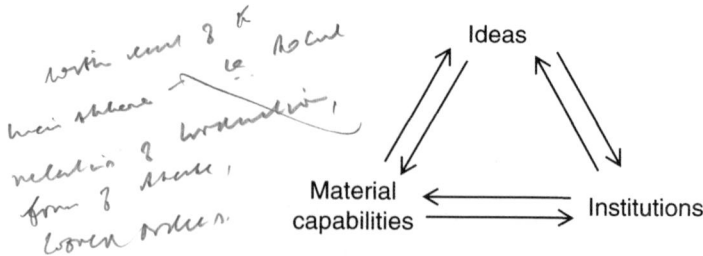

Figure 2.2   The dialectical moment of hegemony

meanings as well as collective images of world order; *material capabilities*, referring to accumulated resources; and *institutions*, which are amalgams of the previous two elements and are means of stabilizing a particular order. These again are represented schematically in Figure 2.2 (Cox, 1981, p. 136).

The aim is to break down over time coherent historical structures – consisting of different patterns of social relations of production, forms of state and world order – that have existed within the capitalist mode of production (Cox, 1987, pp. 396–8). In the following, the main characteristics of the three spheres of activity are outlined.

The social relations of production

According to Cox (1987, pp. 1–9), patterns of production relations are the starting point for analysing the operation and mechanisms of hegemony. Yet, from the start, this should not be taken as a move that reduces everything to production in an economistic sense.

> Production ... is to be understood in the broadest sense. It is not confined to the production of physical goods used or consumed. It covers the production and reproduction of knowledge and of the social relations, morals and institutions that are prerequisites to the production of physical goods. (Cox, 1989, p. 39)

These patterns are referred to as modes of social relations of production, which encapsulate configurations of social forces engaged in the process of production. By discerning different modes of social relations of production it is possible to consider how changing production relations give rise to particular social forces that become the bases of power within and across states and within a specific world order (Cox, 1987, p. 4). The objective of outlining different modes of social relations of production is to question what promotes the emergence of particular modes and what might explain the way in which modes combine or undergo transformation (Cox, 1987, p. 103). It is argued that the reciprocal relationship between production and power is crucial. To examine this relationship a framework is developed that focuses on how power in *social relations of production* may give rise to certain *social forces*, how these social forces may become the bases of power in *forms of state* and how this might shape *world order*. This framework revolves around the social ontology of historical structures. It refers to 'persistent social practices, made by collective human activity and transformed through collective human activity' (Cox, 1987, p. 4). An attempt is therefore made to capture 'the reciprocal relationship of structures and actors' (Bieler and Morton, 2001a; Cox, 1995a, p. 33, 2000, pp. 55–9).

Hegemony is thus understood as a form of class rule linked to social forces, as the core collective actors, engendered by the social relations of production (Overbeek, 1994). Under capitalist social property relations the direct extraction of surplus is accomplished through 'non-political' relations associated with different forms of social power. In capitalist social forms surplus extraction is indirectly conducted through a contractual relation between those who maintain the power of appropriation, as owners of the means of production, over those who only have their labour to sell, as expropriated producers. The direct producers are thus no longer in possession of their own means of subsistence but are compelled to sell their labour power for a wage in order to gain access to the means of production (Wood, 1995, pp. 31–6). Said otherwise, direct producers only have access to the means of production through the sale of their labour power in exchange for a wage, which is mediated by the purely 'economic' mechanisms of the market. The market does not therefore represent an opportunity but a compulsion to which both appropriators and expropriators (capital and labour) are subjected, through the imperatives of competition, profit maximization and survival (Wood, 2002, pp. 96–8, 102).

For Cox, class is viewed as a historical category and employed in a heuristic way rather than as a static analytical category (Cox, 1987, pp. 355–7, 1985/1996, p. 57). This means that class identity emerges within and through historical processes of economic exploitation. 'Bring back exploitation as the hallmark of class, and at once class struggle is in the forefront, as it should be' (Ste. Croix, 1981, p. 57). As such, class-consciousness emerges out of particular historical contexts of struggle rather than mechanically deriving from objective determinations that have an automatic place in production relations (see E.P. Thompson, 1968, pp. 8–9, 1978). Yet the focus on exploitation and resistance to it ensures that social forces are not simply reduced to material aspects, but also include other forms of identity involved in struggle such as ethnic, nationalist, religious, gender or sexual forms. In short, ' "non-class" issues – peace, ecology and feminism – are not to be set aside but given a firm and conscious basis in the social realities shaped through the production process' (Cox, 1987, p. 353).

Forms of state

The conceptual framework, outlined so far, considers how new modes of social relations of production become established. Changes in the social relations of production give rise to new configurations of *social forces*. State power rests on these configurations. Therefore, rather than taking the state as a given or pre-constituted institutional category, consideration is given to the historical construction of various forms of state and the social context of political struggle. This is accomplished by drawing upon the concept of historical bloc and by widening a theory of the state to include relations within civil society.

A historical bloc refers to the way in which leading social forces within a specific national context establish a relationship over contending social forces. It is more than simply a political alliance between social forces represented by classes or fractions of classes. It indicates the integration of a variety of different class interests that are propagated throughout society 'bringing about not only a unison of economic and political aims, but also intellectual and moral unity ... on a "universal" plane' (Gramsci, 1971, pp. 181–2). The very nature of a historical bloc, as Anne Showstack Sassoon (1987, p. 123) has outlined, necessarily implies the existence of hegemony. Indeed, the 'universal plane' that Gramsci had in mind was the creation of hegemony by a fundamental social group over subordinate groups. Hegemony would therefore be established 'if the relationship between intellectuals and people-nation, between the leaders and the led, the rulers and the ruled, is provided by an organic cohesion. ... Only then can there take place an exchange of individual elements between the rulers and ruled, leaders ... and led, and can the shared life be realised which alone is a social force – with the creation of the "historical bloc" ' (Gramsci, 1971, p. 418).

These issues are encompassed within the focus on different forms of state which, as Cox notes, are principally distinguished by 'the characteristics of their historic[al] blocs, that is, the configurations of social forces upon which state power ultimately rests. A particular configuration of social forces defines in practice the limits or parameters of state purposes, and the modus operandi of state action, defines, in other words, the *raison d'état* for a particular state' (Cox, 1987, p. 105). In short, by considering different forms of state, it becomes possible to analyse the social basis of the state or to conceive of the historical 'content' of different states. The notion of historical bloc aids this endeavour by directing attention to which social forces may have been crucial in the formation of a historical bloc or particular state; what contradictions may be contained within a historical bloc upon which a form of state is founded; and what potential might exist for the formation of a rival historical bloc that may transform a particular form of state (Cox, 1987, p. 409n.10). In contrast, therefore, to conventional state-centric approaches in IR, a wider theory of the state emerges within this framework. Instead of underrating state power and explaining it away, attention is given to social forces and processes and how these relate to the development of states (Cox, 1981, p. 128) as well as states in alternative conditions of development (Bilgin and Morton, 2002). Considering different forms of state as the expression of particular historical blocs and thus relations across state–civil society fulfils this objective. Overall, this relationship is referred to as the state–civil society complex that, clearly, owes an intellectual debt to Gramsci.

For Gramsci, the state was not simply understood as an institution limited to the 'government of the functionaries' or the 'top political leaders and personalities with direct governmental responsibilities'. The state presents itself in a different way beyond the political society of public figures and top leaders so that 'the state is the entire complex of practical and theoretical activities with which the ruling class not only justifies and maintains its dominance, but manages to win the active consent of those over whom it rules' (Gramsci, 1971, pp. 178, 244). This alternative conception of the state is inclusive of the realm of civil society. The state should be understood, then, not just as the apparatus of government operating within the 'public' sphere (government, political parties, military) but also as part of the 'private' sphere of civil society (church, media, education) through which hegemony functions (Gramsci, 1971, p. 261). It can therefore be argued that the state in this conception is understood as a social relation. The state is not unquestioningly taken as a distinct institutional category, or thing in itself, but conceived as a form of social relations through which capitalism and hegemony are expressed (this understanding of the state as a social relation will be developed further in Chapter 9). It is the combination of political and civil society that is referred to as the integral state through which ruling classes organize intellectual and moral functions as part of the political and cultural struggle for hegemony in the effort to establish an 'ethical' state (Gramsci, 1971, pp. 258, 271).

Furthermore, different social relations of production engender different fractions of social forces. This means that 'foreign' capital, for example, is not simply represented as an autonomous force beyond the power of the state but instead is represented by certain classes or fractions of classes *within* the constitution of the state apparatus. There are contradictory and heterogeneous relations internal to the state, which are induced by class antagonisms between nationally and transnationally based capital and labour. The state, then, is the condensation of a hegemonic relationship between dominant classes and class fractions. This occurs when a leading class develops a 'hegemonic project' or 'comprehensive concept of control' which transcends particular economic-corporate interests and becomes capable of binding and cohering the diverse aspirations and general interests of various social classes and class fractions (Overbeek, 1990, 1993; van der Pijl, 1984, 1998). It is a process that involves the 'most purely political phase' of class struggle and occurs on a ' "universal" plane' to result in the forging of a historical bloc (Gramsci, 1971, p. 263).

Hegemony and world orders

The construction of a historical bloc cannot exist without a hegemonic social class and is therefore a national phenomenon (Cox, 1983, pp. 168, 174). This is because the very nature of a historical bloc is bound up with how various classes and fractions of classes construct, or contest, hegemony through national political frameworks. Or, put another way, how such classes 'nationalise' themselves through historically specific and peculiar socio-economic and political structures (Gramsci, 1971, p. 241; Sassoon, 1987, pp. 121–2). Yet the hegemony of a leading class can manifest itself as an international phenomenon insofar as it represents the development of a particular form of the social relations of production. Once hegemony has been consolidated domestically it may expand beyond a particular social order to move outward on a world scale and insert itself through the world order (Cox, 1983, p. 171, 1987, pp. 149–50). By doing so it can connect social forces across different countries. 'A world hegemony is thus in its beginnings an outward expansion of the internal (national) hegemony established by a ... social class' (Cox, 1983, p. 171). The outward expansion of particular modes of social relations of production and the interests of a leading class on a world scale can also become supported by mechanisms of international organization. This is what Gramsci (1971, p. 243) referred to as the 'internal and international organizational relations of the state': that is movements, voluntary associations and organizations, such as the Rotary Club, or the Roman Catholic Church that had an 'international' character whilst rooted within the state. 'Italian Catholicism', Gramsci (1985, pp. 220–1) minuted, 'was felt not only as a surrogate for the spirit of the nation and the state but also as a world-wide hegemonic institution, an imperialistic spirit.' Social forces may thus achieve hegemony within a national social order as well as through world order. Hegemony can therefore operate at two levels: by constructing a historical bloc and establishing social cohesion *within* a form of state as well as by expanding a mode of production *internationally* and projecting hegemony through the level of world order. For instance, in Gramsci's time, this was borne by the expansion of Fordist assembly plant production beyond the United States which would lead to the growing world hegemony and power of 'Americanism and Fordism' from the 1920s and 1930s (Gramsci, 1971, pp. 277–318).

Pax Americana and globalization

In more recent times, it has been one of Cox's key objectives to explain additional processes of structural change, particularly the change from the post-Second World War order to globalization. Cox argues that a United States-led hegemonic world order, labelled *pax Americana*, prevailed until the early 1970s. It was maintained through the Bretton Woods system of fixed exchange rates and institutions like the International Monetary Fund (IMF) and the World Bank. Moreover, it was based on the principle of 'embedded liberalism', which allowed the combination of international free trade with the right for governments to intervene in their national economy in order to ensure domestic stability via social security and the partial redistribution of economic wealth (Ruggie, 1982). The corresponding form of state was the Keynesian welfare state, characterized by interventionism, a policy of full employment via budget deficit spending, the mixed economy and an expansive welfare system (Gill and Law, 1988, pp. 79–80). The underlying social relations of production were organized around the Fordist accumulation regime, characterized by mass production and mass consumption, and tripartite corporatism involving government–business–labour coalitions (Cox, 1987, pp. 219–30).[1] The forms and functions of United States-led hegemony, however, began to alter following the world economic crisis of the 1970s and the collapse of the Bretton Woods system during a period of 'structural change' in the world economy in the 1970s. This overall crisis, both of the world economy and of social power within various forms of state, has been explained as the result of two particular tendencies: the internationalization of production and the internationalization of the state that led the thrust towards globalization. As Cox clearly indicated at an early stage, 'it becomes increasingly pertinent to think in terms of a global class structure alongside or superimposed upon national class structures' (Cox, 1981, p. 147).

Since the erosion of *pax Americana* principles of world order in the 1970s, there has been an increasing internationalization of production and finance driven, at the apex of an emerging global class structure, by a 'transnational managerial class'. Taking advantage of differences between countries, there has been an integration of production processes on a transnational scale with Transnational Corporations (TNCs) promoting the operation of different elements of a single process in different territorial locations. It is this organization of production and finance on a transnational level, which fundamentally distinguishes globalization from the period of *pax Americana*. Following the neo-Gramscian focus on social forces, engendered by the social relations of production, as the main actors it is realized that the *transnational* restructuring of capitalism in globalization has led to the emergence of new social forces of capital and labour. Besides the transnational managerial class, other elements of productive capital (involved in manufacturing and extraction), including small- and medium-sized businesses acting as contractors and suppliers and import–export businesses, as well elements of financial capital (involved in banking insurance and finance) have been supportive of this internationalization of production. Hence there has been a rise in the structural power of transnational capital supported and promoted by forms of elite interaction that have forged common perspectives, or an 'emulative uniformity', between business, state officials and representatives of international organizations favouring the logic of capitalist market relations (Cox, 1987, p. 298; Gill, 1995a, pp. 400–1; Gill and Law, 1989, p. 484). Significant contradictions are likely to exist between transnational social forces of capital and nationally based capital. The latter, engendered by national production systems, may oppose an open global economy due to their reliance on national or regional protectionism against global competition. Parallel to the division between transnational and national capital, Cox identifies two main lines of division within the working class. First, workers of TNCs can be in conflict with workers of national companies, shadowing the split of capital. Second and related to this, there may be a rift between established workers in secure employment, often within the core workforce of TNCs, and non-established workers in temporary and part-time positions at the periphery of the labour market (Cox, 1981, p. 235). In other words, globalization in the form of the transnationalization of production has led to a fractionalization of capital and labour into transnational and national social forces alike. During this period of structural change in the 1970s, then, the social basis across many forms of state altered as the logic of capitalist market relations created a crisis of authority in established institutions and modes of governance. Whilst some have championed such changes as the 'retreat of the state' (S. Strange, 1996), or the emergence of a 'borderless world' (Ohmae, 1990, 1996), and others have decried the global proportions of such changes in production (Hirst and Thompson, 1999; Weiss, 1998), it is argued here that the internationalization of production has profoundly restructured – but not eroded – the role of the state. The notion of the internationalization of the state captures the dynamic of state restructuring by referring to the way transnational processes linked to changes in production have been transmitted through the policy-making channels of governments and associated forms of consensus formation. The network of control that has maintained the structural power of capital has also been supported by an 'axis of influence', consisting of institutions such as the World Bank, which have ensured the ideological osmosis and dissemination of neo-liberal economics in favour of the perceived exigencies of the global political economy. As a result, those state agencies in close contact with the global economy – offices of presidents and prime ministers, treasuries, central banks – have gained precedence over those agencies closest to domestic public policy – ministries of labour and industry or planning offices (Cox, 1992, p. 31). Across the different forms of state in countries of advanced and peripheral capitalism, the general depiction is that the state became a transmission belt for neo-liberalism and the logic of capitalist competition from global to local spheres (Cox, 1992, p. 31).[2]

Whilst wider criticisms of the neo-Gramscian perspectives will be outlined and engaged with shortly, it is worth noting at this stage of the discussion that the thesis on globalization and the internationalization of the state has received pertinent critical attention. In particular, Leo Panitch has argued that an account unfolds which is too top-down in its expression of power relations and assumes that globalization is a process that proceeds from the global to the national or the outside-in. The point that globalization is *authored* by social class forces within states is thus overlooked by developing the metaphor of a transmission belt from the global to the national within the thesis of the internationalization of the state (Panitch, 1994, 2000). It has also been added that this is a one-way view of internationalization that respectively overlooks

reciprocal interaction between the global and the local, overlooks mutually reinforcing social relations within the global political economy, or
ignores class conflict within national social formations (Ling, 1996; Baker,
1999; Moran, 1998). The role of the state, following Panitch's (1994, p. 74)
argument, is still determined by struggles among social forces located
within particular social formations, even though social forces may be
implicated in transnational structures. The discussion below will indicate,
however, precisely how the agency of particular social forces is realized in
constituting, reproducing and contesting the globalization of neo-
liberalism (also see Chapters 5 and 7 for comparative accounts of the
constitution and contestation of such processes or how social forces have
authored the globalization of neo-liberalism in different contexts).

From the internationalization of the state
to globalization: further developments

Although the thesis of the internationalization of the state has received
much recent criticism, the work of Stephen Gill has greatly contributed
to understanding this process as part of the changing character of US-
centred hegemony in the global political economy, notably in his
detailed analysis of the role of the Trilateral Commission (Gill, 1990).
Similar to Cox, the global restructuring of production is located within
a context of structural change in the 1970s. It was in this period that
there was a transition from what Gill recognizes as an *international historical bloc* of social forces, established in the post-Second World War
period, towards a *transnational historical bloc*, forging links and a synthesis of interests and identities not only beyond national boundaries and
classes but also creating the conditions for the hegemony of transnational capital. Yet Gill departs from Gramsci to assert that a historical
bloc 'may at times have the potential to become hegemonic', thereby
implying that a historical bloc can be established without necessarily
enjoying hegemonic rule (Gill, 1993, p. 40). For example, Gill argues
that the current transnational historical bloc has a position of
supremacy but not hegemony. Drawing in principle from Gramsci, it is
argued that supremacy prevails, when a situation of hegemony *is not*
apparent and when dominance is exercised through a historical bloc
over fragmented opposition (Gill, 1995a, pp. 400, 402, 412).
    This politics of supremacy is organized through two key processes: the
new constitutionalism of disciplinary neo-liberalism and the concomi-
tant spread of market civilization. According to Gill, new constitutionalism involves the narrowing of the social basis of popular participation

within the world order of disciplinary neo-liberalism. It involves the hollowing out of democracy and the affirmation, in matters of political economy, of a set of macro-economic policies such as market efficiency, discipline and confidence, policy credibility and competitiveness. It is 'the move towards construction of legal or constitutional devices to remove or insulate substantially the new economic institutions from popular scrutiny or democratic accountability' (Gill, 1991, 1992, p. 165). Economic and Monetary Union (EMU) within the European Union (EU) is regarded as a good example of this process (Gill, 2001). New constitutionalism results in an attempt to make neo-liberalism the sole model of development by disseminating the notion of market civilization based on an ideology of capitalist progress and exclusionary or hierarchical patterns of social relations (Gill, 1995a, p. 399). Within the global political economy, mechanisms of surveillance have supported the market civilization of new constitutionalism in something tentatively likened to a global 'panopticon' of surveillance (Gill, 1995b).

The overarching concept of supremacy has also been used to develop an understanding of the construction of US foreign policy towards the 'Third World' and how challenges were mounted against the United States in the 1970s through the New International Economic Order (NIEO) (Augelli and Murphy, 1988). It is argued that the ideological promotion of American liberalism, based on individualism and free trade, assured American supremacy through the 1970s and was reconstructed in the 1980s. Yet this projection of supremacy did not simply unfold through domination. Rather than simply equating supremacy with dominance, Augelli and Murphy argue that supremacy can be maintained through domination *or* hegemony (Augelli and Murphy, 1988, p. 132). As Murphy (1994, p. 295n.8) outlines in a separate study of industrial change and international organizations, supremacy defines the position of a leading class within a historical bloc and can be secured by hegemony as well as through domination. Gramsci (1971, p. 57) himself states, 'the supremacy of a social group manifests itself in two ways, as "domination" and as "intellectual and moral leadership" '. Where the former strain of supremacy involves subjugation by force, the latter involves leading allied groups. Shifts or variations in hegemony therefore characterize conditions of supremacy, which may reveal the limits of organizing the balance between passive and active consent relative to force within world order.

A recent important intervention by van der Pijl (1998) further expands the possibility of using class struggle as an analytical device for the analysis of confrontations beyond those concerned with purely material interests. He distinguishes three areas of capitalist discipline and exploitation: (1) primitive accumulation and resistance to it, mainly relevant during the early history of capitalism; (2) the capitalist production process, referring to the exploitation of labour in the work place; and (3) the extension of exploitation into the sphere of social reproduction, submitting education and health to capitalist profit criteria and leading to the destruction and exhaustion of the environment. It is the latter form of capitalist discipline that has become increasingly relevant during neo-liberal globalization. Resistance to it, be it by progressive social movements and Green Parties, or be it by populist, nationalist movements, can be understood as class struggle as much as the confrontation between employers and employees at the workplace (van der Pijl, 1998, pp. 36–49).

In addition to the neo-Gramscian perspectives discussed so far, there also exists a diverse array of similar perspectives analysing hegemony in the global political economy. This includes, among others, an account of the historically specific way in which mass production was institutionalized in the United States and how this propelled forms of American-centred leadership and world hegemony in the post-Second World War period (Rupert, 1995a). Extending this analysis, there has also been consideration of struggles between social forces in the United States over the North American Free Trade Agreement (NAFTA) and globalization (Rupert, 1995b, 2000). Moreover, there have been analyses of European integration within the context of globalization and the role of transnational classes within European governance (van Apeldoorn, 2002; Bieler, 2000; Bieler and Morton, 2001b; Bieling and Steinhilber, 2000; Cafruny and Ryner, 2003; Holman *et al.*, 1998; Ryner, 2002; Shields, 2003). This has increasingly included a focus on the role of labour in transnational European class formation (Bieler, 2003a, 2003b, 2005; Bieling and Schulten, 2003; Ryner and Schulten, 2003; G. Strange, 2002). The internationalization and democratization of Southern Europe, particularly Spain, within the global political economy (Holman, 1996) and analysis of international organizations including the role of gender and women's movements (Lee, 1995; Stienstra, 1994; Whitworth, 1994) are also covered, whilst a study of the hegemonic formation, consolidation, and role of the Congress for Cultural Freedom (CCF) in the context of US and European relations, between 1945 and 1955, has been undertaken (Scott-Smith, 2002). There has, moreover, been a recent return to understanding forms of US foreign policy intervention within countries of peripheral capitalism. This has included analysing the promotion of polyarchy defined as, 'a system in which a small group actually rules and mass participation in decision-making is confined to leadership choice in elections carefully managed by elites' (W.I. Robinson, 1996, p. 49). Polyarchy, or low intensity democracy, is therefore analysed as an adjunct of US hegemony through institutions such as the US Agency for International Development (USAID) and the National Endowment for Democracy (NED) in the particular countries of the Philippines, Chile, Nicaragua and Haiti and recently extended in relation to the case of Mexico (Morton, 2005a). There are clearly a variety of neo-Gramscian perspectives dealing with a diversity of issues linked to the analysis of hegemony in the global political economy. The next section outlines some of the criticisms levelled against such perspectives and, in conclusion, indications are given of the direction future research might take.

Welcome debate: controversies surrounding neo-Gramscian perspectives

In broad outline, neo-Gramscian perspectives have been criticized as too unfashionably Marxist or, alternatively, too lacking in Marxist rigour. They are seen as unfashionable because many retain an essentially historical materialist position as central to analysis – focusing on the 'decisive nucleus of economic activity' (Gramsci, 1971, p. 161). Hence the accusation that analysis remains caught within modernist assumptions that take as foundational the structures of historical processes determining the realms of the possible (Ashley, 1989, p. 275). However, rather than succumbing to this problem, the fallibility of all knowledge claims is accepted across neo-Gramscian perspectives. A minimal foundationalism is therefore evident based on a cautious, contingent and transitory universalism that combines dialogue between universal values and local definitions within historically specific circumstances (Cox, 1995b, p. 14, 2000, p. 46). Elsewhere, other commentators have alternatively decried the lack of historical materialist rigour within neo-Gramscian perspectives. According to Peter Burnham's classic critique (see Chapter 3) the neo-Gramscian treatment of hegemony amounts to a 'pluralist empiricism' that fails to recognize the central importance of the capital relation and is therefore preoccupied with the articulation of ideology. By granting equal weight to ideas and material capabilities it is argued that the contradictions of the capital relation are blurred which results in 'a slide towards an idealist account of the determination of economic policy'. Hence, the categories of state and market are regarded as opposed forms of social organization that operate separately in external relationship to one another.

In specific response to these criticisms, it was outlined earlier in this chapter how the social relations of production are taken as the starting point for thinking about world order and the way they engender configurations of social forces. By thus asking what modes of social relations of production within capitalism have been prevalent in particular historical circumstances, the state is not treated as an unquestioned category. Indeed, rather closer to Burnham's own position than he might care to admit, the state is treated as an aspect of the social relations of production so that questions about the *apparent* separation of politics and economics or states and markets within capitalism are promoted. Although a fully developed theory of the state is less evident, there clearly exists a set of at least implicit assumptions about the state as a form of social relations through which capitalism and hegemony are expressed (Chapter 9 extends this avenue of critical state theorizing). Moreover, ideas in the form of intersubjective meanings are accepted as part of the global political economy itself. Yet, in contrast to Burnham's claim, they are not regarded as an additional independent variable next to material properties. Rather, the 'material structure of ideology' is the principal emphasis, which demonstrates an awareness of the ideological mediations of the state through libraries, schools, architecture, street names and lay-out (Gramsci, 1995, pp. 155–6).[3] Only those ideas, which are disseminated through or rooted in such structures, linked to a particular constellation of social forces engaged in an ideological struggle for hegemony, are considered to be 'organic ideas' (Bieler, 2001). In Gramsci's own words, only those ideas can be regarded as 'organic' that 'organise human masses, and create the terrain on which men move, acquire consciousness of their position, struggle, etc.'. These are contrasted with ideas that are merely 'arbitrary, rationalistic, or "willed" ', based on extemporary polemics (Gramsci, 1971, pp. 376–7). This indicates an appreciation of the links intellectuals may have, or the wider social function they perform, in relation to the world of production within capitalist society. It offers the basis for a materialist and social class analysis of intellectuals (see Morton 2003b). There is therefore an appreciation of how ideas and intellectual activity can 'assume the fanatical granite compactness of ... "popular beliefs" which assume the same energy as "material forces" ' (Gramsci, 1971, p. 404).

In relation to contentions on the internationalization of state thesis, it will be recalled from the above discussion that the point of departure within a neo-Gramscian approach could equally be changing social relations of production *within* forms of state *or* world order (Cox, 1981, p. 153n.26). Indeed, Cox's focus has been on historical blocs underpinning particular states and how these are connected through the mutual interests of social classes in different countries. Further, following both Gramsci and Cox, the national context is the only place where a historical bloc can be founded and where the task of building new historical blocs, as the basis for counter-hegemony to change world order, must begin. Gill too, although he tends to take a slightly different tack on the application of notions such as historical bloc and supremacy, is still interested in analysing attempts to constitutionalize neo-liberalism at the domestic, regional and global levels (Gill, 1995a, p. 422). Therefore, there is a focus on transnational networks of production and how national governments have lost much autonomy in policy making, but also how states are still an integral part of this process.

Extending these insights (see Chapter 9), it might also be important to recognize that capital is not simply something that is footloose, beyond the power of the state, but is represented by classes and fractions of classes within the very constitution of the state. The phenomenon now recognized as globalization, represented by the transnationalization of production, therefore induces the reproduction of capital within different states through a process of *internalization* between various class fractions within states (Poulantzas, 1975, pp. 73–6). Seen in this way, globalization and the related emergence of transnational social forces of capital and labour has not led to a retreat of the state. Instead, there has unfolded a restructuring of different forms of state through an internalization within the state itself of new configurations of social forces expressed by class struggle between different (national and transnational) fractions of capital and labour (see Chapters 5, 7). This stress on both internalization and internationalization is somewhat different from assuming that various forms of state have become simple 'transmission belts' from the global to the national. Finally, Cox (1992, pp. 30–1, 2002, p. 33) has made clear that the internationalization of the state and the role of transnational elites (or a *nébuleuse*) in forging consensus within this process remains to be fully deciphered and needs much more study. Indeed, the overall argument concerning the internationalization of the state was based on a series of linked hypotheses suggestive for empirical investigation (Cox, 1993/1996, p. 276).

Further criticisms have also focused on how the hegemony of transnational capital has been over-estimated and how the possibility for transformation within world order is thereby diminished by neo-Gramscian perspectives (Drainville, 1995). For example, the focus on elite agency in European integration processes by Gill and van Apeldoorn would indirectly reinforce a negative assessment of labour's potential role

in resisting neo-liberalism (G. Strange, 2002). Analysis, notes André
Drainville (1994, p.125), 'must give way to more active sorties against
transnational neo-liberalism, and the analysis of concepts of control
must beget original concepts of resistance.' It is therefore important, as
Paul Cammack (1999) has added, to avoid overstating the coherence of
neo-liberalism and to identify materially grounded opportunities for
counter-hegemonic action. All too often, a host of questions related
to counter-hegemonic forms of resistance are usually left for future
research, although the demonstrations during the 'Carnival Against
Capitalism' (London, June 1999), mobilizations against the World Trade
Organisation (Seattle, November 1999), protests against the IMF and
World Bank (Washington, April 2000 and Prague, September 2000), and
'riots' during the European Union summit at Nice (December 2000), as
well as the G-8 meeting at Genoa (July 2001), all seemingly further
expose the imperative of analysing globalization as a set of highly contested social relations. Overall, while the point about a lack of empirical investigation into concrete acts of resistance is correct in many
instances, it should not be exaggerated either. It has to be noted that an
analysis of the current power configuration of social forces does not by
itself strengthen this configuration nor does it exclude an investigation
of possible resistance. Rather, the analysis of hegemonic practices can be
understood as the absolutely essential first step towards an investigation
into potential alternative developments; and resistance can only be successfully mounted if one understands what precisely needs to be resisted.
Moreover, several neo-Gramscian attempts dealing with issues of resistance have now been formulated and provide fertile avenues for further
exploration (see Bieler and Morton, 2004; Cox, 1999; Gill, 2000, 2001;
Morton, 2002). The primary task of critical scholarship is, therefore, to
clarify resistance to globalization (Cox, 2002, p. 42).

The final and most recent criticisms arise from the call for a much
needed engagement by neo-Gramscian perspectives with the writings of
Gramsci and thus the complex methodological, ontological, epistemological and contextual issues that embroiled the Italian thinker
(Germain and Kenny, 1998). This emphasis was presaged in an earlier
argument warning that the incorporation of Gramscian insights into IR
and IPE ran 'the risk of denuding the borrowed concepts of the theoretical significance in which they cohere' (H. Smith, 1994, p. 147). To commit the latter error could reduce scholars to the accusation of 'searching
for gems' in the *Prison Notebooks* in order to 'save' IPE from a pervasive
economism (Gareau, 1993, p. 301). To be sure, such criticisms and warn-
ings have rightly drawn attention to the importance of remaining

engaged with Gramsci's own writings. Germain and Kenny also rightly call for greater sensitivity to the problems of meaning and understanding in the history of ideas when appropriating Gramsci for contemporary application. In such ways, then, the demand to remain (re)engaged with Gramsci's thought and practice was a necessary one to make and well overdue. Yet the demand to return Gramsci to his historical context need not prevent the possibility of appreciating ideas both *in* and *beyond* their context. Rather than the seemingly austere historicism of Germain and Kenny's demands, which limit the relevance of past ideas in the present, it is possible to acknowledge the role played by both past forms of thought and previous historical conditions in shaping subsequent ideas and existing social relations (Morton, 2003a). This method pushes one to consider what might be historically relevant as well as limited in a theoretical and practical translation of past ideas in relation to alternative conditions. It is this approach that has also been the backdrop to a fuller engagement across the realms of political and international theory on the thought and practice of Antonio Gramsci (Bieler and Morton, 2006a). Overall, though, what matters 'is the way in which Gramsci's legacy gets interpreted, transmitted and used so that it [can] remain an effective tool not only for the critical analysis of hegemony but also for the development of an alternative politics and culture' (Buttigieg, 1986, p. 15).

Notes

1. It is worth noting that, whilst the Keynesian welfare state form is referred to by Cox as the 'neoliberal state', this precedent is not followed. This is because confusion can result when using his term and distinguishing it from the more conventional understanding of neo-liberalism related to processes in the late 1970s and 1980s, which he calls 'hyperliberalism'.
2. It is noteworthy that the metaphor of a transmission belt has been withdrawn from more recent work (Cox, 2002, p. 33).
3. James Scott (1998) has extended this awareness in an interesting way by encompassing a variety of state naming practices, or 'state simplifications', that enhance the legibility of society.

3
Neo-Gramscian Hegemony and the International Order

Peter Burnham

\१९९१

This chapter was originally published in 1991. The reason for reprinting the original text is not, of course, that it is incapable of improvement but rather that as the first serious engagement with neo-Gramscian theory the piece has a certain cogency and is of interest as it stands. In terms of the further development of the Open Marxist alternative to neo-Gramscian theory, the reader is directed to chapters 4, 6, 8, 10 and 11 in this volume by Peter Burnham and Werner Bonefeld.

Outside the cloistered academic world of American political realism the theory of hegemonic stability is dead. This fatality is the product not only of a sustained theoretical critique, which has questioned its adequacy as a theory of collective action, as a theory of economic behaviour and as a theory of economic decline (see Guerrieri, 1988; Snidal, 1985; S. Strange, 1987). An increasingly large array of historical evidence (Burnham, 1990; Harper, 1986; Milward, 1984) gleaned from recently available primary sources – the so-called revisionist view of reconstruction – has undermined an image of the post-war order as one in which a hierarchy of dominance was established amongst states by the direct exertion of United States hegemony understood in a behaviourist 'power over' or 'crude basic force' sense.

Whilst of course the United States and the Soviet Union have, in the post-war period resorted to direct military intervention to re-establish 'imperialist colonial possession', it is equally clear that America's role in the reconstruction of Western Europe cannot be reduced to the exercise of such dominance. Neither is it feasible to argue that the United States unilaterally imposed its dominance over Western Europe in this behavioural sense through economic leverage rather than direct military intervention. Although clearly an intention of early American foreign economic policy this strategy had largely been abandoned by 1950 in the face of subtle but concerted resistance from the major Western European nations orchestrated primarily by Britain.

In partial recognition of the deficiencies of the realist notion of hegemony when applied to world orders, a sophisticated attempt has been made to reconstitute the concept in a self-consciously Gramscian fashion. The aim of this chapter is to assess the explanatory power of the neo-Gramscian version of hegemony when applied to the study of international orders. I am not therefore interested in tracing the lineage of the concept or the extent to which this usage is a correct reading of Gramsci. The aim is rather to assess whether the application of the neo-Gramscian concepts of hegemony, historic bloc, extended state and civil society as developed by such writers as Robert Cox and utilized by the 'Amsterdam school of international relations'[1] provide the basis for a sophisticated understanding of the global inter-state system.

Beyond international relations theory?

The most rigorous adaptation of Gramsci's thought to the study of the contemporary global political economy has been undertaken by Robert Cox and presented in his impressive analysis of the role of social forces in the making of history (Cox, 1987).

Cox's approach to the study of international relations is informed by a critical philosophy, which aims to identify the potential for structural transformation and the determination of breaking points between successive structures, which would, it is assumed, enable an organized working class to advance the struggle for the overthrow of capitalism. His framework is oriented to a study of strategic consciousness and ideology formation at the ruling class level linking such formation to the historical cycle of successive world orders. This ambitious project is a valuable attempt to escape the theoretical bankruptcy of state-versus-society centred political realist analysis, which as Halliday (1989) plausibly argues, is a Social Darwinism on an international scale, shorn of its explicit racism.

The notion of hegemony developed by Cox out of Gramsci's fragmentary *Prison Notebooks* (Gramsci, 1971) is located within the discourse of 'transnational historical materialism'. This affords a structural concept of power wherein the constitution of a stable order is the result of a manufactured compatibility between dominant ideas, institutions and material capabilities. In a move evocative of the Parsonian model of dyadic interaction structured around 'pattern variables', Cox theorizes that all structure is the outcome of interaction between these three variables (ideas, institutions and material capabilities) each of which possesses a real autonomy – 'no determinism need be assumed' (Cox, 1986, p. 218). Hegemonic structures are distinguished from non-hegemonic inasmuch as those in control of institutions do not predominantly resort to the use of force since the controlled accept the prevailing power relation as legitimate. This acquiescence is strengthened if the controllers make concessions to the dominated and express their leadership in terms of a universal general interest. Whilst the power basis of hegemonic structures is thus implicit, the management of power relations in non-hegemonic orders is always to the forefront.

At the international level, Cox's abstract triad is translated into the historical study of social forces generated by the production process, forms of state derived from state–society complexes and world orders – each level interrelated but with no universal causality assumed. Historical phases are thereby identified when a coherent fit has occurred between material power, the development of collective world images and the administration of an order through a set of institutions claiming universality. These are hegemonic phases – periods of relative stability in the international order – distinguishable from non-hegemonic phases where 'states advance and protect the interests of particular national social classes' (Cox, 1987, p. 8), no single power can establish its legitimacy and international instability is the result.

Initially Cox theorized world hegemony as an outward expansion of internal national hegemony established by a dominant social class. In this reading world hegemony is not simply another order but one in which a dominant mode of production, culture and system of social institutions penetrates all countries within an orbit exploiting subordinate modes of production – 'world hegemony is describable as a social structure, an economic structure, and a political structure; and it cannot simply be one of these things but must be all three' (Cox, 1983, pp. 171–2). As an analysis of the material capabilities (economic and political power) of nation states related to the cycle of *pax hegemonica* the neo-Gramscian approach is barely distinguishable from a sophisticated neo-realist account.[2] It simply yields a reading of the last 100 years as 1845–75 – hegemonic; 1875–1945 – non-hegemonic; 1945–65 – hegemonic; 1965–present – non-hegemonic (Cox, 1983, p. 170).

For its advocates however the real inspiration of this adaptation of Gramsci lies in the exhortation to consider global structural changes and world orders in terms of 'the dynamics and dialectics of their normative (ethical, ideological, practical) as well as their material dimensions' (Gills and Law, 1989). The precursor to the creation of a hegemonic order is therefore the formation of a 'historic bloc' organised around a set of hegemonic ideas – a 'dominant ideology', which temporarily forms the basis for an alliance between social classes. A successful bloc is thereby politically organized through the exercise of 'intellectual and moral leadership' and forms the organic (long-term) as opposed to conjunctural (short-term) link between political and civil society. For neo-Gramscians, the state is held to comprise not only the machinery of government but also aspects of 'civil society' – press, church, mass culture – which stabilize existing power relations. The emergence of a new historic bloc is the result of conscious planned struggle. Employing this 'extended concept of the state' – machinery of coercion plus machinery for the organization of consent (Cox, 1987, p. 409) – it is argued that a new bloc is not established by capturing the state but is established through the articulation of 'persuasive ideas and arguments (Gramsci's 'ethico-political' level), which build on and catalyse its political networks and organisations' (Gill and Law, 1989, p. 476). A hegemonic world order therefore emerges out of the successful formation of an international historic bloc of social forces, which in turn is premised upon the articulation of a dominant ideology accepted by subordinate classes. This international historic bloc is not simply a cross-national alliance of capitalist interests. Its success rests on the incorporation and persuasion of the working class to accept as legitimate a new institutional context and its associated values.

Seen from this perspective the implementation of the post-war Keynesian structure of accumulation rested on the articulation of the ideals of the corporate liberal international historic bloc, which incorporated fractions of capital, the state and labour movement representatives in a trans-Atlantic alliance. Similarly, it is argued that the implementation of a 'new regime of accumulation' depends ultimately on the attainment of a new transnational hegemony organized around the monetarist celebration of capital domination, free enterprise and open markets, inasmuch as 'the broad contours of any new regime of accumulation will be partly shaped by the ideological climate at the national and international levels' (Gill and Law, 1989 p. 489).

Pluralism revisited

The pioneering application of Gramscian concepts to the international level in addition to the related writing of the 'Amsterdam School' (Overbeek, 1990; van der Pijl, 1984) represents an important attempt to re-cast academic international relations on a wider inter-disciplinary footing.

In its present form however, the neo-Gramscian approach in its frantic attempt to escape the twin evils of 'economism' and idealism offers little more than a version of Weberian pluralism oriented to the study of the international order. The Weberian approach to the social order is committed to accepting both the structural variability and the historical specificity of data. Variables which comprise a social order – the economy, the polity and civil society – are given no overall structure but rather each has a real autonomy which precludes over-determination. This position is often championed by neo-Weberians as offering a methodology, which has no preconceived image of society or its patternings and thus displaces both reductionism and theoreticism. Weber usefully summarizes his 'middle way' between economism and idealism when he says that 'not ideas but ideal and material interests directly govern men's conduct. Yet very frequently the "world images" that have been created by "ideas" have, like switchmen, determined the tracks along which action has been pushed by the dynamic of interest' (Weber, 1948, p. 280). This factor approach is reflected in Cox's analysis to the effect that in the interaction between material capabilities, ideas and institutions, no determinism exists, and relationships are reciprocal. The question of lines of force is a historical one to be answered by a study of the particular case. *(Weberian .)*

However laudable in theory, the true consequence of this position is to produce a pluralist empiricism which lacks the power to explain either the systematic connection between values, social relations and institutions or the extent to which the historical appearance of capital as a social relation transforms the social order in such a way that all relations are subsumed under the capital relation as the basis of the valorization process. The Weberian framework is rooted in an analysis of social action, which leads to an understanding of individual meanings and motives and the development of a typology of motivational characteristics. Actions are classified not only in terms of typical value orientations but also according to the types of means and end to which they are directed – hence types of action and corresponding organizations must be analysed independently of one another. This approach cannot grasp the complexity of an increasingly interdependent global political economy in which, governed by the law of value, social relations between people take the form of relations between things. The social form of capitalist relations of production invalidates an approach, which simply begins from the individual. The principal substantive defect of Cox's unwitting restatement of pluralist analysis on an international level is that the *species differentia* of capitalism is obscured and the theory therefore remains fundamentally non-propositional allocating equal weight to each and any 'variable'.

An analysis of the inter-state system which recognizes the centrality of the capital relation need not however be conflated with base-superstructure reductionism. The social relations of production are not simply another 'sphere' or 'factor' to be considered alongside normative or ethico-political 'levels'. The capital relation is the basis of valorization process on which the entire edifice of capitalism is constructed. The relations of production are not therefore the economic 'level'. Rather as Marx clarifies in *Wage Labour and Capital* 'the relations of production in their totality constitute what are called the social relations, society and specifically, a society at a definite historical stage of development' (Marx and Engels, 1977, p. 212). The consequence of taking Gramsci's 'revision' of Marx at face value is to end up however unwittingly in the 'post-Marxist' camp struggling to escape an economism which in reality owes more to the Second and Third Internationals than to Marx. In so doing the neo-Gramscian approach displaces an analysis rooted in the contradictions of the capital relation with a pre-occupation on the articulation of ideology. To what extent however is the restructuring of capital, the restoration of the conditions for profitability, or the development of a new 'regime of accumulation', dependent on the articulation of a 'dominant ideology' accepted by subordinate classes in the context of a wider historic bloc?

Ideology and accumulation: the case of post-war reconstruction

An analysis of how the current inter-state system developed in the crucial period of postwar reconstruction leaves little doubt that a neo-Gramscian factor approach necessarily leads to an overestimation of the importance of ideology in economic policy formation. A recent analysis of the pattern of post-war reconstruction inspired by Cox for instance suggests that a Gramscian approach with its emphasis on ideas and culture is better placed to explain certain aspects of inter-state relations than is realist theory (Gill and Law, 1988, p. 79). These authors argue that in terms of a rational calculus of long-term costs and benefits for the United Kingdom, it is difficult to explain the priority given by the United Kingdom to relations with the United States and the Commonwealth at a time when a historic opportunity arose in the shape of the emerging European Community. This apparently irrational choice of policy, they suggest, is fully explained through a 'Gramscian analysis of the nature of the consciousness of the British leadership' (ibid., p. 79). An argument is therefore constructed that the path of British post-war reconstruction was determined largely by the 'world-view of the British ruling classes' with 'Anglo-Saxon cultural chauvin-ism' (perpetuated at institutions such as Harrow) 'at the heart of this world-view' (ibid.). Gill and Law therefore conclude that a congruence existed between hegemonic ideas – the consciousness of the British leadership – dominant material forces (which they document as a pat-tern of British foreign investment and trade focused largely on the United States and the Colonies) which shaped British foreign policy at this time. Similarly, their recent study of the structural power of capital is paradoxically an analysis of the 'tenacity of normative structures' (Gill and Law, 1989, p. 480), which leads to the suggestion that a new regime of accumulation has its roots in the theories of 'organic intellectuals'.

The accentuation of this dimension of neo-Gramscian theory repli-cates the errors identified by Tomlinson (1981) in his discussion of the relation of economic policy to economic theory. The familiar presenta-tion of the rise of a Keynesian accumulation regime, with which neo-Gramscian theory is in accord, suggests that it was introduced as a result of the Keynesian 'revolution' in economic theory cemented by the pub-lication of the General Theory in 1936, overturning the previously dom-inant 'Treasury View' (Howson, 1975). Tomlinson points out that this presentation to which Keynes himself adhered (witness the infamous remark that 'practical men ... are usually the slaves of some defunct economist') implies that economic policy is derived from theory, that 'the history of policy is the history of theory (with lags)' (Tomlinson, 1981, p. 77).

This accentuation of the role of ideology formulated by organic intel-lectuals in determining economic regimes carries with it the proposition that policy is conditioned by the consciousness of the policy maker. The barrier to the implementation of a new regime is the construction and articulation of a new ideology around which a new historic bloc can emerge. At the heart of neo-Gramscian analysis is therefore a slide towards an idealist account of the determination of economic policy. Alternatively, an analysis rooted in the capital relation approach has lit-tle recourse to invocations of the 'nature of consciousness'. Constraints on public expenditure and deficits are not to be conceived as the prod-uct of the ideology of decision makers (Tomlinson, 1981, p. 85). Britain's preference in 1945 for an Atlantic and Commonwealth trading system had little to do with the consciousness of policy makers or the articula-tion of a persuasive ideology. Whilst it is true to suggest that British foreign investment in the United States increased in the latter half of the nineteenth century, this increase mirrored the general growth of the City of London as the world's major commercial and financial centre and the ability of sterling to finance approximately 60 per cent of world trade between 1860 and 1913 (Williams, 1968). The growth of British foreign investment and the extension of British banks into the banking structure of a number of foreign nations, not simply the United States, were concomitantly very high. Joslin (1963) indicates for instance that by 1914 British banks controlled a third of the deposits of the Brazilian banking system and over a quarter of those lodged in Argentina and Chile. Second, with regard to the pattern of British trade it is misleading to claim that 'most of it was in the United States' and the Commonwealth with very little directed to Continental Europe (Gill and Law, 1988, p. 79). Whilst of course following the 1931 crisis in the international monetary system Britain continued to trade heavily with the nations of the Sterling Bloc and, following the outbreak of hostilities in 1939, with the nations of the Sterling Area. Britain from 1910 to 1952 sold no more than 6 per cent of its domestic exports in the United States compared with a figure averaging almost 30 per cent of United Kingdom exports to Western Europe (Milward, 1984 tables 39 and 40). By 1938 the United Kingdom had an import surplus with every European country (except Greece and Turkey) with the flow in particular of European food-stuffs (with grain an exception) chiefly directed to the United Kingdom, who drew 22 per cent of her total food imports from Europe (Burnham, 1990, p. 19).

A neo-Gramscian emphasis on ideas and culture, with the scant and misleading addition of 'dominant material forces', cannot adequately explain the pattern of European post-war reconstruction. The restructuring of accumulation occurs in a context of inter-imperialist rivalry in which nation states seek temporarily to overcome the contradictions of the capital relation, which are manifest in uneven development. A neo-Gramscian approach submerges this focus on the contradictions of the capital relation and leads to the assertion that ideas are to be accorded equal weight to 'material capabilities'. However, continuing the example of post-war reconstruction, it is evident that the primary barrier to rapid accumulation in 1945 was the uneven development of world capitalism, which had produced disequilibrium in production and trade between the Eastern and Western hemispheres. To generate economic growth in 1945 Western Europe needed to construct an international payments system, which would facilitate trade and secure regular import of essential commodities and raw materials. The British state's economic strategy therefore turned on finding a solution to its balance of payments problems which were a manifestation of this disequilibrium. To expand the economy the state had to meet its existing balance of payments deficit (huge sterling balances and other accumulated liabilities since 1939) in addition to finding extra dollars to pay for imports of essential materials abundant only in the United States. The need to maximize accumulation was thus translated into the need to accumulate world currency. Britain's strategy was to construct an international payments system, which allowed maximum commodity trade in inconvertible sterling whilst minimizing the outflow of dollars needed for purchases in the United States. The British state's path to 1951 through the Washington Loan Agreement, the 1947 Convertibility crisis, the Marshall Plan, sterling devaluation in 1949 and Korean rearmament in 1950, was thus one bound by material constraints, which were themselves products of uneven world development. These constraints – expressed directly in balance of payments crises – ruled out the viability of taking the European route. This is clearly shown in the episode of the Washington agreement where, in response to Richard Clarke's suggestion (from the Overseas Finance Division of the Treasury) to build a European group instead of accepting a US loan, Keynes sardonically observed: 'from which countries can we expect to borrow what we have failed to obtain from the United States? ... the alternative is to build up a separate economic bloc which excludes Canada and consists of countries to which we already owe more than we can pay, on the basis of their agreeing to lend us money they have not got and buy from us and from one another goods we are unable to supply' (Keynes, 1979).

It was not therefore contending theories but fluctuations in the balance of payments, which determined at what pace the British state would adopt multilateral trade and payments arrangements. European integration and the scrapping of Commonwealth relationships were materially inconceivable for the state since the viability of this route rested on the slow restructuring of production and trade to support generalized currency convertibility. The British state's strategy was a response to the particular nature of uneven material development as it stood in the world economy in 1945. Strategic options were tightly circumscribed by this uneven development. The international restructuring of accumulation occurs in a context of inter-imperialist rivalry in which nation states struggle to overcome the contradictions of the capital relation. In obscuring this point the professed strength of neo-Gramscian analysis is in fact its greatest weakness. Taking the case of reconstruction as an example it is clear that when assessing the determinants of restructuring the starting point remains Marx's injunction in the *1859 Preface* that,

> just as our opinion of an individual is not based on what he thinks of himself, so can we not judge ... a period of transformation by its own consciousness; on the contrary, this consciousness must rather be explained from the contradictions of material life, from the existing conflict between the social forces of production and the relations of production. (Marx and Engels, 1987, p. 263)

The attempt to move beyond 'economism' has the result that ideas, institutions and material capabilities are accorded equal weight. Analysis is thereby, reduced to a pluralist factor study, which offers a misleading appraisal of how capitalist social relations are reproduced and how capitalist crises are resolved. If it is believed that the transition from one 'regime' to another is largely a matter of constructing a historic bloc this obscures that the basis for the resolution of crisis is laid in the sacrifice of inefficient capitals as the means to further accumulation – as Weeks clarifies, 'the same process that makes crisis necessary also provides for recovery, renewed accumulation' (Weeks, 1981). The foundation for a theory of the inter-state system lies therefore in a study of the material conditions, which foster restructuring.

To put the point simply, capital does not wait for the articulation of the ideology of monetarism before restructuring. The articulation of ideology is important for the political legitimization of a set of policies that by and large have already been implemented. The contradictions of the capital relation and the nature of competition in the world market determine the path and the pace of particular state strategies. They are not determined by groups of organic intellectuals gathered in cloistered circles, who then produce a policy, which state officials decide to implement. This latter idealist account of policy implementation is a type of pluralism, which sees the state as at the behest of external pressure groups; only, in this case, membership of the groups is restricted solely to fractions of the ruling class. In neo-Gramscian analysis, the focus is shifted from identifying the specific form of the contradictions of the capital relation to the question of how a ruling class fraction can articulate an ideology to win the hearts and minds of other capital fractions, the working class and key state personnel. Aside from the realization that accumulation regimes are simply different 'modes of domination' (London Edinburgh Weekend Return Group, 1979) in which the working class are either 'included' merely on an ideological level or transparently excluded as in the monetarist form, the structural dynamics of capitalism make recourse to the role of ideas clearly subordinate in an analysis of restructuring. Neither, as sociology has striven to grasp for the last 25 years, does the systemic integration of capitalism depend on the social integration of individuals.

Capitalist reproduction, ideology and integration

In presenting the argument that the historic bloc is the organic link between structure and superstructure organized around a set of hegemonic ideas comprising the dominant ideology (Gill, 1986, p. 210), the neo-Gramscian framework falls foul not only of a mechanistic interpretation of Marx but offers a version of normative functionalism long discarded even by academic sociology. The major contribution for instance of Erving Goffman is to show that there is a considerable potential separation between the practices individuals sustain in day-to-day social reproduction and the overall symbolic order normatively sanctioned by dominant groups. As Giddens (1981, pp. 65–6) usefully summarizes, the taken-for-granted cannot inevitably be equated with the accepted-as-legitimate.

Drawing on Althusser, Giddens' account of ideology carries a sophistication, which eludes the neo-Gramscian presentation. Cox (1986, p. 218) sees ideology as a set of shared notions of the nature of social relations or as collective images of the social order. However an analysis of 'beliefs about' how society is constituted obscures a focus on the ideological effects of material practices. The notion of a 'dominant ideology' consisting of shared beliefs legitimating a social order is thoroughly discredited on both empirical and theoretical grounds (see e.g. Abercombe *et al.*, 1980). In its place is the understanding that in principle some of the most potent forms of ideological mobilization 'do not rest upon shared beliefs (or shared normative commitments); rather they operate in and through the forms in which day to day life is organised' (Giddens, 1981, p. 68). This understanding of the ideological effects of material practices has its roots in Marx's observation that capitalist reproduction is achieved largely through the 'dull compulsion of economic relations'. Marx's ironic double freedom, whereby as a free individual, a worker can dispose of his/her labour power as his/her commodity, whilst on the other hand he/she has no other commodity for sale – a worker is 'free of all the objects needed for the realisation of his labour-power' (Marx, 1976a, p. 273) – clearly indicates that capitalism

does not rely on the *social* integration of individ·
exists only as a capacity of a mortal individual wh
poses the daily reproduction of the means of subsiste.
labour power must therefore appear continuously in the ⅃
only means within capitalism of securing material reproductiσ.
the importance of Marx's prefatory methodological remark thaι
standpoint from which the development of the economic formation oι
society is viewed ... can less than any other make the individual responsible for relations whose creature he remains ... however much he may
subjectively raise himself above them' (ibid., p. 92). Individuals are to be
theorised primarily as bearers of social relations, and it is only by utilizing this framework, crudely and incompletely constructed by Ricardo,
that Marx could elaborate a sophisticated labour theory of value
whereby the creation of new value takes place not by the virtue of the
particularities of labour (spinning, joinery, jewel-making), but because it
is labour in general, abstract social labour – 'and we see also that the
value added is of a certain definite amount, not because his labour has a
particular useful content but because it lasts for a definite length of time'
(ibid., p. 308).

The systemic integration of capitalism is achieved as the working
class, as bearers of social relations, sell their labour power in order to
meet their subsistence requirements. Theories of incorporation and integration, of which the dominant ideology thesis is one, rely on the
famous 'over-socialised concepts of man' (see the still-pertinent essay by
D. Wrong, 1961). The working class have no normative commitment to
capitalism, there is no social integration beyond the brittle bond of the
callous 'cash nexus' which is liable to snap in recession. The explanatory
power of the concept of an international historic bloc pales therefore
before the twin realization that recovery from crisis is inherent in the
process of capitalist reproduction and that the systemic integration of
capitalism is not dependent on the internalization of shared norms
understood in terms of a dominant ideology.

Conclusion: towards a theory of the international state

The neo-Gramscian approach to the world order seeks to replace state-
centred frameworks with a study of class forces and their operation in
national–international contexts. Nevertheless, the international order
is still primarily one of politically constructed nation states, which
provide both the domestic political underpinning for the mobility of
capital and offer rudimentary institutional schemes aimed at securing

ernational property rights as a basis for the continued expansion of apital (Chase-Dunn, 1981). Whilst during the twentieth century the dominant force for global economic internationalization has been the transnational corporation (see Picciotto, 1988, 1990), TNCs clearly favour an inter-state system founded on nation state imperialist rivalry. TNCs rely not only on the services provided by nation states in terms of internal security and the reproduction of a compliant working class; they also favour competition between nation states to enhance the structural power of transnational capital. The scramble of nation states to attract TNCs to their shores highlights this structural power which is further evidenced in the 'political and economic risk analysis' undertaken by TNCs in appraising concessions and inducements offered by nation states.[3]

It is a fallacy therefore to suppose that the importance of the nation state in the world order has diminished with the rapid internationalization of capital. The starting point for a productive analysis of the international order is thus the recognition of the durability of the nation state – in other words, it is incumbent upon analysts to develop a theory of the international state. The elements of such a theory are not to be found in Weberian pluralism or Realist transhistorical pronouncements on the nature of power. Rather they are to be developed from the capital relation approach to the state (see Holloway and Picciotto, 1977, 1978b), which recognizes that historically the 'apparent separation' of the polity and the economy is bound up with the rise of capitalism as a distinct set of social relations. Whilst there remains an urgent need for a detailed historical analysis of the rise of Western European states, the strength of the capital relation position is that it dispenses with the tautologous relative autonomy debate and posits both logically and historically (insofar as present research allows) the internal and necessary implication of the state in the social relations of production. This is not however to conflate state and capital in the manner characteristic of neo-Gramscian approaches as developed in their most sophisticated form by the 'Amsterdam school' of international relations.

Drawing on Gramsci, both van der Pijl (1984) and Overbeek (1990) develop the notion of a 'comprehensive concept of control', which represents the unity of a critical mass of interests forming the basis for a new programme and the constellation of (national and international) economic and class forces providing the structural context in which interests are politically articulated. A concept of control, therefore represents a bid for hegemony: a project for the conduct of public affairs and social control which transcends narrowly defined fractional interests and which 'combines mutually compatible strategies in the fields of labour relations, socio-economic policy and foreign policy on the basis of a class compromise entailing specific economic and/or ideological rewards for the dominated classes and class fractions involved' (Overbeek, 1990). In essence such 'concepts' are similar to Gramsci's notion of a historic bloc. Serving as the rallying point for a fraction of the ruling class and capable of attracting a mass following, a concept is potentially hegemonic if it combines satisfactory blueprints for the handling of relations between fractions of capital. For the Amsterdam theorists, concepts of control can be defined 'from certain ideal-types related to the functional perspective of specific capital fractions' (van der Pijl, 1984 p. 8). These ideal types reflect the vantage point of circulating and productive capital respectively and are developed as the 'money-capital' and the 'productive-capital' concepts of control from which 'historically specific, and increasingly synthetic, strategies for adjusting bourgeois rule and international relations to the ongoing process of internationalisation were developed' (ibid., p. 9). By way of concrete example, van der Pijl argues that when productive capital is in crisis the money-capital concept presents itself as the obvious, rational solution – 'it is this correspondence between the objective state of capitalist society and the particular solution proposed by a single class-fraction (in this case the bankers and owners), which allows the rest of capitalist society a view of the whole which under other circumstances only bankers have; hence, which makes for bankers' class consciousness to crystallise and gain the upper hand' (ibid., pp. 33–4).

Consequently, this neo-Gramscian approach apparently renders a theory of the state redundant. A new accumulation strategy is the result again of conscious planned struggle organized by intellectuals from the vantage point of capital fractions articulating a particular ideal, which incorporates other elements of the ruling class, the state and the representatives of the working class. Both state and working class struggle therefore recede from view in this approach since state strategy is explained as the outcome of fractional struggles, which take place in cloistered ruling class circles by invitation only, such as the meetings of the Trilateral Commission, the Mont Pelerin Society and the Bilderberg conferences. The consequence of this approach is the view that an accumulation strategy pursued by the state can be explained as the outcome of a fractional struggle. As Clarke (1990) identifies, this merely moves pluralism one step further back since the restructuring of the forms of the state and of political representation are seen as the result of class and fractional conflicts which take place outside of the confines of the existing institutional forms of politics, so that there is a kind of 'state behind the state'.[4] This type of fractionalist account is beset with the familiar problems of representation and calculation.[5] Put briefly, whilst fractional interests may be represented in policy making, this process can never simply be reduced to such representation. Similarly, the way in which any group conceives of its interest is always ambiguous and open to revision. The analysis of post-war reconstruction cited above highlights the inadequacy of attempting to understand the development of an accumulation strategy in terms of the primacy of the political rather than one rooted in the imperatives which accumulation imposes on the particular form of the capitalist state.

The state as an aspect of the social relations of production must be seen at one remove from the interests of particular capitals since the form of the state dictates that its role is to address the contradictory foundations of accumulation in the guise of meeting the interests of capital-in-general. The conceptual distinction between particular capitals and capital-in-general is as Rosdolsky (1977, pp. 51–3) points out, not only the key to understanding the *Grundrisse* and *Capital*, it also represents first and foremost a blueprint without which Marx's entire economic system could not have been developed. It is clarified in the *Grundrisse* that 'capital-in-general is no mere abstraction. If I regard the total capital of, for example, a nation, as distinct from total wage labour (or landed property), or if I regard capital as the general economic basis of a class as distinct from another class, then I regard it in general' (Marx, 1973, p. 852). The Gramscian inspired view that state policy is the result of ruling class fractions deciding a line which is then either forced on or chosen by state officials sanctions an autonomous view of the state released from the constraints inherent in its form as an aspect of the social relations of production. The example of post-war reconstruction clearly indicates that the state is neither autonomous nor external to accumulation as is implied by Cox (1987, p. 5) when he argues that the state is 'content empty' and can, 'consecrate a type of production relation as the dominant, legitimate, hegemonic form'. State strategy cannot be at the behest of a capital fraction, since the state embodies the power of capital-in-general against the direct demands of particular capitals. 'Just because individuals seek only their particular interest, which for them does not coincide with their communal interest ... the latter will be imposed on them as an interest "alien" to them, and "independent" of them, as in its turn a particular, peculiar "general interest" ' (Marx, 1964, pp. 45–6).

In terms of the overall circuit of capital, although there is an inter-dependence between capitals both in production and circulation this relationship is obscured in competition – the locomotive force of the bourgeois economy in which everything is presented in an inverted fetishised form – as capitals seek by whatever means to secure the highest rate of return. The conflictual interests of particular capitals in competition are mediated through the mechanism of the market. The reproduction of total social capital (and paradoxically of particular capitals) therefore depends on the subordination of all particular capitals to the authority of the market. In this way, the state meets the interest of capital-in-general by enforcing the discipline of the market through the rule of law and the rule of money.[6] The significant point is that within the capitalist system there is no other basis for the formation of the general interest other than the state. The state therefore does not have a political autonomy. Rather its role is to express the general conditions of accumulation and devise overall economic strategy. Whilst this may favour particular capitals, at specific points, this is an unintended consequence of policy and there is no necessary relation to their political representation. If we take a further example from the post-war period, it is often argued[7] that the City of London forced its policies on the state to the long-term detriment of productive capital. But this overlooks the fact that the restoration of sterling was essential to restore productive capital, and far from acting as the fifth columnist it was the City and the Treasury with an interest in the restoration of sterling that offered the most resistance to American multilateral objectives. State strategy was therefore directed to restoring the conditions for general profitability.

The form of the capitalist state therefore delineates its role as removing barriers to accumulation – barriers realised as financial crises. In developing a strategy to expand accumulation the limits of state action are determined by the fact that such a strategy is constrained by an existing pattern of economic development, which is a legacy of uneven world development. The neo-Gramscian analysis of the international order at face value seems to hold out great potential for an insightful analysis of the inter-state system. On closer inspection however it simply offers a pluralist analysis of global capitalism, which overemphasizes the role of ideology in economic policy and regime formation, illegitimately invokes the dominant ideology thesis and fails to specify its implicit fractionalist theory of the state. By contrast, the capital relation approach to the state provides the elements from which a theory of the international state can be formulated as the basis for understanding the contemporary global inter-state system.

Notes

1. For an overview of the 'Amsterdam' perspective on international relations see van der Pijl (1984) and Overbeek (1990).
2. See for instance a similar account of *pax hegemonica* cycles in Keohane (1984) and Gilpin (1987).
3. Gill and Law (1989) p. 484 provide some interesting observations on this 'political and economic risk analysis'.
4. For a more general critique of fractionalism, see Clarke (1978).
5. Tomlinson (1981) discusses such problems.
6. This interpretation of Marx is rigorously presented by Clarke (1988).
7. An example of this misconceived argument is found in Fine and Harris (1986).

4
Social Constitution and the Spectre of Globalization
Werner Bonefeld

Introduction

Adam Smith was certain in his own mind that capitalism creates the wealth of nations and noted that

> 'the proprietor of stock is properly a citizen of the world, and is not necessarily attached to any particular country. He would be apt to abandon the country in which he was exposed to a vexatious inquisition, in order to be assessed to a burdensome tax, and would remove his stock to some other country where he could either carry on his business, or enjoy his fortune more at his ease' (1981, pp. 848–9).

Ricardo (1995, p. 39) concurred, adding that 'if a capital is not allowed to get the greatest net revenue that the use of machinery will afford here, it will be carried abroad' leading to 'serious discouragement to the demand for labour'. According to Hegel, the accumulation of wealth renders those who depend on the sale of their labour power for their social reproduction, insecure in deteriorating conditions. He concluded that despite the accumulation of wealth, civil society will find it most difficult to keep the dependent masses pacified, and saw in the form of the state the means of reconciling the social antagonism, containing the dependent masses. This containment might be advanced by 'successful wars' to prevent 'the civil broils' (Hegel, 1896, §324). Marx developed this insight, arguing that the political character of bourgeois society is concentrated in the form of the state and that the rule of equality, of equal rights, is in its social contents a right of inequality: 'The power which each individual exercises over the activity of others or over social wealth exists in him as the owner of *exchange value*, of *money*. The individual carries his social power, as well as his bond with society, in his pocket' (Marx, 1973, pp. 156–7). What is the contemporary meaning of these insights?

Globalization has come to the fore as the key concept of contemporary analyses. Some see globalization to amount to a decline in state authority (Strange, 2004), for others state authority is indispensable to its success (Wolf, 2004). Strange argues that globalization has undermined the autonomy of the state to regulate economic relations on the basis of the national interest, and Wolf that the free economy requires the strong state to depoliticize social relations on the basis of the rule of law. Leaving aside the political implications of these contrasting views, both agree that globalization has restrained the democratic character of the liberal-democratic state to its liberal foundation.

Neo-Gramscian definitions of globalization do not fare much better. For example, Robinson (2004, p. 2) sees globalization as an 'epochal shift' towards a new capitalist formation. He agrees with Gill (2003, p. xii) that this formation is characterized by the 'creation of the world market'. Whereas in the past the national state enjoyed 'relative autonomy' over its economy (cf. ibid., p. 109), globalization effectively cancels such a state-centric regime of accumulation, and instead of a nationally anchored capitalism of 'Keynesian redistribution' (cf. Robinson, 2004, p. 42), globalization indicates a capitalism where the 'power of capital attains hegemonic status' (Gill, 2003, p. 105). As Robinson (2004, p. 11) explains, the phase of a purely national economy that served 'national interests' had been superseded by an international economy where national economies were intertwined through state-sponsored relations of trade and commerce. Now this inter-national system is replaced by a truly global economy that substitutes the many national economies with a single economy, the global economy. Thus, it becomes impossible to discern the national interest, everyday activity becomes dependent on global forces, and people are enmeshed in global networks of 'complex connectivity' (ibid., p. 2). This, then, is the so-called transnationalization of capitalist social relations, which is the 'result of clear agency, operating with the structural conditions of transnational production and finance' (Bieler and Morton, 2004, p. 309). The agency in question is the transnational class: 'a group of people who share a common relationship to the process of social production and reproductions, constituted relationally on the basis of social power struggles' (Robinson and Harris, cited in ibid.). In short, 'the globalizing elites' are seen as the 'directive element in globalizing capitalism' (Gill, 2003, p. 154) and they thus embody capital's attainment of hegemonic status.

In the past, the state was the 'political determinant of class formation' (Robinson, 2004, p. 42) and the political master of 'intra-class as well as inter-class struggle' (Gill, 2003, p. 179). Leaving aside Gill's notion of capitalist competition as class struggle between capital and capital, globalization changes the role and function of the state. It no longer formulates 'national policies' and instead administers 'policies formulated through supranational institutions' (Robinson, 2004, p. 101). Thus, helped on by 'transnational cadres' (ibid.), it now serves the 'general needs of the new pattern of global accumulation' (ibid., p. 75). Still, this new pattern is contested by 'emerging forms of political agency associated with struggles over the nature and direction of globalization that I call "the Post-modern Prince" ' (Gill, 2003, p. 211). The post-modern attribute of this new dialectics of transnational structure and transnational agency is well captured by Bob Jessop. He argues that 'globalization is best understood to denote a multicentric, multiscalar, multitemporal, multiform, and multicausal process' whose scales are 'no longer ... in a neat hierarchy' but are 'co-existing and interpenetrating in a tangled and confused manner'. As a consequence, globalization is 'multicausal because it results from a complex, contingent interaction of many different causal processes ... the complex, emergent product of many different forces operating on many scales'. In sum, the global economy is the 'fast economy' that 'privileges the executive over the legislature and the judiciary, finance over industrial capital, consumption over long-term investment' (Jessop, 2001). While Jessop's view is clear at least in its representation of 'complex connectivity', Gill summons myth. As he sees it, post-modern refers to 'new forms of political agency whose defining myths are associated with the quest to ensure human and intergenerational security on and for the planet, as well as democratic human development and human rights' (Gill, 2003, p. 211). Why Gill should see these important human values as 'mobilizing myths' (ibid., p. 221) is difficult to discern – unless his summons is read as a salute to Althusser's (1996) post-Stalinist view that the human subject exists, if it exists at all, only as myth.

Gill's and Jessop's accounts echo Robert Cox's earlier formulation according to which globalization transforms the state into a 'transmission belt' (Cox, 1992, p. 32; see also Robinson, 2004, pp. 109, 124, 125). Although Cox (2002) no longer uses this metaphor, and in their contributions to this volume, Andreas Bieler and Adam Morton appear to distance themselves from it, the debate on the transnational state owes its inspiration to it (see Burnham, 2000).[1] As Cox put it, the state has become 'a transmission belt from the global to the national economy, where heretofore [before the onslaught of globalization] it had acted as the bulwark defending domestic welfare from external disturbances' (Cox, 1992, p. 31). The transnationalization of the state entails its transformation into a 'competition state' (Cerny, 1990) – a state that is charged with providing comparative advantages of 'exploitative conditions' (cf. Gill, 2003, p. 102). In the past, it seems, the state had relative autonomy over the economic and the economy was national in character and was regulated by state on the basis of the national interest. Now that the economy has 'globalised' itself, the economy is said to have autonomy over the political.[2] Again, Robert Cox provides the succinct formulation upon which this insight rests: The competitive logic of capital on a world scale entails the

'subordination of domestic economies to the perceived exigencies of a global economy. States willy-nilly became more effectively accountable to a *nébuleuse* personified as the global economy; and they were constrained to mystify this external accountability in the eyes and ears of their own publics through the new vocabulary of globalization, interdependence, and competitiveness' (Cox, 1992, p. 27).

Cox thus argues that domestic relations, including the national state, have become accountable to something invisible – to a *nébuleuse*. Cox's view has much to commend it by, especially his conception of the global economy as a *nébuleuse*. He does however not show the social constitution of this invisible mist. The *nébuleuse* is not a category of critical reason. Just like the deist conception of the market as something regulated by an invisible hand, his attempt to discover the practical meaning of misty principles ends up as an irrational exercise because what needs to be understood is presupposed as something beyond the grasp of reason and thus comprehension. This presupposition thus precludes understanding of capital as a social relationship of 'Man himself in his social relations' (Marx, 1973, p. 600); and instead purports that human social practice unfold within an extra-mundane framework that is both objectively given and invisible. What, then, is the social constitution of this invisible world?

The question of social constitution is of central importance. It does not ask how capital manages to 'attain hegemonic status' in a capitalist society. Rather, it asks about its social constitution. It thus does not affirm the existence of human beings as mere agents of abstract social laws. Instead, it asks about the social constitution of these laws and it thus asks why humanity exists as a mere personification or agent of abstract laws. It seeks to determine what Adorno (1971) called the 'constituted conceptuality' of social laws, including the law of capital and its state. It conceptualizes the dynamic of capitalist development not as some sort of periodic shedding and attainment of new capitalist formations. Instead it takes the dialectics of dynamic and stasis seriously and it therefore focuses on the dialectics of social law: 'The law is what remains in disappearance' (Gadamer, 1976, p. 42). Whatever the specific historical form of capitalism, the law of value remains, as does the law of capital and its state.[3] The chapter focuses on the 'social law' of the world market. It does not challenge the notion that the capital relation is a global relation. It asks about its social constitution. The next sections introduce Marx's account on the world market and analyse his critique of fetishism as a critique of the world market. The final section examines the relationship between the world market and crises, and the conclusion summarizes the argument in relation to the role and function of the state.

Marx and the world market

Marx never wrote his planned books on the state and the world market. Nevertheless, his writings and a brief look at various outlines of his work reveal that both, the state and the world market are always present. In his outline of 1857, the world market is posed as the final and concluding part of his investigation, coming after the international relation of production and 'the concentration of bourgeois society in the form of the state' (Marx, 1973, p. 108). Furthermore, the anticipated examination of 'crises' is associated with the projected study of the world market. The theme, then, is 'the world market and crises'. Moreover, following his outline, the world market is distinct from the inter-national relations of production. His outline suggests that capitalist crises can be conceptualized adequately only in a global dimension and that the global relations of capital do not equate with the inter-national relations between states.

For Marx, the projected study of the 'world market and crises' is more than just the final book of his investigation. Rather, it is the conclusion where all contradictions of bourgeois society come into play and as such manifest themselves in their most concrete materiality. This view is supported by Marx's conceptual argument that 'as a rule, the most general abstractions arise only in the midst of the richest possible concrete development, where one thing appears as common to many, to all. Then it ceases to be thinkable in a particular form alone' (Marx, 1973, p. 104). In other words, all and everything subsists not only in relation to the world market but, fundamentally, in and through the world market. Marx's critique of political economy points, time and time again, towards the world market as the proper mode of existence and movement of the capital relation. As he argues in volume III of *Capital*, the world market is 'the basis and the vital element of capitalist production' (Marx, 1966, p. 110). It is the presupposition and result of the reproduction of capitalist social relations.

The notion of the world market as the 'basis' of capitalist production raises the question of the distinctive difference between the 'international' relations of interdependency and world market relations. The insight that capitalist production is unthinkable without foreign trade (Marx, 1978, p. 456) seems to suggest that the 'world market' is coterminous with the inter-national state system. However, the 'relations of industry and trade within every nation are dominated by their intercourse with other nations, and are conditioned by relations with the world market' (Marx, 1968, p. 149), and 'money' takes off its 'national uniform' when it reaches the world market (Marx, 1983, p. 125). This suggests that the world market is not the sum of many states and their 'national economies', but that it is instead the condition through which exists the inter-national relations between states. The world market is thus posed as the universal form of capitalist existence, and that is, nationally located industry acquires its livelihood as capitalist industry only through the world market form. The world market is posed as the 'categorical imperative' of capitalist production within national borders, between national borders and beyond national borders. Furthermore, as such an imperative, trade and industry within national borders amount, at the same time, to trade and industry beyond national borders. The productivity, then, of 'domestic' labour acquires its livelihood in and through the world market. It is this market that suffuses, confirms and contradicts the 'domestic' exploitation of labour and it is in and through the world market that labour acquires validity as socially necessary labour. Therefore, 'the entanglement of all people in the net of the world market, and with this, the international character of the capitalist regime' (Marx, 1983, pp. 714–15) entails that whoever wants to speak about the division of labour has to speak about the world market (Marx, 1977, p. 550). The domestic division of labour entails the global division of labour, the former cannot be conceived of without the latter: the domestic division of labour subsists through the global division of labour.

Marx's account of the global division of labour does not depend on Ricardo's idea of 'comparative advantages'. Ricardo seeks to render the 'complexity' of the inter-national relations of production coherent and capable of rational organization through schemes of a mutually advantageous national specialization of production. Marx does not focus on inter-national comparative advantages but, rather, on the equalization of the rate of profit on a global scale. This equalization 'compares' the productive labour set to work within industry with the productive labour of all other industries, leading to the determination of an average rate of profit. This average rate of profit obtains as the average world market rate of profit. This equalization and averaging entails the unleashing of the 'heavy artillery' of cheaper prices (cf. Marx and Engels 1997, p. 17) upon national states should the exploitation of labour within their jurisdiction fall below the average world market rate of profit. This heavy artillery makes itself felt through pressures on the exchange rate, the accumulation of balance of payments deficits and drains on national reserves. It is through the movement of money capital that the global conditions of accumulation impinge on 'national economies'. World money is not only a means of exchange or a means of payment; it obtains, fundamentally, as a power that polices the effectiveness of the 'domestic' exploitation of labour (see Bonefeld, 1996).

The circumstance that the equalization of the rate of profit obtains at the world market means that the domestic productivity of labour is valid in terms of value only in and through the 'global' conditions of exchange. The existence of the world market, then, presupposes 'a very developed totality of real kinds of labour, of which no single one is any longer predominant' (Marx, 1973, p. 104). This general 'indifference' towards any specific kind of labour' means that the category of labour has become in reality 'the means of creating wealth in general, and has ceased to be organically linked with particular individuals in any specific form' (ibid.). In sum, the emergence of labour in its most simple form as abstract labour not only 'requires the fullest development of the most modern society' (ibid., p. 105) it, also, establishes the world market as the basis, premise and continuously reproduced result of the capitalist relations of production. In short, 'the tendency to create the world market is directly given in the concept of capital itself' (ibid., p. 408). The commodity, as Marx (1981b, p. 128) argues, is in and for itself beyond every religious, political, national and linguistic barriers. Its language is 'price' and its community is the abstract wealth that money represents. Thus, capital, whether in terms of commodity capital, money capital, or productive capital, does neither have a national character nor a patriotic affiliation. Its patriotism is money and its language is profit, and that is, 'the private interest within each nation divides itself into as many nations as it has "fully grown individuals" ' (Marx, 1973, p. 159). The 'market', then, does not obtain as a 'national' market but, and with necessity, as a world market (see Marx, 1981b, p. 128).

The term 'bourgeois society' does not stand, and has never stood, for a 'national' society. The attribute 'national' indicates some sort of homogeneity of interest and shared values, a homogeneity that is neatly summoned by the metaphor of the 'one national boat' (cf. Reich, 1991). Much analysis of globalization does indeed rest on the idea that such an integrated 'national' society existed before globalization started a process of economic 'denationalisation', leading to a society that is 'increasingly fractured on socio-economic lines' (Hirsch, 1997, p. 46).[4] However one might wish to assess, *inter alia*, Reich's image of a one-national past, the metaphor of a one national boat stands, since Roman times, for a conservative conception of an 'organic' or 'corporate' society where everybody regardless of 'position' fulfils socially valid tasks: the majority rowing the minority navigating. The notion, then, that globalization undermines the inter-national state system of 'one national economies' that are governed by the one-national states in the pursuit of their respective national interests makes as little sense as the idea that globalization fractures and divides the once nationally integrated society along 'class lines' (cf. Bonefeld, 2000).

The term 'bourgeois society' stands, from its inception, not only for a class-divided society but, also and because of this, for the global freemasonry of capital. Following Marx, 'just as money, general exchange, subsists as world money, as global exchange, so the owner of commodities, the bourgeois, is a cosmopolitan' (cf. Marx, 1981b, p. 128). In the *Communist Manifesto*, the life of the bourgeoisie is portrayed in terms of the global existence of capital: old industries are destroyed and replaced by new industries whose introduction is a question of survival within the global system of production and the division of labour, 'giving a cosmopolitan character to production and consumption in every country' (Marx and Engels, 1997, p. 16). The notion, then, of a 'national economy' makes little sense; it is a regressive concept that lends itself, at best, to ideas of national developmental methods associated with the theory and practice of economic nationalism (List, 1904) or, at worst, to the reactionary and romantic ideas and practices of nationalism (cf. Bonefeld, 2005b). Of course, protectionism was and still is a very powerful device to protect a 'national economy'. However, neither is the national economy independent from the world market nor does it merely exist in relation to the world market. Rather, the national economy subsists in and through the world market. Protectionism, then, amounts merely to a 'measure of defence *within* free trade' (Marx and Engels, 1970, p. 78).

Marx's investigation shows that the first moment of the capitalist state is also the first moment of generalized commodity production.

Generality, however, obtains only as universality. The emergence of 'capital' as the dominant production relation entails the emergence of a world where separate and distinct histories become subsumed and condensed into a single world history 'insofar as it made all civilised nations and every individual member of them dependent for the satisfaction of their wants on the whole world' (Marx and Engels, 1970, p. 78). Marx's projected book on the world market as the conclusion of his critique of political economy indicates, then, that the world market is the presupposition, premise and result of the capitalist exploitation of labour.

In sum, capital has been from 'its birth a global power' (Clarke, 1988, p. 178). This insight is of fundamental importance because it highlights that 'the world market, international capitalism, the global system of social relations that has grown up for the first time in history' emerged at the same time as the national state (Barker, 1978/1991, p. 205). In this way, then, 'the question of the national integration of the state could not be divorced from that of the integration of the international state system' (Clarke, 1988, p. 179). The emergence of the national state 'originated as an international system of states' (Picciotto, 1991a, p. 218), a 'system' of inter-state relations that is founded on 'the international relations of production; international division of labour; international exchange and import; rate of exchange' (Marx, 1973, p. 108). Furthermore, this inter-state system existed, from its inception, within the 'global context of production and exchange' (von Braunmühl, 1978, p. 163). In other words, the 'world market is integrated into the national economy' (ibid., p. 168). The world market is not the sum of distinct national economies. Nor is it a recent force that has undermined the integrity of national economies. Such 'integrity' never existed inasmuch as the world market is the 'categorical imperative' of 'national economies'.

World market and fetishism

The previous section argued that the world market is a historical precondition of capitalist social relations. The 'creation in the 16th century of a world-embracing commerce and a world-embracing market' laid the 'historical ground-work' from which the capitalist social relations emerged (Marx, 1983, p. 145). Once capital was established as the dominant production relation, the historical precondition of its genesis transformed into the presupposition and result of its continued reproduction. 'The expansion of foreign trade, although the very basis of the capitalist mode of production in its infancy, has become its own product, however, with the further progress of the capitalist mode of production, through the innate necessity of this mode of production, its need for an ever-expanding market' (Marx, 1966, p. 237). The world market forms the 'basis for this mode of production'; it is the historical foundation of capital as well as its continued result (ibid., p. 333).

However, the capital relation 'can spring into life only when the owner of the means of production and subsistence meets in the market with the free labourer selling his labour-power' (Marx, 1966, p. 167). The separation of labour from its means is the constitutive presupposition of capitalist social relations (cf. Bonefeld, 2002b). Behind the liberation of the social individual from relations of personal dependency, the rule of objective conditions obtains: 'Individuals are now ruled by *abstractions*' and these abstractions subsist in the form of objective world market conditions that 'are independent of the individual and, although created by society, appear as if they were *natural conditions*, not controllable by individuals' (Marx, 1973, p. 164). The divorce, then, of labour from its conditions entails not only the complete independence of the individuals from one another but, also, their complete dependence on the seemingly impersonal relations that the world market presents. Thus, the independence of the individual is an 'illusion, and so more accurately called indifference' (ibid., p. 162). Their independence is that of atomized market individuals that are 'free to collide with one another and to engage in exchange within this freedom' (ibid., pp. 163–4); and their indifference to each other is that of human factors of production whose social existence as individuals appears to derive from objective conditions and their laws of development. Their connection as social individuals appears to be constituted by impersonal relations, by the things themselves. The world market, then, appears to create a 'spontaneous interconnection, a material and mental metabolism which is independent of the knowing and willing of individuals, and which presupposes their reciprocal independence and indifference' (ibid., p. 161). The liberation of the social individual from feudal relations of personal dependency is thus overcome in as much as these relations of personal dependency are transformed into relations of objective dependency.

The commodity-form appears as the substitute for the missing self-conscious organization of social labour. It appears to produce the interconnection between 'the individual with all' other individuals (Marx, 1973, p. 161). Social cooperation appears, thus, in the form of objective relations of dependency. Although produced by them, their cooperation appears in a form that is independent from and beyond the control of individuals. As Marcuse (1988, p. 151) put it, 'the constitution of the world occurs behind the backs of the individuals, yet it is their work'.‖ Marx conceived of the world market as the most developed form of individual interconnectedness and interdependence. The apparent autonomization of the value form acquires, then, a livelihood in the apparent 'autonomisation of the world market' (Marx, 1973, p. 160) from the social individual. The 'general foundation of all industry comes to be general exchange itself, the world market, and hence the totality of all activities ... of which it is made up' (Marx, 1983, p. 141). The world market includes thus not only 'the activity of each individual' (ibid.) it is, also, '*independent* of *this connection from the individual*' (ibid., p. 161). Human social practice appears thus as a vanishing moment of a social reality that it itself produces but over which it has no control. Social reality appears thus to be constituted by the actions of the things themselves, as if these were a person apart. This appearance is real. Human social practice does indeed disappear in the substance of its own perversion, and appears thus as a mere agency or personification of economic categories (cf. Bonefeld, 1995, 2001b).

Nevertheless, the notion of the world market as an objective coercive force makes sense only on the assumption that the appearance of social objectivity entails the 'immediate and direct proof of the general laws' of capitalist social relations. The conception of the world market as a thing in-itself abstracts 'from the *conditions, the conditions of existence* within which these individuals enter into contact' (Marx 1969, p. 106). It is therefore 'an insipid notion to conceive of this merely *objective bond* as a spontaneous, natural attribute inherent in individuals and inseparable from their nature. ... This bond is their product. It is a historic product' (Marx, 1973, p. 162). Thus, to conceive of the world market in terms of objectively given relations of dependency, and of individuals as mere agents of economic categories, is to derive human social practice from hypothesized social structures whose social constitution remains a mystery – a *nébuleuse* (cf. Cox). Like in the religious idea of God, an incomprehensible but irresistible object assumes subjective power over the social individual, as if it were a person apart. This object needs to be deciphered on a human basis to bring its social constitution to the fore, and that is, the reified world gives back to Man what Man has put into it.

The social individual is indeed subjected to constant coercive pressures emanating from the world market. At the same time, however, these pressures are 'brought out of him by his labour'. Free labour, commodified labour, is capital's presupposition, a presupposition that shows itself as '*alien wealth*' (ibid., p. 541). Capital does not compete with capital for nothing. 'Capital can not confront capital if capital does not confront labour, since capital is only capital as non-labour' (Marx, 1973, p. 288). The understanding, then, of the global relations of capital can not go forward through the rationalization of the strategic calculations of particularly transnational banks and multinational companies. It has to go forward through an examination of the relations of exploitation and that is through an understanding of the dependence of capital on labour. Capital cannot liberate itself from labour; it has to confront labour by imposing necessary labour on the world's working classes. Labour 'is and remains the presupposition' of the 'law of capital ... to create surplus labour' (ibid., p. 399). This, then, is the law of capital: to avoid the threat of its own capital-punishment, it is condemned to exploit labour (cf. ibid.). For capital, then, to assert itself as 'non-labour' it has to posit necessary labour (cf. ibid., p. 288). In other words,

'capital forces the workers beyond necessary labour to surplus labour. Only in this way does it realise itself, and create surplus value. But on the other, it posits necessary labour only *to the extent* and *in so far as* it is surplus labour and the latter *realisable* as *surplus labour*. It posits surplus labour, then, as the condition of the necessary, and surplus value as the limit of objectified labour, of value as such. As soon as it cannot posit value, it does not posit necessary labour; and, given its foundation, it cannot be otherwise' (ibid., p. 421).

The world market, then, obtains in and through the capitalist tendency 'to make human labour (relatively) superfluous, so as to drive it, as human labour, towards infinity' (ibid., p. 399). Capital, then, exists in antithesis to necessary labour and at the same time only in and through the imposition of necessary labour. It cannot posit surplus labour without positing necessary labour (cf. ibid.). Labour creates surplus value (cf. Marx, 1966, p. 823) at the same time as it obtains as a wage-labouring commodity that, on the basis of free and equal exchange relations, is at the disposal of capital as the owner of the means of production.

The affirmation of capital as a thing endowed with objective coercive force obscures the social constitution of capital. It does not include '*human* natural force' (Marx, 1973, p. 330). The social character of labour 'does not show itself except in the act of exchange' (Marx, 1983, pp. 77–8) at which time the concrete materiality of capital 'disappears' (Marx, 1987a, p. 497). Capital, as Marx insists, 'only appears *afterwards*, after already having been presupposed as capital – a vicious circle – as *command over alien labour*' (Marx, 1973, p. 330). Exploitation is not visible in the act of equivalence exchange. The disappearance of labour and the appearance of money as the form of self-reproducing value are two sides of the same process that validates social labour by converting it into its opposite, 'into a social hieroglyphic' (Marx, 1983, p. 79). This conversion is a world market conversion. 'It is only in the markets of the world that money acquires to the full extent the character of the commodity whose bodily form is also the immediate social incarnation of human labour in the abstract' (Marx, 1983, p. 141). However destructive to the environment and the worker, capital always carries with it its dependence on labour. Each individual capital is at the same time *the* capital (cf. Reichelt, 2005). Capital posits itself as expanding value in circulation only on the condition that it extracts value from social labour (cf. Marx, 1983, p. 555).

The act of exchange does not explain the generation of the 'thing' that is being exchanged, nor does it explain why the individual producers exist in the way they do. Thus, at best, Ricardo's labour theory of value, following Negri (1992, p. 70), merely shows that 'the development of social labour produces either a process of accumulation of value or a complex norm of distribution'. The secret of the social constitution of value remained unresolved because 'value' was merely conceived as a 'thing' and not as a social relationship. As such a thing, the movement of value manifests itself as an 'automatic' movement, 'acting with the force of an elemental natural process' as if it were an 'independent thing' (Marx, 1978, p. 185) that is historically active and stands above and so structures social relations, and that therefore appears as an irresistible force in its own right. However, 'value' is this independent thing only if looked at merely in terms of its formal mode of movement, that is in terms of the 'fetishism of capital, as a value-creating-thing' (Marx, 1966, p. 829). This fetishism is due to the circumstance that 'all of labour's social productive force appear to be due to capital, rather than labour as such' (ibid., p. 827). There is no doubt that human social practice subsists in and through the world of commodities where 'the person objectifies himself in production [and] the thing subjectivies itself in the person' (Marx, 1973, p. 89). There is, however, no 'form' without 'content' (Marx, 1983, p. 78, 1966, p. 392). To argue that form exists without content is to say that 'form' is external to its own social constitution. Like the notion of the world market as an objectively coercive thing, the notion of 'value' as a 'form' without 'content' espouses the religion of bourgeois society: commodity fetishism.

Marx's critique of fetishism shows that the derivation of human social practice from 'the action of objects' (Marx, 1983, p. 79) reformulates the doctrine of the invisible hand. That is, social existence obtains within a framework of objective economic laws whose rationality structures and imposes itself 'objectively' on the protagonists and sets in motion the decisive conditions of economic adjustment, but whose social force appears to derive from uncontrollable extra-mundane properties. Social reality appears thus to be governed by something beyond comprehension and that is, social practice is derived from something that transcends human understanding and transformative power. Cox's idea of the world market as a *nébuleuse* and Gill's summons of myth as the mobilizing force of human agency are two sides of the same coin. As Horkheimer (1985, p. 84) has argued, one of the blind spots of dogmatic thought is the separation of genesis from existence. Indeed, if capital is endorsed as a constituted thing, its dynamic appears to derive from a blind and impersonal 'system-logic' to which the social individual has to accommodate and conform in order to stay alive. Dogmatism refuses to understand the social world we live in as a world constituted in and through human social practice, however perverted this practice might be in the form of capital. The reality in which the social individual moves day in and day out has no invariant character, that is, something which exists independently from it. Thus the critique of political economy amounts to a conceptualized praxis (*begriffene Praxis*; cf. Schmidt, 1974), that is, an understanding of the totality of human social practice, which constitutes and contradicts the world of capital.

Therefore, in order to understand the working of the world market, one has to descend from its objective coercive existence (*Dasein*) to an analysis of the social relations of production; from the sphere of circulation to the constitution of value; from the object-less existence of labour to the relationship between necessary and surplus labour; and from the exploitation of labour to capital's dependency on labour's value-creating power. One thus has to conceptualize the displacement of production towards the world market and, conversely, the constitution of the world market as the perverted (*ver-rückte*) form of human social practice, a practice in which humanity exists in the mode of being denied and that is, it vanishes in its own social world and appears as a personification of economic categories.[5] This vanishing appearance of Man as a mere object of his own social world lies at the heart of the law of capital. In short, the existence of the social individual as an exploitable resource is as real as the circumstance that capital is nothing without human social practice.

Capital, in short, is a 'living contradiction' (Marx, 1973, p. 421). The entire development of '*human productive forces*, i.e., wealth' (Marx, 1966, p. 540), 'proceeds in a contradictory way' (ibid., 541). Its universal mode of existence is the world market, and it is through the world market that labour's productive power acquires validity in the form of value. The world market is thus the form 'in which production is posited as a totality together with all its moments, but within which, at the same time, all contradictions come into play. The world market, then, forms the presupposition of the whole as well as its substratum' (ibid., pp. 227–8). As such a substratum, the world market hides the constitution of value through labour and, in fact, shows the direct opposite of this constitution. It is as if 'Monsieur le Capital and Madame le Terre do their ghost-walking as social characters and at the same time directly as mere things' (Marx, 1966, p. 830).

In sum, understanding the world market as a global space founded on the separation of labour from the means of production (and emancipation), entails that the world market constitutes the 'totality of the activities, intercourse, needs, etc., of which it is made up' (ibid., p. 426). The category of the world market is, thus, not a category amongst others. It is 'at once the pre-condition and the result of capitalist production' (Marx, 1972, p. 253). As such it is the substratum through which all other categories of Marx's critique of political economy subsist (von Braunmühl, 1978). 'The world market is the presupposition of all and the support of the whole' (Negri, 1984, p. 63). The presupposition of the world market is human labour whose productive power exists against itself in the form of relations between things. However, these relations are not an objectively given. Instead, the 'abstraction of the category of "labour", "labour as such", labour pure and simple, becomes true in practice' (Marx, 1973, p. 105) in these relations. Thus, and as the next section argues, the world market is like a screen upon which the contradictory constitution of capital, its crisis-ridden dependency on labour, is magnified, long before it comes to the surface domestically.

World market and crises

The circumstance that the equalization of the rate of profit obtains at the 'level' of the world market means that the individual capitalist 'always has the world-market before him, compares, and must constantly compare, his own cost-prices with the market-prices at home, and throughout the world' (Marx, 1966, p. 336). In order to preserve its existing capital-value, each capitalist has constantly to expand 'his capital, in order to preserve it, but extend it he cannot, except by means of progressive accumulation' (Marx, 1983, p. 555). The risk is bankruptcy. Thus, mediated through competition capital is spurred into action.[6] 'Fanatically bent on making value expand itself, [the personified capitalist] ruthlessly forces the human race to produce for production's sake' (ibid.). The sacrifice of 'human machines' on the pyramids of accumulation entails that

'labour capacity has appropriated for itself only the subjective conditions of necessary labour – the means of subsistence for actively producing labour capacity, i.e. for its reproduction as mere labour capacity separated from the conditions of its realization – and it has posited these conditions themselves as *things, values*, which confront it in an alien, commanding personification' (Marx, 1973, pp. 452–3).

Capitalist crisis is, however, not simply a crisis of overproduction or underconsumption, nor is it merely a crisis of capitalist overaccumulation where too much 'capital' confronts saturated world markets (see, Clarke, 1994). What restricts capitalist production 'is not commerce (in so far as it expresses the existing demand), but the magnitude of employed capital and the level of development of the productivity of labour' (ibid., p. 336). The investment required to put labour to work increases the cost price of production, which, even under conditions of a rising rate of exploitation, tends to decrease the rate of profit. This is so because of the rising value of constant capital (means of production) relative to variable capital (labour power).

Capital is thus 'limited by its very nature' inasmuch as the '*development of human productive forces*' (Marx, 1973, p. 540) liberates social labour relative from production through the revolutionizing of its productive force. Thus, capital contradicts itself because it 'restricts labour and the creation of value … and it does so on the same grounds as and to the same extent that it posits surplus labour and surplus value. By its nature, therefore, it posits a *barrier* to labour and value-creation, in contradistinction to its tendency to expand them boundlessly' (ibid., p. 421). The contradiction between the relations and forces of production subsists, thus, in the '*relation between necessary labour and surplus labour* that is … the relation between the constitutive parts of the working day and the class relation which constitutes it' (Negri, 1984, p. 72). While capital can do no other than revolutionize the productive power of labour in order to preserve itself as capital, the increase in labour's productive power renders capitalist accumulation crisis-ridden. Although the worker 'regards the development of the productive power of his own labour as hostile to himself' (Marx, 1969, p. 573), it is the development of labour's productive power that sets limits to the preservation of capital through expanded accumulation.

To recap, the revolutionizing of labour's productive power entails a 'relative decrease of the ratio of variable to constant capital' (Marx,

1966, p. 249). This decrease indicates the development of the social productivity of labour (ibid., p. 213). Less living labour is needed to produce
the same amount of commodities. While labour's productive power
increases, the cost price of production grows in terms of constant capital relative to variable capital, the value constituents representing necessary labour. The tendency of the rate of profit to fall, including the
countertendencies to its fall, 'is identical in meaning' (Marx, 1973,
p. 749) with the development of the productive power of labour. Crisis,
then, signals not just the overaccumulation of capital but, also and
importantly, expresses the 'contradiction between the capitalist tendency to develop the forces of production without limits, and the need
to confine accumulation within the limits of the social relations of
production' (Clarke, 1989, p. 142). A fall in the rate of profit can, of
course, be compensated by the devaluation of capital, the bankruptcy
of producers, liquidation of so-called excess productive capacity, mass
unemployment, the concentration and centralization of capital in fewer
and fewer 'hands', and through an 'ever expanding market' (Marx,
1966, p. 237).

There is, thus, the tendency of capital to create ever more and more
points of exchange and to develop the world market further through the
'exploration of all of nature in order to discover new useful qualities in
things; new universal exchange of the products of all alien climates and
lands; new (artificial) preparations of natural objects by which they are
given a new use-value. The exploration of the earth in all directions'
(Marx, 1973, p. 409). Furthermore, this exploration goes hand-in-hand
with attempts to annihilate space through time. In distinction to contemporary ideas that globalization is driven by some sort of law inherent in modern technology, the formation of new technology that
replaces space by time is a social process. 'Circulation time is a barrier to
the reproduction of labour – an increase in necessary labour time – a
decrease in surplus labour time' (ibid., p. 539). Thus, the development of
more and more modern means of communication in order to be present
in all markets at all time. Equally, the expansion of credit-relations
allows the creation of 'ever more surplus labour' (ibid., p. 408) by reducing the time productive capital is suspended in circulation or by bridg-
ing the gap between the investment requirements of productive capital
and the profits acquired in exchange.

A fall in the rate of profit can also be offset by an increase in the mass
of profits. Such an increase requires the realization of a growing mass of
commodities – the 'economics of scale' is a countertendency to 'declining' rates of profits. This insight is emphasized by the debate on globalization in terms of the worldwide operation and power of multinational

companies. However, capital is capital only as non-labour and that is, 'the means of production become capital only in so far as they have become separated from the labourer and confront labour as an independent power' (Marx, 1963, p. 408). In the course of capitalist reproduction, the separation of labour from its conditions is a continuously reproduced separation. The separation 'begins with primitive accumulation, appears as a permanent process in the accumulation and concentration of capital, and expresses itself finally as centralisation of existing capitals in a few hands and a deprivation of many of their capital (to which expropriation has now changed)' (Marx, 1966, p. 246). The circumstance that big fish eat small fish does not render obsolete the understanding of capital as a definite social relation 'entered into by individuals in the process of reproducing their life' (ibid., p. 819). It merely shows that the terror of separation, of capitalism's original beginning, weighs like a nightmare on human social practice.

Capitalist crises assert themselves in the form of 'unemployed' capital that has become divorced from productive engagement, and that has therefore spilled over into speculative channels seeking profitable returns through interest-bearing investment or currency speculation, etc. 'The so-called plethora of capital always applies essentially to a plethora of the capital for which the fall in the rate of profit is not compensated through the mass of profit – this is always true of newly developing fresh offshoots of capital – or to a plethora which places capitals incapable of action on their own at the disposal of the managers of large enterprises in the form of credit' (Marx, 1966, p. 251). It is this plethora of capital that, for Susan Strange (1997a, 1998) and others, characterizes the new faced capitalism of globalization. However, the so-called predominance of finance capital represents an accumulation of capital that cannot be converted into direct productive activity. Hence, 'unemployed capital at one pole and unemployed workers at the other' (Marx, 1966, p. 251). The sustaining of overaccumulation through credit-expansion implies a potentially disastrous speculative deferral of 'economic' crisis on a global scale. This is because money capital accumulates in the form of a potentially worthless claim on future surplus value. The solidity and very existence of money capital is endangered insofar as a progressive deterioration of the relation between credit and exploitation renders capital, in its elementary form of money, potentially 'meaningless' (see ibid., p. 393).[7] In sum, the divorce of monetary accumulation from productive accumulation obtains as a mortgage on the future, a speculative gamble over the future exploitation of labour. This gamble indicates that the strength of the tie between capital and

labour is loosening: the less credit-expansion is supported by the generation of surplus value through the exploitation of labour in the present,
the more the credit-structure is at risk of losing its grip on the very source
that renders it valid as a form of abstract wealth.

There is, then, no doubt that capital can divorce itself from labour.
However, this divorce is more ideal than real. The contradictory unity of
surplus value production reasserts itself in 'M ... M' – 'the meaningless
form of capital, the perversion and objectification of production relations in their highest degree, the interest-bearing form, the simple form
of capital, in which it antecedes its own process of reproduction' (Marx,
1966, p. 392). It appears, then, as if the 'social relation is consummated
in the relation of a thing, of money, to itself' (ibid., p. 392). However,
'interest is only a portion of the profit, i.e. of the surplus-value, which
the functioning capitalist squeezes out of the labourer' (ibid.). In sum, in
the form of money capital assumes the form of an 'automatic fetish' and
we see 'only form without content' (ibid.). However, although in
'M ... M' the relation to labour as the substance of value is seemingly
eliminated, the expansion of monetary accumulation exists as a 'claim
of ownership upon labour' (Marx, 1966, p. 476), that is as a claim on a
portion of future surplus value. The divorce, then, of monetary accumulation from productive accumulation indicates the crisis of capital's
innate necessity of imposing necessary labour on the working class on a
global scale. The circumstance that capitalist production is sustained by
credit-expansion and debt, including its recycling, indicates the speculative dimension of capitalist accumulation, and that is, the fictitious
integration of labour into the capital relation itself. Monetary panic and
industrial crash are two sides of the same coin.

Capital, then, might well go beyond its dependency on necessary
labour. However, 'from the fact that capital posits every such limit as a
barrier and hence gets *ideally* beyond it, it does not by any means follow
that it has *really* overcome it' (Marx, 1973, p. 410). Thus, the world market represents '*an ever broader process of the constitution of the average
rate of profit* and it is here that the contradiction inherent in profit, the
antagonism of its constituted forces, imposes itself' (Negri, 1984,
p. 120). The world market is the terrain where the contradictory constitution of capital, its dependence on and anti-thesis to necessary labour,
asserts itself as a crisis of credit, as speculative pressure on national currencies, and in terms of financial turmoil and industrial crisis. The other
side of the divorce of monetary accumulation from production accumulation is the potentially irredeemable accumulation of unemployed capital, of debt. Marx (1966, p. 438) characterized this situation as 'the

abolition of the capitalist mode of production within the capitalist mode of production itself'. Within capitalist society, this contradiction can be contained only through force (*Gewalt*) including not only the destruction of productive capacities, unemployment, worsening conditions and widespread poverty but, also, the destruction of human life through war and starvation. Thus,

> 'society suddenly finds itself put back into a state of momentary barbarism; it appears as if famine, a universal war of devastation had cut off the supply of every means of subsistence; industry and commerce seem to be destroyed; and why? Because there is too much civilisation, too much means of subsistence; too much industry, too much commerce. The productive forces at the disposal of society no longer tend to further the development of the conditions of bourgeois property; on the contrary, they have become too powerful for these conditions, by which they are fettered, and so soon as they overcome these fetters, they bring disorder into the whole of bourgeois society, endanger the existence of bourgeois property. The conditions of bourgeois society are too narrow to comprise the wealth created by them. And how does bourgeois society get over these crises? On the one hand by enforced destruction of a mass of productive forces; on the other, by the conquest of new markets, and by the more thorough exploitation of the old ones' (Marx and Engels, 1997, pp. 18–19).

'Globalization' does indeed represent such a forceful process of 'adjustment'. It is therefore hardly surprising that its advocates demand better and stronger states to guarantee its safe conduct through 'honest and organized coercive force' (Wolf, 2001).

Conclusion

The chapter has argued that the purpose of capital is to make profit and that the state is the political expression of this purpose. The debate on the transnationalization of the state is based on the presupposition that the state had relative autonomy over 'its' national economy in the past. It is on the basis of this presupposition that the novelty of globalization is discussed. This presupposition is based on misleading premises. First, it suggests that exploitation of labour within a nationally organized space is based on some sort of 'national harmony' of interest: the 'national interest'. The claim that the 'national relations of exploitation' constituted a national harmony should be dismissed as, at best, nonsense or, at worst, deceitful publicity. Second, it assumes that the 'limits' to 'national harmony', to 'national wealth', are *not* constituted in and through capital's dependence on labour, that is, the dialection between the forces and relations of production. Rather, 'national wealth' is seen to be limited by external forces that disrupt the integrity of 'national economies'. Thus, 'disharmony' is merely 'imported' from the outside. In his critique of Carey's economic nationalist ideas, Marx argues forcefully that 'these world-market disharmonies are merely the ultimate adequate expressions of the disharmonies which have become fixed as abstract relations within the economic categories, or which have a local existence on the smallest scale' (Marx, 1973, p. 887). In other words, global 'disharmony' exists in and through 'domestic relations' and *vice versa*. Capitalist relations of exploitation do not exist in terms of two sets of relations, that is as relations of domestic harmony and, distinct from these, as relations of global disharmony. As the quote from Marx makes clear, the 'world-market form' is the mode of existence of domestic relations, and conversely, domestic relations subsist in and through world market relations. Thus, the concept of 'national wealth' makes no sense. Wealth is not created to 'enrich the state' or the 'nation'; nor is it the purpose of the state to produce wealth (cf. Marx, 1973, p. 108). The purpose of the state is entailed in its form – it is a capitalist state, and because of this, it represents the 'common good' of a capitalistically constituted form of social reproduction. Regardless of its historically changing forms (Agnoli, 1997; Clarke, 1992), the function of the capitalist state has always been to secure the 'common interests' of a capitalistically organized form of social reproduction: capital accumulation.

The national state, then, is the 'harmonies' last refuge' (Marx, 1973, p. 886) – the harmonies of abstract equality, abstract freedom, Bentham and liberty. The wage relation subsists through these harmonies, and the state is their concentrated political force. It is charged with eliminating any doubt about their veracity. The depoliticization of bourgeois society as a society of private interests entails the concentration of its political character in the form of the state. The divorce of labour from the means of production appears thus not only in the form of bourgeois freedom, that is in the form of contractual relations between formally equal partners in exchange, but also in the form of the state that guarantees and sanctions the equality of each individual regardless of the inequality in property. Behind the relations of liberty, equality, freedom and Bentham, lays the doubly free labourer and the concentration of the means of production and subsistence in the hands of capital. Behind the guarantee of formal freedom and abstract equality lies the guarantee of exploitation – once the wage contract is signed, the factory floor beckons.

In sum, the nation state cannot be understood in abstraction from the world-market society of capital (cf. Burnham, 1996, and chapter 3 in this volume). Neither is the state an 'independent being which possesses its own *intellectual, ethical and libertarian bases* (Marx, 1968, p. 28), nor can its class character be 'defined in national terms' (Clarke, 1992, p. 136). Its class character is entailed in its form-determined purpose to protect the capitalist law of property and contract. This protection secures the freedom of labour from the mean of production and it does so by safeguarding its freedom as wage-labour – a living commodity. That is, the 'sine qua non of the existence of capital' – the 'perpetuation of the labourer' (Marx, 1983, p. 536) – attains political existence in the form of the state. In distinction to the idea that state purpose depends on the balance of class forces, the state is not a state in capitalist society. It is a capitalist state. Finally, it makes no sense, as John Holloway (2003) has pointed out, to see capital as a thing that can be owned, exchanged, moved from one place to another, applied in that industry or in another, transformed into money and moved from one country to another. Such affirmation of capital as a 'thing' and of the state as an 'actor' that is either accountable to or in control of this 'thing', leads to nowhere except to the view that the state has somehow become 'accountable to a *nébuleuse* personified as the global economy'. Roset Cox focuses the constituted fetish of the world market well but cannot tell us what it is.

Notes

1. Their 'distancing' is however only one of degree. As they see it, the state pursues a neo-liberal agenda not because of emergent structural 'transnationalisations' or 'global economic structures' but because the 'transnational nucleus' of a given national society (cf. Morton, Chapter 7) is said to have captured the national state. Politically, they thus agree with Panitch's (1994) notion that a shift in the balance of class forces is required to overcome neo-liberal globalization in favour of labour (see Bieler and Morton, Chapter 2). The state is thus central, especially since its relationship to society is deemed to be fundamentally neutral: depending on the balance of class forces it can be used for capitalist purposes or socialist purposes. Once the purpose of the state is thus determined, it operates as the public authority of these interests, 'authoring' (Panitch) either 'neo-liberal globalisation' or 'redistribution in favour of labour'. The state is thus central because it is deemed to be a 'transmission belt': it allows the 'transmission' of particular social or class interests that have captured the state to society as a whole.
2. For a critique of conceptions of 'relative autonomy', see Clarke (1991b), Holloway and Picciotto (1978b) and Bonefeld (1992).

3. For a critique of periodization along these lines, see Bonefeld and Holloway (1991), Clarke (1992).

4. In contrast, some other commentators, for expample Boyer and Drache (1996), Hirst and Thompson (1999) Ruigrok and van Tulder (1995), Weiss (1998) and Panitch (1994, 2000) argue in favour of what Radice (2000) has termed 'progressive nationalism' – a state-centric account of globalization as something that remains state-dependent, and according to Panitch is authored by states, and where the state therefore retains the power to hold the global down. Of these authors, it is only Panitch who argues for a decisive socialist strategy. He calls upon the Left to 'reorient strategic discussions … towards the transformation of the state' (Panitch, 1994, p. 87), so as to achieve 'a radical redistribution of productive resources, income and working time' (ibid., p. 89). Panitch envisages a form of economic development that combines national protectionism with economic planning and redistribution of wealth from capital to labour. His socialist version of a domestic Keynesianism appears persuasive – yet appearances are often deceptive and on closer inspection tend to reveal themselves as myth (Radice, 1984).

5. On the meaning of 'perversion' as a movement where the subject vanishes in the object of its creation, see Backhaus (1992, 2005).

6. See Brenner (1998, 2002) for an argument that competition, rather than mediating, is in fact at the heart of capitalism's crisis-ridden development. For critique, see Bonefeld (1999) and Lebowitz (1999), amongst others.

7. In the German original, Marx uses the term *begriffslose* form. In the English edition of *Capital*, *begriffslos* is translated as 'meaningless'. This translation is misleading. I use the term from here in terms of 'losing its grip' on labour – a loss that renders money as a form of value fictitious. On this, see Bonefeld (1996).

Part II
State, Capital and Labour

5
European Integration and Eastward Enlargement
A Historical Materialist Understanding of Neo-liberal Restructuring in Europe
Andreas Bieler

Introduction

From the mid-1980s onwards, European integration experienced a drastic revival around the Internal Market and Single European Act (SEA) as well as the Treaty of Maastricht. Enlargement rounds including Austria, Finland and Sweden in 1995 and the accession of additional ten countries from Central and Eastern Europe as well as the Mediterranean area in 2004 intensified European integration further. Neo-Gramscian perspectives were initially applied to concerns around structural change and hegemony in the global economy within the disciplinary confines of International Political Economy (IPE). Since the early to mid-1990s, however, they have also been increasingly applied to questions relating to European integration. After first attempts by Cox (1993), Gill (1992) and Holman (1992), more comprehensive neo-Gramscian analyses of individual instances of integration followed (van Apeldoorn, 2002; Bieler, 2000; Bieler and Morton, 2001b; Bieling and Steinhilber, 2000; Cafruny and Ryner, 2003). Within the general Open Marxist literature too, considerable work has recently been directed towards understanding the processes underlying European integration (see, for example, the contributions in Bonefeld, 2001c; Carchedi, 2001; Moss, 2000). In close relation to the overall purpose of this book, a neo-Gramscian analysis of the revival of European integration will be developed in this chapter through a critical engagement with Open Marxist explanations of these events. In the analysis of the deepening as well as widening of European integration since the mid-1980s, specific emphasis is placed on the social purpose underlying these processes.

From early on, the study of European integration has been dominated by neo-functionalist and intergovernmentalist theories. Neo-functionalism assumes that European integration is a self-sustaining, almost automatic process of further integration, following a rationale of spill-over, where integration in one sector requires the integration of related sectors to achieve the full gains of the first step of integration (Tranholm-Mikkelsen, 1991, pp. 4–6). Strongly influenced by neo-realist International Relations (IR) theory, intergovernmentalist approaches, including liberal intergovernmentalism, on the other hand, argue that states are the most important decision makers in the EU. Integration only takes place as the result of a convergence of national interests (Hoffmann, 1966; Moravcsik, 1998). These mainstream approaches have three fundamental problems. Firstly, neo-functionalist and intergovernmental approaches are ahistoric. The former focus on the rational, utility-maximizing individual, aggregated into interest groups, as the most important actor. It leads to the notion of an automatic process of further integration rooted in the process of spill-over and implies a teleological, economic deterministic account, which overlooks the open-endedness of any political development (Bieler, 2000, p. 4). Similar to neo-functionalism although in a different way, intergovernmentalists deny the open-endedness of history. Due to their basic state-centric assumption, intergovernmentalist approaches view the EU's future as a kind of strengthened intergovernmental arrangement by default. No developments beyond state-centrism are conceivable. Secondly, mainstream approaches concentrate on the form of integration at the expense of the social purpose underlying integration. Neo-functionalists' assumption that integration leads to the formation of a new, supranational state implies a focus on form as does intergovernmentalists' insistence that the EU's future would be intergovernmental (van Apeldoorn, 2002, pp. 35, 40). In short, integration theories in general, according to Smith, are based on two related institutionalist fallacies. 'Institutionalist fallacy number one is the tendency to narrow down the subject of inquiry in respect of European integration to the study of how the institution makes its decision. Institutionalist fallacy number two is the conflation of the study of European integration with the institutional practices defined by policy-makers' (H. Smith, 2002, p. 265). It is not asked what type of integration occurs. Finally, by overlooking the social relations of production, mainstream approaches do not comprehend the historic specificity of capitalism. Instead, they take the separation of the state and market, characteristic of capitalism, as their ahistoric starting point of investigation. As a result, the inner connection between the political and the economic cannot be problematized by these approaches. 'Instead the "state" is fetishised whilst "the market" is dehistoricised and viewed as a technical arena in which the "external" state "intervenes" ' (Burnham, 1995a, p. 136). Change beyond the capitalist mode of production cannot be conceptualized.[1]

In the following, it will be analysed how Open Marxist and neo-Gramscian perspectives overcome these problems. This will illustrate their similarities, but also core differences, indicated already in Part I of this volume. Open Marxism's understanding of European integration is introduced as a historical materialist alternative to established approaches in the next section. While its focus on class struggle is welcomed, its lack to conceptualize concrete instances of transnational class formation at the international, European level is criticized. This sets the stage for an outline of an alternative historical materialist approach to European integration drawing on neo-Gramscian perspectives and conceptualizing class struggle as a transnational phenomenon in times of globalization. Then, the deepening and widening of European integration since the mid-1980s will be analysed from a neo-Gramscian perspective, before the conclusion summarizes the results of the analysis and provides an outlook on potential resistance to neo-liberal restructuring.

Open Marxism and the analysis of European integration

In contrast to established approaches, Open Marxism starts an analysis through a focus on the social relations of production. Thus, the state and market are not fetishised as ahistoric 'things', but they are regarded as different forms expressing the very same social relations of production. As production in capitalism is organized around wage labour and the private ownership of the means of production, it is realized that the extraction of surplus value is not politically enforced, but the result of the 'free' sale of labour power by those, who are excluded from the means of production (see Chapters 3 and 4). The resulting apparent separation of 'state' and 'market' in capitalism does not imply, however, that there is no internal link between the two. Rather, the former secures the functioning of the latter through the guarantee of private property, the contractual relationship between employer and employee and the process of commodity exchange (Burnham, 1995a, p. 145; see also H. Smith, 2002, p. 262). Furthermore, Open Marxism avoids economic determinism through a focus on open-ended class struggle (Burnham, 1994, p. 225).

This emphasis on open-ended class struggle and on overcoming the separation of the political and the economic is expressed in the recent Open Marxist contributions to the analysis of European integration. In his investigation of Economic and Monetary Union (EMU), Bonefeld makes clear that 'politics is understood, here, as class politics. Conventional accounts deny the importance of class politics through their premise that the economic and political are two distinct forms of social organisation' (Bonefeld, 2001c, p. 66). From an Open Marxist perspective, EMU signifies the attempt to ensure that monetary policy remains removed from politics. This should not, however, be understood as a separation of the economic from the political. Rather, by isolating neo-liberal economic policies and abolishing the possibility of devaluation through the introduction of a single currency, those countries with lower rates of productivity can only compete with more productive countries through the extraction of more surplus value at the point of production; that is a higher level of worker exploitation through lower wages, longer working days and labour market flexibilization (Bonefeld, 2001c, p. 89; Carchedi, 1997, pp. 95–101). Thus, EMU represents a shift from a politicized, discretion-based to a depoliticized, rules-based management of labour. The low inflation policy is not the responsibility of governments, but the task of the independent European Central Bank (ECB) with its primary goal of price stability. Capital's profitability is restored through an externalization of the imposition of financial discipline (see Burnham, Chapter 6 of this volume). By indicating that it is actually labour, which bears the costs of EMU, it is also clear how a class analysis 'helps reveal the true nature of the project' (Carchedi and Carchedi, 1999, p. 128), that is the social purpose underlying monetary union. According to Bonefeld, from its very foundation in the 1950s, the EU had the purpose to further a free market economy, initially in combination with national welfare states, to stifle potential resistance by workers:

> There is the attempt to integrate the working class into the capital relationship through the promises of full-employment and welfare, and the acceptance of the mass democratic rights of political participation. And there is the insulation of the 'political' from mass democratic influence through the creation of a European anchor in support of this insulation. (Bonefeld, 2002a, p. 129)

EMU is simply regarded as a continuation of this policy in the changed circumstances after the end of the Cold War and the global crisis of capitalist accumulation. 'In short, EMU merely provides a supranational anchor for the purpose of a politics of austerity' (Bonefeld, 2002a, p. 134). Thus, the intensification of exploitation of labour in order to secure the continuation of capitalist accumulation is identified as the social purpose visible in the revival of European integration.

This rationale is also underlying other policy areas. In an analysis of the Treaty of Amsterdam, Smith argues that the promotion of individual rights actually serves the smooth functioning of capitalist accumulation. 'The system of legal and political norms developed in the EU specifically formalises an abstract conception of the individual as self-interested monad who relates to the European Union in a way which is seemingly separate from any class location with capitalist social relations' (H. Smith, 2002, p. 274). Social policy innovation, closely linked to the rights agenda, is similarly geared towards optimizing the competitive conditions for European capital through creating, for example, a level playing field by countering social dumping (H. Smith, 2002, p. 271). In the EU's external commercial policy, neo-liberalism is represented by the drive of pushing other countries to open up their markets to free competition, thereby providing new opportunities for European companies. 'Since Maastricht, and to a large extent before, no external agreement has been signed without the partner having to commit itself to developing its internal polity along liberal market lines' (H. Smith, 1998, p. 165). Ultimately, however, and this indicates the open-ended nature of Open Marxism as an analytical approach, whether the renewed strategy of continuing capitalist accumulation, as represented by EMU, works, depends on class struggle. 'The failure of one member state to contain "its" working class has costly consequences for all the other member states' (Bonefeld, 2002a, p. 135).

Nevertheless, Open Marxism's ability to account for structural change, the third problem identified in relation to mainstream integration theories, is limited. As argued in detail in Chapter 9, while the character of the accumulation of capital and, thus, class struggle is considered to be global in substance, the conditions of exploitation are standardized at the national political level. The form of class struggle at the global level is the interaction of states, which 'are interlocked internationally into a hierarchy of price systems' (Burnham, 1995a, p. 148). Hence, Open Marxism's analysis of international relations in general and European integration in particular remains rather abstract and fails to comprehend the new dynamics of transnational class struggle underpinning the revival of European integration since the mid-1980s against the background of globalization. For example, Carchedi analyses capitalist accumulation as the result of competition between different national capitals, competing with each other for the extraction of surplus value at the international level. The future form of the EU 'will continue to be shaped by inter-capitalist rivalries (centring upon the relations among Germany, France and the United Kingdom)' (Carchedi, 1997, pp. 108–9). Moss applauds Moravcsik's state-centric explanation of European integration and only recommends that his analysis of domestic preference formation should be amended with a focus on geopolitics, political ideology and class (Moss, 2000). It is also not surprising that this emphasis on national class formation can only recommend a concentration on the state for the development of alternatives. The state 'is still the principle framework for both the organisation and contestation of capitalist hegemony' (Moss, 2001, p. 130). Carchedi (2001) is the only contribution, which recognizes that the EU itself may actually be the ground of class struggle taking place in form beyond state borders. This is, however, expressed in the rivalry between the capitalist enterprises of the EU countries, the imperialist relations of the EU as a whole with developing countries as part of a dominated bloc and is then further extended to the imperialist rivalry between the EU and the United States. The latter centres on the competition between the Euro and the Dollar for being the dominant international currency (Carchedi, 2001, pp. 114–17, 144–60). This rivalry is also invoked in the analysis of European integration by Carchedi and Carchedi (1999), where the EU is analysed as an imperialist actor on the world stage. This, however, again restricts the analysis of class formation to distinctive boundaries, only this time they are regional instead of national borders. Class struggle across borders is not conceptualized. In sum, globalization as processes of structural change and transnational class formation cannot be conceptualized by Open Marxism.

A neo-Gramscian perspective on European integration

As outlined in Chapter 2, neo-Gramscian perspectives conceptualize the historical specificity of capitalism by taking the sphere of production as the starting-point of their analysis. Similar to Open Marxism, state and market are comprehended as two different forms of the same social relations of production. The separation between the political and the economic is overcome. Moreover, the social relations of production are considered to engender social forces as the most important actors. Thus, a neo-Gramscian analysis is open-ended through an emphasis on class struggle 'as the heuristic model for the understanding of structural change' (Cox with Sinclair, 1996, pp. 57–8). Due to this open-ended focus on class struggle, understood as resistance to exploitation, neo-Gramscian perspectives are a critical theory, which 'does not take institutions and social and power relations for granted but calls them into question by concerning itself with their origins and how and whether they might be in the process of changing' (Cox, 1981, p. 129). Hence, the analysis of class struggle goes beyond an analysis of form in that it implies an investigation of the social purpose underlying various social forces' activities (Bieler, 2000, p. 8; van Apeldoorn, 2002, pp. 11–13). In short, the three main defects of integration theories, outlined in the introduction, are overcome.

The capitalist mode of production is organized around wage labour and private property. This leads to the opposition between the bourgeoisie, the owner of the means of production, on the one hand, and workers, who can only sell their labour power, on the other. The partial transnationalization of national production and financial systems due to globalization (Cox, 1993, pp. 259–60), however, and here neo-Gramscian perspectives go beyond Open Marxism, implies that there is not only class struggle between capital and labour at the national level, but also between national capital and labour and transnational forces of capital and labour (van Apeldoorn, 2002, pp. 26–34). In other words, transnational classes are involved in class struggle across borders. National capital and labour can be further subdivided in nationally oriented social forces, engendered by production processes organized at the national level producing predominantly for domestic consumption, and internationally oriented social forces, stemming from national production, which is geared towards export markets (Bieler, 2000, pp. 9–14). European production and finance have become increasingly transnationalized. While the annual average of inward FDI flows into the EU between 1989 and 1994 was $76634 millions, inward FDI in 2000 was $617321 millions (UN, 2001, p. 291). The corresponding figures for outward FDI are $105194 millions as annual average between 1989 and 1994, and $772949 millions in 2000 (UN, 2001, p. 296). Overall, there were 33249 parent corporations and 53753 foreign affiliates located in the EU in 2000 (UN, 2001, p. 239). As a result, we can expect transnational social forces of capital and labour as core collective actors in addition to national forces of capital and labour. At the European level, it can additionally be distinguished between European transnational forces, engendered by production structures organized across borders within Europe, and global forces of capital and labour, stemming from production structures across the world (Holman, 1992, pp. 15–16; van Apeldoorn, 2002, p. 47). European transnational forces may favour strong internal integration combined with some protection against outside competition, while truly global social forces may prefer fully open borders. National social forces, it can by hypothesized, may be extremely reluctant about European integration in the first place, whether this is combined with protectionist barriers to the global economy or not, because they are likely to depend on direct state assistance.

Understanding globalization along these lines allows us to unmask the agency behind transnational restructuring instead of viewing globalization as a set of external pressures, which inevitably leads to an ahistoric separation between national states and the global market. It opens up the possibility for a dialectical understanding of the relationship between structure and agency, acknowledging the impact of the social relations of production, forms of state and world order, resulting from strategies in the past, on agency in the present, while comprehending at the same time the open-endedness of agency in turn. 'Structure ceases to be an external force which crushes man, assimilates him to itself and makes him passive; and is transformed into a means of freedom, an instrument to create a new ethico-political form and a source of new initiatives' (Gramsci, 1971, p. 367; see also Bieler and Morton, 2001a, pp. 16–29). Nevertheless, an analysis of the production structure only allows the identification of the core actors and the formulation of research hypotheses. The uncovering and explanation of actual strategies of social forces remains the task of an empirical investigation. The position within the sphere of production shapes the behaviour of social forces, it does not determine it. The latter would imply an economism, which Gramsci firmly rejected in all its different forms (Gramsci, 1971, pp. 158–68).

The rejection of economism and the related focus on open-ended class struggle also highlights the independent role Gramsci attributed to ideas. As he points out, 'it is on the level of ideologies that men become conscious of conflicts in the world of economy' (Gramsci, 1971, p. 162). Two different functions of ideas can be distinguished. On the one hand, they are considered to be a part of the overall structure in the form of 'intersubjective meanings'. Hence, ideas establish the wider frameworks of thought, 'which condition the way individuals and groups are able to understand their social situation, and the possibilities of social change' (Gill and Law, 1988, p. 74). On the other hand, ideas may be used by actors as 'weapons' in order to legitimize particular policies and are important in that they form part of a hegemonic project by organic intellectuals (see below). Constructivist approaches, increasingly applied to European integration, can also account for ideas as part of the overall structure. Ben Rosamond, for example, argues that the Commission is behind the social construction of the category 'European competitiveness', in order to justify neo-liberal restructuring and an expansion of its policy competencies within the EU institutional set-up (Rosamond, 2002, pp. 162, 171). Why this is done via a neo-liberal offensive, however, instead of an argument in favour of EU social policies and stronger European regulation, able to provide protection against the disruptive aspects of globalization, cannot be accounted for. It is only when Rosamond refers to the close relationship between the Commission and the European Round Table of Industrialists (ERT), thereby referring to a neo-Gramscian analysis by van Apeldoorn (Rosamond, 2002, p. 170), that the material interests and power behind the neo-liberal project come to light.

In contrast to constructivism, neo-Gramscian perspectives emphasize the material structure of ideas (Bieler, 2001, p. 97). The connection between human masses, that is social forces, and ideas is provided by organic intellectuals, emerging from and representing particular fractions of social forces (Gramsci, 1971, p. 5). They do not simply produce ideas, but they concretize and articulate strategies in complex and often contradictory ways, which is possible because of their class location, that is proximity to the most powerful forces in production. It is their task to organize the social forces they stem from and to develop a 'hegemonic project', which is able to transcend the particular economic-corporate interests of their social group by binding and cohering diverse aspirations, interests and identities into a historical bloc. Once successful, a historical bloc establishes a position of hegemony, where its rule relies predominantly on the consent of the ruled, not on open force (see Chapter 2). This focus on the role of ideas as part of a hegemonic project further highlights the way neo-Gramscian perspectives can address the issue of the social purpose underlying European integration. In the next section, the core social forces in European integration and the different projects related to them are identified. Then, the question of the social purpose underlying the revival of European integration since the mid-1980s will be analysed, before the investigation is extended to the enlargement of the EU.

The deepening of European integration since the mid-1980s

When analysing the social purpose underlying European integration since the mid-1980s, a struggle over the future EU model of capitalism can be identified. Van Apeldoorn's (2001 and 2002) detailed analysis of the different projects behind the Internal Market programme reveals that there were three rival projects underlying the revival of European integration in the mid-1980s and early 1990s, when the SEA paved the way towards the Internal Market and the Treaty of Maastricht was signed including plans towards EMU. Firstly, there was the neo-liberal project with an emphasis on market-led, negative integration and close connection with globalization through the opening of the EU to the global economy. It was argued that the loss of competitiveness of European production was due to expansive welfare systems and labour market rigidity. To increase competitiveness, internal deregulation and liberalization should not be accompanied by the establishment of barriers to the global economy. This project was mainly supported by big TNCs, European and US, with production sites in the EU, which had established themselves as players on the global market, that is the globalist fraction of European capital. Secondly, there was a neo-mercantilist project supported mainly by transnational European firms, which predominantly produced for the European market, but were still not fully global players. Considering the success of their US and Japanese counterparts, these companies regarded the fragmentation of the European market as the main cause of their lack of competitiveness. 'A strong European home market was expected to serve as both a stepping-stone to conquer the world market as well as a protective shield against outside competition' (van Apeldoorn, 2001, p. 75). It was, therefore, hoped that the completion of the Internal Market would be complemented with a European industrial policy helping the creation of European champions, ready to face competition on the global market. Finally, there was a social democratic project, especially supported by Jacques Delors, social democrats and a whole range of trade unions. For social democrats, the European level offered the possibility of re-regulation of the market at a higher level and thus the opportunity to regain some control over capital lost at the national level. The next section will look at the social purpose of the Internal Market and EMU to identify the project that was successful at the end of this struggle.

The Internal Market programme and Economic and Monetary Union

In 1985, the Commission published its famous White Paper 'Completing the Internal Market', which proposed 300 (later reduced to 279) measures designed to facilitate progress towards the completion of the Internal Market by 1992 through the abolition of non-tariff barriers. The SEA of

1987, which institutionalized the Internal Market programme, spelled out the goals of the four freedoms, that is the freedom of goods, services, capital and people. While tariff barriers had been abolished by the end of the 1960s in the EU, there had been many non-tariff barriers, which had impeded free trade. This was now to be remedied. The rationale underlying the Internal Market programme was clearly of a neo-liberal nature (Grahl and Teague, 1989). A bigger market was supposed to lead to tougher competition resulting in higher efficiency, greater profits and eventually through a trickle-down effect in more general wealth and more jobs. National markets should be deregulated and liberalized, national companies were to be privatized. An emerging common competition policy was to secure that the market was no longer disturbed through state intervention or ownership even in areas such as telecommunications, public procurement and energy. As for the EU financial system, legislation led to the creation of a European financial area, which moved the EU 'decisively in the direction of a more transnationalised, marketised, and desegmented financial system based on a single legislative framework' (Underhill, 1997, p. 118). This goes hand in hand with developments at the global level and the general transnationalization of finance.

The Treaty of Maastricht was signed in 1991. Amongst other changes, it laid out the plan for EMU, including a single currency to be administered by a supranational and independent ECB. In January 1999, 11 member states carried out this step, when they irrevocably fixed their exchange rates. The underlying rationale of EMU is embodied in the statutory role of the ECB and the convergence criteria. As for the former, a common monetary policy is now dealt with by the independent ECB. The sole target of the ECB and its interest rate policy, as spelled out in the Treaty of Maastricht, is the maintenance of price stability and low inflation. Economic growth and employment are only secondary objectives, subordinated to price stability. In relation to the institutional set-up of the ECB, we experience, what Stephen Gill calls a 'new constitutionalism', which 'seeks to separate economic policies from broad political accountability in order to make governments more responsive to the discipline of market forces' (Gill, 2001, p. 47).[2] As for the convergence criteria, most importantly, the criteria obliged member states to have a government budget deficit of no more than 3 per cent of GDP and government debt of no more than 60 per cent of GDP. They do not include a criterion on unemployment. This is of secondary importance and thought to be solved through the trickle-down effect. The EMU member countries, in order to meet the criteria, had to implement tough austerity budgets in the run-up to EMU. Within EMU, continuation of neo-liberal budget policies is ensured through the Stability and Growth Pact, adopted at the Amsterdam European Council summit in June 1997. It commits members to stay within the neo-liberal convergence criteria even after the start of EMU on 1 January 1999 and, through the requirement to adhere to the Broad Economic Policy Guidelines including a general commitment to a balanced budget, further emphasizes the overriding focus on low inflation (Jones, 2002, pp. 37–40).[3] In sum, both the Internal Market and EMU firmly put the EU on the road towards a neo-liberal model of capitalism.

The European Round Table of Industrialists (ERT) has played a crucial role in the revival of European integration. It was founded in 1983 and has currently about 45 captains of industry from European TNCs as members. They 'come from huge corporations with a combined turnover of 800 billion euro and more than 4 million employees worldwide' (Balanyá *et al.*, 2000, p. 26; see also van Apeldoorn, 2002, pp. 83–114). The ERT only maintains a small office in Brussels to co-ordinate its activities. The main strategy is the direct lobbying of the Commission and individual governments by the CEOs. Its main objective is to increase competitiveness via benchmarking of best (neo-liberal) practice, further deregulation, flexible labour markets and transport infrastructure investment. In January 1985, the ERT chairman Wisse Dekker (Philips) published the report 'Europe 1990: An Agenda for Action'. Three days later, the new President of the Commission Jacques Delors gave a speech to the EP with very similar contents. In fact, the Commission White Paper on Completing the Internal Market, published in June 1985, resembles very much Dekker's report. The only real difference is the postponement of the deadline from 1990 to 1992 (Balanyá *et al.*, 2000, p. 21; see also van Apeldoorn and Holman, 1994, p. 11). The role of the ERT in the Treaty of Maastricht was less pronounced than in the Internal Market programme, but the timetable for EMU implementation in 1991 is very similar to the timetable for EMU in an ERT report of the same year.

As van Apeldoorn outlines, the struggle between mercantilist and neo-liberal ideology was also conducted within the ERT. Initially, the former was stronger, which is why several global corporations, Unilever, Shell and ICI, left the ERT in the early 1980s. As the discussion of the social purpose above, however, indicates, transnational social forces in favour of neo-liberalism and the corresponding model of an open Europe won over their neo-mercantilist rivals, partly due to the fact that several core member states such as Britain, Germany and the Netherlands were against the introduction of protective external barriers, partly because the European firms themselves had been involved in further transnational restructuring and had, thus, become more globally oriented in the late 1980s and early 1990s. Additionally, some of their concerns for a European industrial policy had been met in the chapters on 'Trans-European [infrastructure] Networks' and 'Research and Technological Development' of the Maastricht Treaty. The Social Chapter, finally, signified a concession to the social democratic project and incorporated social democratic forces and trade unions into the compromise (van Apeldoorn, 2001, pp. 81–2). In short, the eventual outcome of the struggle between these three projects constituted a compromise, aptly labelled 'embedded neo-liberalism' by van Apeldoorn (2001, p. 82). It is predominantly neo-liberal in content, but also includes some mercantilist and social policy side aspects to widen the social basis of support.

When analysing the ERT from a neo-Gramscian perspective, it is important that it should not be misunderstood as a lobby group next to other lobby groups such as environmental or human rights groups. Rather, the ERT is an institution which provides a platform for organic intellectuals, who formulate a coherent hegemonic project for transnational European capital, which is at the same time able to transcend the particular interests of this capital fraction in order to attract wider social forces towards the formation of a historical bloc (van Apeldoorn, 2002, pp. 104–7). Embedded neo-liberalism can be understood as the hegemonic project of transnational European capital. The fact that it is so influential is not because the ERT is the more effective lobbying machine, but firstly because the neo-liberal ideas, underpinning embedded neo-liberalism, corresponded positively to the general shift towards neo-liberalism, itself a part of the structural change of globalization since the mid-1970s, early 1980s (Gamble, 2001). Secondly, embedded neo-liberalism has gained predominance within the EU, because this project has been backed up by increasing structural power of transnational capital as expressed in the increasing levels of outward and inward FDI noted above. In other words, it was firmly rooted in the material structure.

Neo-liberal restructuring and EU enlargement

European integration since the mid-1980s has not only been characterized by deepening, but also widening of the EU. In 1995, Austria, Sweden and Finland joined the EU as new members, and ten further countries from Central and Eastern Europe (CEE) and the Mediterranean area acceded in May 2004. In accordance with neo-Gramscian perspectives, this section focuses on the social purpose underlying enlargement as well as the social forces pushing this purpose.

The 1995 EU enlargement

Traditionally, Austria and Sweden rejected the EU for two main reasons. First, they considered membership in a supranational economic organization to be incompatible with their status as neutral countries. Second, they both considered their economic-political system based on traditional social democratic values such as equal opportunity, redistribution, gender equality in the workplace, a generous welfare system and full employment, to be superior to the EU, dominated by Christian Democratic parties and big capital. The paradox here is why did they join the EU in a moment, when the EU had moved even further away from the European social model? The answer can be found by analysing these countries' accession to the EU against the background of global structural change (Bieler, 2000). Partly due to structural pressure, especially exemplified in Sweden through the relocation of production units and investment by Swedish TNCs to locations in the EU, and partly due to a change in hegemonic ideas away from a Keynesian towards a neo-liberal understanding of the economy, the neo-liberal drive underlying the revival of European integration became suddenly an attractive option in times of severe domestic economic recession in the late 1980s, early 1990s. In Austria, it was even argued that EU membership would provide the external pressure from Brussels necessary for restructuring the heavily protected agricultural and food processing sectors of the economy (Bieler, 2000, pp. 53–65). In Sweden, representatives of transnational capital pointed out that the traditional Swedish model of capitalism had already been abandoned in the early 1990s. Nonetheless, some argued that membership was important in that it foreclosed any possible future return to policies different from the general neo-liberal course (Bieler, 2000, p. 107). At the material level, the increasing transnationalization of Swedish manufacturing gave both transnational capital and labour a strong position in the yes-campaign of the referendum.

In Austria, by contrast, the production structure was hardly transnationalized. Instead, there was a split between internationally oriented capital and labour, engendered by export-oriented domestic production, on the one hand; and nationally oriented capital and labour of domestic production sectors supplying the domestic market, on the other. As a result, it was the Federation of Austrian Industrialists (VÖI), organic intellectuals of internationally oriented capital, which devised a hegemonic project including neo-liberal ideas, which started the process in 1987, which eventually led to Austria's application to the EU in 1989. While neo-liberal economics reflected closely the material interests of internationally oriented Austrian capital, the VÖI realized, nonetheless, that the main obstacle to membership could be Austria's status of neutrality. It, consequently, commissioned a study by two experts of international law, which concluded that membership was compatible with neutrality. Two more publications dealing with the economic and constitutional aspects of membership followed soon afterwards. The goal of these publications was to establish a basis for discussion on membership, which had not existed before. The VÖI's strategy did not lead directly to membership. Nonetheless, it provided a coherent hegemonic project around which various fractions of social forces could rally and which ultimately allowed for the successful establishment of a pro-EU historical bloc. Opposition forces to membership, on the other hand, neither had the material backing, nor were their economic alternatives credible in an environment, where neo-liberal economics had become part of the overall structure, to mount a successful challenge (Bieler, 2000, pp. 53–69).

Eastward enlargement in 2004

In 1989 and 1990, in an atmosphere of great euphoria, the so-called communist regimes collapsed across CEE. In the ensuing transformation processes, the CEE countries were fully exposed to neo-liberal globalization (Holman, 1998). The so-called shock therapy was most directly applied in Poland in 1990, but across the whole of CEE transformation was characterized by deregulation, privatization, the opening-up to foreign direct investment and a general focus on price stability and low inflation. As an immediate result, economic growth stagnated and went into negative figures and GDP levels declined drastically. In the case of Poland, the Czech Republic and Hungary, GDP levels declined by 7, 11.5 and 11.9 per cent respectively. While economic growth had recovered by 1998, unemployment rates remained high at 10.4, 7.5 and 9.1 per cent respectively (Bieler, 2000, pp. 140–8). The result has been social hardship for large parts of the population (Pollert, 1999, pp. 76–80), which can potentially lead to political instability.

In CEE, the decision on application to the EU was taken by cadre elites within state institutions, who secured neo-liberal economic restructuring externally in a strategy labelled by Gramsci as 'passive revolution' (Gramsci, 1971, pp. 105–6; see also Chapter 7 of this volume). Structural change was not driven by domestic coalitions of social forces, but through the incorporation of international ideas and foreign production methods in tandem with an internalization of transnational social forces in the national CEE forms of states (Bieler, 2002, pp. 588–9; Bohle, 2000). Importantly, this does not signify that transnational restructuring has been enforced on CEE countries from the outside. According to Holman, 'the state forms the political framework within which internationally operating concepts of control can be synthesised with particular national political cultures, attitudes, constitutional arrangements and so on, or, conversely, the very medium through which hegemonic concepts of control can transcend national frontiers' (Holman, 2001, p. 169). Transnational forces of capital have become internalized within the CEE forms of state through their co-operation with state elites and their participation in the transnationalization of these countries' production structures via FDI (see Chapter 9).

The transnationalization of CEE countries' production structure differs, however, from country to country, as does the way neo-liberal restructuring is internalized in the various forms of state. First detailed case studies have been carried out. Shields outlines well how in Poland, clearly a front-runner of restructuring due to its shock therapy, a group of neo-liberal economists around Leszek Balcerowicz with international links to the IMF and World Bank had emerged during the 1980s. In an intellectual climate, where communism was totally discredited and neo-liberal economics had become part of the overall structure at the global level, they were seen as presenting the only viable alternative and put in charge of economic restructuring from 1989 onwards. Regarding existing Polish groups as problems, Balcerowicz and his group did not seek the support of the Polish population for their reforms, but initially anchored restructuring externally via the IMF, the World Bank and a range of neo-liberal consultancy firms (Shields, 2003, pp. 228–37). When domestic hardship got out of hand, EU membership was regarded as the ideal external anchor, because it promised future riches and a cultural return to the heart of Europe in exchange for current poverty.

Another good example of the internalization of transnational social forces in national forms of state is provided by Bohle and Husz (2005, pp. 87–96) and their analysis of the Hungarian–EU negotiations on membership. During the negotiations, Hungary pushed the Commission to accept 1 January 2003, a date much later than initially sought by the Commission, as the date for the transfer of Hungary's fiscal aid to foreign TNCs into regional investment aid, compatible with EU regulations. Hungary's strong stance – although it actually implied that the Hungarian government sustained considerable tax losses and undermined its national small- and medium-sized enterprises and although it is clear that these subsidies were not the main factor behind attracting FDI – is explained through a detailed analysis of how the interests of transnational capital, those forces benefiting from the generous state subsidies, had become internalized in state policy. Close contacts between business organizations and here especially the American Chamber of Commerce (AmCham) and the Hungarian government, direct negotiations between TNCs themselves and government ministers and the Hungarian chief negotiator plus direct structural pressure of possible exit and legal challenges by TNCs led to a convergence of interests between the Hungarian government and its major foreign investors in a process of transnational class formation. This implied a direct impact of transnational capital on the formation of the Hungarian negotiation position, in which the Hungarian government mediated between transnational capital and the Commission on behalf of the TNCs (Bohle and Husz, 2005, pp. 94–6).

The EU itself also realized that the young CEE democracies were not consolidated enough to accommodate the political risks inherent in the transformation process towards a neo-liberal market economy (Cecchini *et al.*, 2001, pp. 157–9). Hence, the promise of membership and future wealth can be regarded as a way of keeping the CEE countries on track with transformation. The promise of membership was made at the 1993 European Council summit in Copenhagen. It systematically pushed CEE countries towards adopting the neo-liberal economic-political model of the EU (Holman, 2001, p. 178). It was stated that potential new members had to achieve a stable democracy, a functioning market economy, the ability to withstand competition within the EU, and to take on the full *acquis communautaire* including the aims of political, and economic and monetary union (Gower, 1999, p. 7). Thus, the elements of the enlargement strategy of the EU clearly demanded adaptation to EU rules and thus measures of liberalization and deregulation. As Holman sums up, 'it is no exaggeration to conclude that the Commission's pre-accession strategy is basically about disciplining the candidate members in terms of free market integration' (Holman, 2001, pp. 180–1). This enlargement strategy was strongly supported by transnational European capital. Once the ERT had formed an internal consensus on neo-liberalism, it became strongly involved in the Commission's accession strategy for CEE applicants. From 1997 onwards, the ERT intensified its lobbying urging the EU to reform its institutional structure in order to facilitate enlargement and to work closely together with the governments of applicant countries towards meeting the EU conditions for membership (Holman, 2001, pp. 174–8). The ERT's engagement for further EU enlargement is again a reflection of developments at the structural level. In a recent FDI report by the UN, it is pointed out that the rapidly rising level of 'outward FDI of the EU is increasingly directed towards countries in Central and Eastern Europe, in pursuit of favourable business opportunities in the EU candidates, and driven by privatisation' (UN, 2001, p. 18).

In short, EU enlargement with the social purpose of securing and intensifying neo-liberal restructuring in CEE fulfiled the objectives of both CEE state elites, who want to secure restructuring externally, and of the EU and European transnational capital, who want to expand capitalist accumulation to CEE.

Conclusion

This chapter has shown that if an analysis focuses on the contents of European integration, the deepening and widening of the EU from the mid-1980s onwards are driven by neo-liberal restructuring of European social relations of production. Clearly, in securing neo-liberal restructuring of CEE the process of future EU enlargement strengthens the neo-liberal restructuring in the EU itself. As Bohle (2003, p. 3) points out, 'in contrast to the project of embedded neo-liberalism shaping the deepening of the EU, the mode of incorporating Eastern Europe up to now has resulted in the export of a much more "market-radical" variant of neo-liberalism'. Eastward EU enlargement does not extend substantial financial aid, the free movement of labour, nor the full amount of subsidies available to farmers within the Common Agricultural Policy to the new members (Bohle, 2003, pp. 15–17). This, in turn, may imply further pressure on the old EU members to cut back existing social policies. As also Open Marxist approaches outline, European integration has become a neo-liberal anchor for domestic austerity.

Nevertheless, it needs to be kept in mind that neo-liberal restructuring differs from country to country. An analysis of restructuring in Slovenia by Lindstrom and Piroska (2003) demonstrates that while the Slovenian government had to sign up to deregulation and liberalization of its economy in the negotiations with the EU, domestic pressure nonetheless severely hindered, if not blocked, the selling of Slovenian banks and brewery companies to foreign investors. In other words, Europeanization is not only constraining, but also enabling, leaving room for countries to avoid full-scale liberalization and privatization of their economies. Moreover, a hegemonic situation is never solid, but constantly contested. It is alleged in some quarters that trade unions would have succumbed to neo-liberalism, expressed in their support for the

Internal Market and EMU (e.g. Bieling and Schulten, 2003; Ryner and Schulten, 2003). Empirical evidence, however, indicates that trade unions still question 'embedded neo-liberalism' (Bieler, 2006). Several German unions continue to contest 'embedded neo-liberalism' and demand the development of active employment programmes at the national and European level, even if this implies the softening of the convergence criteria. For this purpose, a common fiscal policy is regarded as the essential counterpart to the common monetary policy (Bieler, 2003a, pp. 34–6). In Britain, criticism of the neo-liberal EMU is even more outspoken. Trade unions which organize workers in national production sectors, such as the public sector union UNISON, strongly oppose EMU, because it would limit national expenditure on public services and have a negative impact on growth and employment levels. The lack of democratic accountability of the ECB is also highlighted. These criticisms are echoed by general unions such as the GMB, which organize workers in the public and manufacturing sector and therefore understand the relevance of both positions (Bieler, 2003a, pp. 31–4). In fact, British pro-EMU unions have always demanded an expansion of the EU's macro-economic competence and a focus on high levels of employment as a precondition for their support (G. Strange, 1997, pp. 21–3). To facilitate this, they have adopted Euro-Keynesian macro-economic management as a new project, based on an ultimately centralized fiscal and monetary policy in a federal union and combined with EU social partnership industrial relations (G. Strange, 2002, pp. 356–7). At the European level, it is the European Metalworkers' Federation, which has taken the lead in organizing intra-union co-ordination of national collective bargaining rounds in order to avoid a downward competition between different national unions. As long as the union demands in all national bargaining rounds follow the formula of inflation plus productivity increase, the damaging competition for higher levels of national competitiveness is avoided (Bieler, 2005).

Of course, trade unions are not by default part of counter neo-liberal movements. A recent analysis of Swedish unions' and their positions on EMU has made clear that peak associations and transnational sector unions have started to accept core neo-liberal assumptions – such as that the main policy focus needs to be on low inflation and that wage for-mation is responsible for a stable economy – against the background of economic growth, falling unemployment and re-established collective bargaining at the sectoral national level. Hence, they are much less committed to European-wide, counter neo-liberal strategies (Bieler, 2003b). Moreover, Eastward enlargement has opened the danger of deep divisions between West European and East European trade unions over the issue of free movement of labour. It was West European trade unions, which through the Economic and Social Committee of the EU, in research by the European Trade Union Confederation, as well as through pressure by the German DGB and Austrian ÖGB on their respective governments, pushed successfully for a transition period of up to seven years in relation to the free movement of labour. Arguing that immediate granting of this fundamental right could undermine the development of social Europe due to the large income gap between East and West and intensify public fears and thus fuel right-wing parties, or simply trying to protect Western privileges in a welfare chauvinist strategy, trade unions strongly lobbied for a transition period (Bohle and Husz, 2005, pp. 102–6). Western labour won, partly also because transnational capital sustained only minor economic losses, if any at all, due to this concession. Nevertheless, as Bohle and Husz make clear, this political victory based on a lack of transnational solidarity may turn out to have disastrous consequences for labour in general in that it may result in long-term divisions between the Eastern and Western labour movements and thereby weaken European labour overall (Bohle and Husz, 2005, pp. 108–9). To conclude, the outcome of the struggle over the future EU model of capitalism is open-ended. Neither is the neo-liberal model without its critics, nor is a successful challenge to this model guaranteed. A neo-Gramscian perspective on transnational class formation will allow us to follow and understand this struggle closely.

Notes

1. For a more detailed criticism of mainstream integration theories, see van Apeldoorn *et al.* (2003) and Bieler (2000, pp. 3–8).
2. The neo-Gramscian notion of 'new constitutionalism' resembles closely the Open Marxist assumption of depoliticized economic management (see above). The difference is, however, that while the former argue that this is a unique new feature of capitalism, Open Marxism is historically more sensitive in that it acknowledges that rules-based approaches have been employed before.
3. It has recently been argued that the Stability and Growth Pact would no longer be in operation, due to the fact that Germany's and France's failure to meet the criteria remained unpunished (e.g. Bonefeld, 2004b). Nevertheless, as in practice all governments still make attempts to fulfil the criteria, it is too early to speak about the demise of the Pact.

6
The Politics of Economic Management in the 1990s
Peter Burnham

Introduction

It is commonly argued that the central, and indeed the defining, question of the discipline of international political economy, concerns the nature of the relationship between political authority and market power (or in less sophisticated parlance, states and markets) (Gilpin, 1987, pp. 8–11; Underhill, 1994, pp. 17–44). In fact, Susan Strange goes so far as to argue that the study of 'the close relation of political power and the ways market economies function is the essence of Polanyi's claim – and of Schumpeter's – to be fathers of modern International Political Economy' (Strange, S., 1997b, pp. 242–3). Given the popularity of this view it may seem somewhat peculiar to argue that the 'political' needs to be put back into international political economy. However, a close inspection of most international political economy (IPE) literature reveals the absence of politics in at least two respects. First, in a rush to avoid the charge of conflating politics with government, much contemporary 'heterodox' international political economy with its focus on social movements, single issue campaigns, fractured identities and policy communities, fails to conceptualize the role of the modern state in capitalist reproduction. It is argued, by Foucauldian sleight of hand, that power is everywhere, exercised from innumerable points, and thus a detailed painstaking study of central government with its internal hierarchies and politics of policymaking is obsolete. It is simply unnecessary to engage with the traditional preoccupations of political science since those who pursue analysis of 'government in one country' are clearly behind the times in this age of globalization. In its extreme liberal transformationist guise, this argument posits the end of the nation-state and the creation of a borderless, stateless world dominated by empowered individuals and footloose capital with unlimited global options.[1] Whilst most measured assessments question both this internationalist claim and the realist assertion that nothing much has changed, IPE's rejection of the study of the politics of government means that most of its practitioners fail to go beyond this point and specify exactly what changes have occurred in the role of the modern state.

The second sense in which much mainstream international political economy literature eschews the 'political' is in respect of its conceptualization of labour. This is most evident in popular treatments of the state–market dichotomy. Although some neo-Gramscians take seriously Polanyi's assertion that markets are political creations (Gill, 1994, pp. 75–88; Underhill, 1994, p. 19), in general markets are fetishised as discrete, technical, economic arenas and the overwhelming tendency is to view them in terms of trade, finance and the application of new technology. Not only are labour markets generally ignored, but much more significantly, the category of labour itself is often viewed as external to state/economy restructuring and is equated simply (in a pluralist sense) with trade union bargaining power. In other words in orthodox (and much heterodox) international political economy there is no systematic conceptualization of the internal relations between state, labour and capital. This contrasts sharply with methodologies derived from Marx, which indicate that the marketization of social relations presupposes the separation of workers from land and property in the conditions of production. The presupposition of bourgeois society is not money, trade or 'markets'. Rather, the dominance of the commodity-form is itself dependent on the prior establishment of bourgeois class relations which begin with 'primitive accumulation', and which are maintained through continuous struggles to achieve the subordination of labour through the imposition of work (Marx, 1976a, p. 874).[2] In summary therefore this chapter argues that the politics of the state and the politics of labour should be centre-stage in radical international political economy if we are to make sense of the changing relations between political authority and market power, and prevent the 'discipline' becoming an off-shoot of business studies.

The argument of the chapter is developed in two sections. First, I indicate briefly how a methodology can be developed, derived from Marx, which offers a theorization of the internal relations between state and labour and highlights the significance of the politics of economic restructuring. Second, and in more detail, the chapter offers a tentative characterization of the new politics of restructuring in terms of the shift from *politicized* to *depoliticized* forms of state management of labour power and money.

States, markets and labour: international political economy and Marxian methodologies

For the last decade, a debate has raged within international political economy over the role of the state in the era of globalization. Despite some dissent (Hirst and Thompson, 1996), the general view within the discipline is that states have lost significant power to markets since the breakdown of the so-called Bretton Woods system in the early 1970s. This conclusion has been expressed in various forms ranging from literature on the 'hollowing out' of the state (Jessop, 1994, pp. 13–37), to discussions of the 'competition state' (Cerney, 1993a, pp. 3–19), and the creation of a new global order associated with the terminal decline of the state (Held, 1995; S. Strange, 1996). Of all the recent attempts to understand the changing character of the state, the most thought-provoking is that provided by Robert Cox who coined the phrase, the 'internationalisation of the state' (Cox, 1987, pp. 253–65; Cox and Sinclair, 1996).

Cox argues that we are witnessing the transformation (the reorganization of structure and role both internally and externally) not the destruction of the state. His position rests on three points. First, that states historically have acted as buffers/bulwarks protecting national economies from disruptive external forces in order to sustain domestic welfare/employment. Since 1973 this priority, he notes, has shifted to one of adapting domestic economies to the perceived exigencies of the world economy. Second, this shift has affected the structures of national governments. Agencies that act as conduits for the world economy have become pre-eminent within governments (ministries of industry and labour are now subordinate to ministries of finance). Finally, we have a transnational process of consensus formation (OECD, IMF, G7) that transmits guidelines to dominant state agencies which in turn enact national policies. The state's role is therefore one of helping to adjust the domestic economy to the requirements of the world economy. The state is a transmission belt from world to domestic economy – it has become 'internationalised' from the 'outside-in'. It is a tributary to something greater than the state, orchestrating 'governance without government'.

Cox's bold thesis provides suggestive themes for future research. However, in typical international political economy fashion it is largely silent on the issue of labour. This is, of course, somewhat paradoxical given that, as Sinclair notes, 'Cox's work stands outside the usual parameters of international relations theory', insofar as Cox develops a critical and historicist epistemology which sought initially to integrate labour into mainstream international political economy (Sinclair, 1996, p. 3). However, the relationship between 'problem solving' and 'critical' theory in Cox's work (and the difficulties involved in combining Weberian and Marxian methodologies) have not been adequately addressed or resolved and in many respects Cox seems to endorse the view that different methodologies can be selected legitimately to study different chronological periods (even since 1945) (Cox with Sinclair 1996, pp. 88–90). Although therefore Cox seems to offer a critique of mainstream international political economy, his stance of methodological pluralism produces the same conceptual disaggregation of state and market, and theorization of labour as external to restructuring, which is present in mainstream IPE. This is reflected in much of his empirical work, which for instance in the case of the cycle of hegemonic stability, is barely distinguishable from sophisticated neo-realist accounts.[3] In respect of the internationalization of the state, class relations (and by implication, struggle) are viewed as external to the process of restructuring, and labour and the state itself are depicted as powerless, passively responding to the demands of the post-Fordist economy. In addition, Cox's thesis fails to convince on historical grounds (when since 1900 did states pursue domestic welfare as their central priority?), in terms of a theory of policy making (Cox sanctions a somewhat simplistic fractionalist view of policy making at the behest of fractions of finance capital), and it underplays the extent to which 'globalization' may be authored by states (Panitch, 1994, pp. 60–93; Wolf, 1997, p. 20) and regarded by state agents (both liberal market and social democrat) as one of the most efficient means of restructuring labour–capital relations to manage crisis in capitalist society.[4] Although Cox's analysis promises a critical edge his failure to develop a coherent theory of the state and its relationship to class, has important implications for his conceptualization of the global system. In short, by viewing the state and the market as opposed forms of social organization (with globalization tipping the balance in favour of the market against the state), Cox and most other IPE approaches follow implicitly the liberal–realist position which separates social reality into rigid categories and looks for external linkages between artificially disaggregated phenomena.[5] In this way, much IPE resembles not a progression from classical political economy but a reversion to what Marx termed 'vulgar economy' (Marx, 1976a, pp. 174–5n.34). The endless tautological accounts of 'state' and 'market', of 'interdependencies', 'interactions', 'influences' and 'autonomies' fail to grasp the complex organic set of social relations, which is the global political economy.

In contrast to the classical tradition of political economy, which set itself the task of conceptualizing the internal framework of capitalist relations of production, vulgar economists are vilified by Marx for 'floundering around within the apparent framework of those relations', ceaselessly ruminating on the materials long since provided by scientific political economy, and seeking there plausible explanations of the crudest phenomena. The charge that modern orthodox IPE confines itself to 'systematising in a pedantic way' (Marx, 1974a, pp.74–5n.34) can again be illustrated from Gilpin's 'magisterial' account where despite the obvious centrality of the concepts of 'state' and 'market', the author notes, 'whether each developed autonomously, the market gave rise to the state, or the state to the market are important historical issues whose resolution is not really relevant to the argument of this book' (Gilpin, 1987, p. 10). If IPE theorists seriously wish to analyse the relationship between political authority and market power, it is difficult to see which historical and conceptual issue could be more relevant.

Marx of course developed his own organic conception of capitalist society through a thorough-going critique and reformulation of the theories of classical political economy. Marx's early economic and philosophical studies led him to question, by method of immanent critique, the naturalistic basis of classical political economy. The error of the classical writers was to naturalize (or present as universal) the historically specific social relations of capitalist society. Behind the formal abstractions of classical political economy (land, labour and capital producing rent, wages and profit) lay an unexamined historically specific postulate, private property. Only by taking for granted the existence of private property could the classical writers assume that classes were derived technically from the division of labour. The best exponents of classical political economy for Marx provided an analysis of value and its magnitude (however incomplete) but failed to ask the vital question, 'why this content has assumed that particular form' (Marx, 1976b, p. 174). In fact, as Holloway points out, Marx saw the question of form as being the crucial dividing line between his theory and bourgeois approaches, for which the question of form is meaningless (Holloway, 1991a, p. 73). Marx's monumental study of *Capital* begins therefore with an analysis of the commodity-form in order to emphasize, in contrast to the classical writers, that the products of labour only become commodities in historically specific and thereby transitory forms of society. On this historical and materialist basis, Marx builds a theory of capitalist society rooted in the concepts of value, surplus value and class. The isolated individual of liberalism is parodied since private interest is itself already a socially determined interest and the symmetrical exchange relation is shown to conceal exploitation thereby exploding Smith's theory of a harmony of interest existing between classes. Capitalist society is based on a particular social form of production within which the production of useful goods is subordinated to the expansion of surplus value. Although therefore Marx agrees with the classical writers that 'the anatomy of civil society is to be sought in political economy', his total reformulation of the classical concepts inaugurated a revolution in social science the results of which have yet to be assimilated by those who wish to develop a radical IPE.

Rather, therefore, than viewing the relationship between states and markets as external and contingent, an alternative methodology rooted in Marx's work is to start from the premise that the relationship is internal and necessary (although of course the institutional form of this relationship varies given the historical character of the class struggle). States are an aspect of the social relations of production (a differentiated form of those relations) and their 'power' derives from their ability to reorganize labour–capital relations within (and often beyond) their boundaries to enhance the accumulation of capital both domestically and globally.[6] This interpretation of Marx's approach to the state has been developed most consistently under the auspices of the Conference of Socialist Economists (and in its journal, *Capital & Class*). Rooted in Marx's account of the 'fetishism of commodities', this approach dissolves the state as a category and sees it as a 'rigidified' or 'fetishised' form of social relations (Holloway, 1994, pp. 23–49). National states exist as political 'nodes' or 'moments' in the global flow of capital and their development is therefore part of the antagonistic and crisis-ridden development of capitalist society. Recent changes in the GPE are thus predominantly about reorganizing (rather than by-passing) states and this recomposition is undertaken actively by state managers as part of a broader attempt to restructure, and respond to, a crisis of labour–capital relations (manifest in national terms as fiscal crisis, declining productivity, lack of competitiveness etc.).

This framework understands the 'state' as an aspect of the social relations of production, and in particular directs attention to the social determination of labour, which forms the starting point for Marx's analysis, 'it is the general light tingeing all other colours and modifying them in their specific quality; it is a special ether determining the specific gravity of everything found in it' (Marx and Engels, 1986, p. 43). For Marx the importance of the social relations of production, and the disposition of power, which thereby obtains between the working class and the ruling class throughout history in class-divided societies, cannot, be overemphasized. By rooting his study in the analysis of the direct relationship of the owners of the conditions of production to the immediate producers, Marx offers a unique theorization of the entire social edifice and, thereby, its changing political form. In capitalism, as Ellen Meiksins Wood points out, the disposition of power between the individual capitalist and worker has as its condition the political configuration of society as a whole – the balance of class forces and the powers of the state which permit the expropriation of the direct producer, the maintenance of private property for the owner, and his control over production and appropriation (Meiksins Wood, 1981, pp. 69–95).

This approach suggests that the apparent solidity of the 'state' masks its existence as a contradictory form of social relationship. The state is not only an institution but a form-process, an active process of forming social relations and therefore class struggles channelling them into non-class forms – citizens rights, international human rights – which promote the disorganization of labour (Holloway, 1991a, pp. 75–6). The key to comprehending capitalist society is that it is a social system based on the imposition of work through the commodity-form (Cleaver, 1979, pp. 71–86). The reproduction of bourgeois social relations at all levels (from the overseer, to the managing director, state managers, international agencies and alliances between states) rests upon the ability of capital (in all its forms and guises) to harness and contain the power of labour within the bounds of the commodity-form. The struggles, which ensue over the imposition of work, the regulation of consumption through the commodification of labour time as money and the confinement of the production of use values within the bounds of profitability produce constant instability and crisis. It is the everyday struggles in and against the dominance of the commodity-form, which are manifest as 'national' economic crises or balance of payments problems or speculative pressure on currency. Thus, Marx's approach does not reject the 'state' as a category in favour of social movements but rather it sees relations between national states in terms of the social relationships, which constitute states as moments of the global composition of class relations.

In contrast therefore to mainstream IPE, Marx's methodology draws attention to the state as an aspect of the social relations of production and highlights that the management of labour and money are the central axes of state 'intervention' in capitalist societies. In many instances, as de Brunhoff (1978, p. 2) points out, monetary policy as a form of managing crisis has functioned as a means of organizing recession in order to establish a new subordination of labour to capitalist command. Discussions of government policy however should not be taken to indicate that the state 'controls' the 'economy' or that it is able always successfully to regulate class conflict. In this sense, 'it is not necessary to confuse the ideology of economic policy with its actual practice as a capitalist strategy even if the practices require such an ideology' (ibid., p. 64). The 'apparent separation' of the state from civil society which defines the capitalist character of the state (Clarke, 1988, pp. 120–54; Holloway and Picciotto, 1977, pp. 76–101), places the management of labour power and money as central to the process of capitalist reproduction. The remainder of this chapter will indicate how this approach can be used to conceptualize recent changes in state–labour–capital relations understood in terms of a shift in the politics of management from politicized to depoliticized state strategies. Although the following analysis will focus on the experience of the British state, many of the depoliticized strategies discussed have been adopted in varying degrees around the globe.

From politicized to depoliticized forms of economic management

The characterization of the politics of state management in the 1990s in terms of the notion of depoliticization is best approached by drawing a contrast with the politicized management approach, which dominated economic policy during the period 1945–76. Table 6.1 indicates the principal features of the politicized mode of economic management. Table 6.2 introduces the notion of depoliticized management.

Throughout the period 1945 to the mid-1980s, the British state adopted a politicized strategy to manage labour and money, which required increasingly elaborate government intervention to persuade business, trade unions and others to moderate wage demands. In the context of relatively full employment (the product largely of fortuitous structural conditions as the Treasury was later to admit),[7] successive governments sought to regulate labour through moral exhortation (in the national interest), increasing the exercise of centralized authority over wage determination and through the creation of new surveillance and guidance machinery. In many key respects the story of state policy in the postwar period confirms the views of Kalecki (1971, p. 141), that lasting full employment is unsound from the government's point of view, causing particular social and political problems and that large-scale unemployment is in many important respects 'an integral part' of the smooth operation of the capitalist economy.

Table 6.1 Politicized Management (Discretion-based)

1. Government publicly adopts primary responsibility for economic management.
2. Emphasis on direct intervention and conciliation/co-option in the management of labour, capital and finance.
3. Government takes immediate credit if policies are successful but perceived 'economic' crisis can quickly become a 'political' crisis of the state.

Characteristic mode of economic management 1945–76, principal features

- Direct controls (production, consumption, exchange);
- Incomes policies (formal, informal);
- Downgrading of exchange rate management (political control of Bretton Woods);
- Fiscal/monetary 'autonomy' (no significant interlinking);
- Centralization of policymaking (including trade union representation);
- Direct control of expanded public sector – political disputes given the nature of the 'state as employer';
- International co-operation (rather than integration).

Table 6.2 Depoliticized Management (Rules-based)

Not the 'end of politics'. Not the wholesale evacuation of politics from policy-making (the act of depoliticization is itself highly political). Rather, there is an attempt to *place at one remove the political character* of decision-making. Three important aspects are as follows:

1. The reordering or reassignment of tasks from the party in office (operational independence, 'managerial 'state);
2. Increased accountability, transparency and external validation of policy (Fiscal Code; IMF Code of Good Practice);
3. Acceptance of binding 'rules' limiting government room for manoeuvre (ERM, WTO Dispute Settlement Mechanism).

Overall aim is to enhance government control and shield party in office from unpalatable consequences of policies.

Characteristic mode of management in the 1990s, principal features

- Centrality of exchange rate management – preference for fixed rate systems (ERM/Convergence criteria/EMU);
- Institutional realignment to enhance policy credibility (central bank independence, Fiscal Code);
- Interlinking of fiscal, monetary and exchange rate policy;
- Devolution of policymaking;
- Deregulation (re-regulation of financial markets);
- Legislative marginalization of trade unions (redrawing of boundaries between the 'industrial' and the 'political'; switch focus from government to law courts);
- Recomposition of management hierarchies within states (managerial state);
- From international co-operation, to forms of regional integration (EU, NAFTA, APEC, etc.).

By 1975, it was clear to the state that the politicized management of labour since 1945 had been far from successful. A Special Treasury Study of government wages policy concluded,

> it can hardly be argued that Incomes Policy has kept our degree of inflation lower than that of our neighbours, and until very recently it could not be plausibly asserted that import price problems had unfairly prejudiced our success. Moreover it cannot be said that the policy has found a formula for a fair or efficient distribution of incomes. Nor is there, in spite of the National Board for Prices and Income's efforts, any evidence that 'restraint' assisted either economic growth or economic efficiency. Incomes Policy, must therefore, to date, be judged a failure'. (UK Treasury (1976), *PRO T267/28*)

A central contradiction inherent in the politicized strategy (Clarke, 1988, p. 298–9) was that it sought to restore the profitability of capital by developing institutional forms of regulation of the working class, which at the same time strengthened and unified the representatives of working class interests. Expectations of increases in wages without regard to productivity were institutionalized in the form of incomes policies. Thereby from its very inception this strategy led to rises in wages and increases in public expenditure that exacerbated pressure on profits so undermining the attempt of the state to 'stimulate investment by encouraging optimistic expectations of profitability on the part of capitalists' (ibid., p. 299). Paradoxically, incomes policies tended to increase inflationary pressure as stronger groups of workers forced the pace on wage settlements. Governments responded through deflationary measures, which further politicized policy culminating in Heath's abortive attempt to subordinate class relations directly to the rule of money and law.

In terms of broad macro-economic management, the gradual relaxation of direct controls in the late 1940s initially placed a greater burden on fiscal policy. Although during the 1950s monetary policy played an enhanced role, in the form of credit restrictions and movements in short-term interest rates, the Radcliffe Report of 1959 confirmed the view that interest rates were an uncertain tool for demand management (Dimsdale, 1991, p. 89; Hatton and Chrystal, 1991, p. 68). However, balance of payments difficulties experienced particularly under Wilson in the 1960s led to increased reliance on monetary restriction to stabilize the external balance. The collapse of Labour's politicized strategy in the mid-1970s saw monetary policy, in the form of one-year targets for monetary aggregates, assume centre stage in macro-economic policy. By the early 1980s, the government gave a clear signal that it would no longer adjust demand to accommodate inflation. The credibility of this strategy, as Hatton and Chrystal (1991, p. 74) emphasize, was established by the imposition of cash limits, by the commitment to medium-term budgetary objectives and by the refusal to reflate the economy using fiscal policy in the early 1980s. Whereas in general in the 1950s and 1960s changes in monetary and fiscal policy were not closely related, the adoption of targets for monetary aggregates led to explicit coordination in the 1980s and the increased importance of exchange rate considerations dominating monetary policy (Dimsdale, 1991, pp. 137–40).

Depoliticization and governing strategies in the 1990s

By the early 1980s, it was clear that the economic circumstances that had given rise to relatively full employment in Western Europe had changed. The return of large-scale unemployment, fiscal crisis and the volatility introduced by the switch to floating exchange rates and the re-regulation of financial markets enabled the British state to reassess its approach to the regulation of labour and money. Kalecki had argued in the early 1940s, 'the assumption that a government will maintain full employment in a capitalist economy if only it knows how to do it is fallacious' (Kalecki, 1971, p. 138). Under a regime of permanent full employment, 'the sack' ceases to play its role as a disciplinary measure and the stronger bargaining power of the workers is likely to increase political instability and lead to problems associated with 'political overload' and 'ungovernability'. The ability of the state to successfully pursue anti-inflationary policies in conditions of relatively full employment is circumscribed fundamentally by the relationship that can be established between government, unions and employers associations (and the relationship between the latter groups and its members). In such circumstances the implementation of anti-inflationary policies will always threaten to heighten class conflict and ultimately risk the danger that an 'economic/industrial' crisis will become a crisis of political authority itself (Goldthorpe, 1978, pp. 186–214). This occurred explicitly in the British case with the state's attempt to reconcile the conflicting aspirations of capital and the working class resulting increasingly in struggles over the form of the state.

One of the most important lessons of the 1920s (from the viewpoint of state managers) was that the onset of recession paradoxically gave governments greater room for manoeuvre in devising strategies to regulate the economy. Switching from a politicized (discretion-based) system to a depoliticized (rules-based) approach enabled the government to 'externalize' the imposition of financial discipline on labour and capital. The stronger (and more distant) the set of 'rules', the greater manoeuvrability the state would achieve, increasing the likelihood of attaining objectives. This was the logic behind Britain's return to the Gold Standard in spring 1925 at the pre-war parity of £1 = \$4.86. The move was subjected to a devastating critique by John Maynard Keynes who argued that the pre-war parity was too high and would impose painful and useless deflation on the British economy (Block, 1977, p. 17). Leading supporters of the return to gold, in particular John Bradbury and Otto Niemeyer in the Treasury, were adamant that the gold standard would make the British economy 'knave-proof', free of manipulation for 'political or even more unworthy reasons' (Rukstad, 1989, p. 440). In effect, it was judged that the gold standard with its 'automatic corrective mechanisms' was the best guarantee against inflation. Similar arguments were employed by critics of the Conservatives' regime of politicized management in the 1950s. Supporters of the Operation Robot plan[8] argued that the rule of the market should prevail over interventionist management and 'if the workers, finding their food dearer, are inclined to demand higher wages, this will have to be stopped by increasing unemployment until their bargaining power is destroyed'.[9] The experience of the 1920s and the criticism voiced in the 1950s were finally heeded in the 1990s in a context where the re-regulation of financial markets strengthened arguments favouring the implementation of depoliticized rules-based policies.

The re-regulation of financial markets (increased capital mobility and the creation of a genuinely integrated global market) which began in earnest in October 1979 with the abolition of the 40-year old system of exchange controls in Britain, has undoubtedly affected the fiscal and monetary choices open to governments.[10] Since foreign exchange dealers prefer to hold currencies backed by anti-inflationary policies, the search for counter-inflationary credibility is of paramount importance both rhetorically and materially. Whilst in the post-war era, as Helen Thompson (1995, pp. 1100–11) indicates, currency markets were driven largely by current account imbalances, now interest rate differentials are the prime determinant of exchange rate movements. The 1980s and 1990s have seen a general convergence in interest rates and any state, which adopts a significantly looser monetary policy than the prevailing level risks a depreciation in its currency. Since the sheer scale of flows in the foreign exchange markets rules out reserve intervention as anything more than a short-term policy, monetary policy is, for the moment, inextricably tied to exchange rate management. The net result of this fiscal and monetary environment is that governments have a clear incentive to enhance their counter-inflationary credibility (Hirst and Thompson, 1996, pp. 143–51; H. Thompson, 1995, p. 1103).

Whilst it is common to view these developments as giving 'power' to markets over states, an alternative would be to see the re-regulation of financial markets as providing the strongest possible public justification governments can muster for maintaining downward pressure on wages to combat inflation and thereby achieve price stability (state managers were of course responsible for the creation of the Eurocurrency markets that developed largely out of inter-state rivalry focused on finance (van Dormael, 1997). In many key ways therefore, the re-regulation of financial markets enhances the 'power' of the state vis a vis the working class since it can be argued forcefully that price stability really is the crucial determinant in the GPE and lack of 'competitiveness' translates directly into a loss of jobs and profits. 'Globalization' in this sense is far from being 'merely' an ideology.

In this environment where the maintenance of price stability is publicly acknowledged as the first objective of monetary policy (and high wage settlements are seen as a major cause of inflation) governments across the world in advanced capitalist states have attempted to control inflation by adopting 'rules-based' rather than 'discretion-based' economic strategies.[11] 'Rules-based' approaches attempt to build counter-inflationary mechanisms into the economy by re-ordering part of the government's responsibility for economic policy onto non-governmental bodies. This can be achieved in two ways; first, by reassigning tasks onto an international regime, usually an international monetary mechanism, which sets definite rules (Gold Standard, ERM). This attempts to build 'automaticity' into the system formally limiting government room for manoeuvre. Second, by reassigning tasks to a national body which is given a definite role in statute and thereby greater independence from the government (for example moves towards central bank independence, complemented by fiscal responsibility codes). Whereas 'rules-based' strategies are attempts to 'depoliticise' the government's economic policymaking (thereby shielding the government from the political consequences of pursuing deflationary policies), 'discretion-based' approaches are highly politicized since national governments play the central role in controlling inflation, usually through formal incomes policies.

In the 1990s the shift to depoliticization strategies has been pronounced and can be illustrated further with reference to the British state's management of labour and money. It is important to be aware that the term 'depoliticisation' as used in this chapter should not be taken to mean the direct removal of politics from social and economic spheres or the simple withdrawal of political influence. Rather, depoliticization is a governing strategy and in that sense remains highly political. In essence, depoliticization as a governing strategy is the process of placing at one remove the political character of decision making. In many respects state managers retain arms-length control over crucial economic processes whilst benefiting from the distancing effect of depoliticization. Furthermore, depoliticization strategies invariably require the public rejigging of bureaucratic practices to achieve their primary aim, which is to change expectations regarding the effectiveness and credibility of policymaking. In this sense depoliticization is not simply an ideology (unrelated to material practice) but rather is one of the most potent forms of ideological mobilization reflecting changes in the form in which state policymaking is carried out (capitalizing thereby on the ideological effects of changed material practices).

As a governing strategy, depoliticization has taken three main forms in Britain in the 1990s. First, there has been a reassignment of tasks away from the party in office to a number of ostensibly 'non-political' bodies as a way of underwriting the government's commitment to achieving objectives. The most obvious example in this regard is the government's move to grant 'operational independence' in the area of monetary policy to the Bank of England. On the 8th October 1992, in a memo to the House of Commons Treasury and Civil Service Committee, Norman Lamont set out the policy framework, which would replace the ERM. Counter inflationary credibility would now be sought by restructuring the institutional relationship between the Treasury and the Bank of England in order 'to make the formation of policy more transparent and our decisions more accountable' (Jay, 1994, pp. 169–205). In November 1992 Lamont set an inflation target of 1–4 per cent and asked the Bank to assess inflation prospects in quarterly independent reports. With Kenneth Clarke as Chancellor in May 1993, the Bank was given the right of deciding the timing of interest rate changes. Finally, in February 1994, Clarke outlined a new framework for monetary policy decision making: decisions concerning interest rates would be taken at meetings between the Chancellor and the Governor and minutes would be published with some time delay. Well-publicized disputes between the Chancellor and the Governor during the Major administration questioned the extent to which these halting moves towards central bank independence constituted an effective counter-inflationary anchor. The response of the government in 1995 was to review recommendations to enshrine price stability in statute as the primary objective of monetary policy and follow the Bank of France by creating an independent Monetary Policy Committee within the Bank to oversee the making of policy. In the wake of Blair's victory in May 1997, 'New Labour' completed the reforms begun by Lamont and Clarke. The move to introduce 'operational independence', broadly along the lines of the New Zealand model, has now left the Bank 'free' to pursue an inflation target laid down by a nine-person Monetary Policy Committee (Bonefeld and Burnham, 1998, pp. 32–52; *The Sunday Times* (15 March 1998, p. 6)). In respect of the management of labour, the reassignment of tasks away from the party in office is evident first in the legislative marginalization of trade unions, second in government-sponsored union use of the legal system which switches attention away from government to the law courts and third in the reorganization of the public sector and the emergence of so-called New Public Management. Since most attention in industrial relations has been focused on the use of restrictive legislation, I will focus this brief discussion on the reorganization of labour in the public sector.[12]

The politicized management of public sector labour established in line with the Whitley procedures of interest representation, which underwrote the increased relevance of trade unionism to state workers, resulted in mass union militancy by state workers in the 1970s.[13] As Peter Fairbrother (Fairbrother, 1994, pp. 1–32) points out, for union leaders this meant a direct engagement with state policy and a questioning not only of incomes policies but of other state policies concerned with the provision of state services. For successive governments the dilemma was how to implement state policies on public services as well as incomes policies without creating the conditions for direct challenges from increasingly active state sector unions.

The result in key areas of state administration has been the recomposition of managerial and worker relations through the establishment of marketized state labour processes. Moving beyond definitions of privatization where the emphasis is on ownership and the transfer of assets, a range of public sector functions have been externalized and out-sourced. The consequence is that the public sector is defined by 'a permeable set of relations, where there is a mix of responsibility between public sector enterprises and the private sector for the provision of public sector functions' (Fairbrother, 1998, p. 1). In short we are witnessing the creation of 'managerial states' as part of the process of depoliticizing labour–management relations in the public sector, as responsibility for the operational activity of state bodies shifts away from direct government involvement and is placed in the hands of managers who represent a more distant and disembodied form of regulation via financial control and restriction (Carter, 1997, pp. 65–85; Pollitt, 1990).

The second form in which depoliticization has been manifest as a governing strategy in Britain in the 1990s is in the adoption of measures to ostensibly increase the accountability, transparency and external validation of policy. Recent moves to establish a Code for Fiscal Stability (based on the fiscal responsibility codes created in New Zealand) and the government's intention to create, in conjunction with the World Bank and the OECD, a Code of Good Practice for openness and transparency in macro-economic policy both exemplify this trend. In July 1997 the Blair government tied fiscal policy to two rules. First, over the economic cycle, the government would only borrow to invest (public consumption would therefore be paid for by taxation). Second, the government would ensure that the level of public debt as a proportion of national income would be held at a stable and prudent level (UK Treasury (1998), *A Code for Fiscal Stability* (HMSO)). Building on this framework, the government announced in March 1998 that its fiscal rules must be seen to represent a 'credible commitment in the eyes of the public' (Ibid. p. 2). To make this commitment visible the chancellor proposed that the code be enshrined in legislation, 'to rule out the possibility of profligate fiscal behaviour and so that governments can be held accountable for their policy decisions' (ibid., p. 3). At the heart of the Code stand five principles of fiscal policy management: *transparency* in the setting of fiscal objectives, implementation of policy and presentation of results; *stability* in policymaking and the impact of fiscal policy; *responsibility* in the management of public finances; *fairness* not least between generations; and *efficiency* in managing both sides of the public sector balance sheet.

To achieve these objectives, and more importantly to indicate in public how specific policies relate to declared principles, the government has drawn up plans to recast the Financial Statement and Budget Report (to include its key operating assumptions and explain discrepancies between outcomes and previous budget forecasts) and to introduce an Economic and Fiscal Strategy Report (reconciling short- and long-term fiscal strategy). In addition, to enhance accountability and transparency the government proposes a closer involvement of the National Audit Office to police key assumptions and conventions underpinning economic policy. In short, through these measures, justified in terms of openness and accountability, the government aims to both alter expectations of key actors (in particular public sector trade unionists) and insulate itself from the consequences of tight fiscal policies.

Finally, depoliticization strategies have been pursued in an overall context favouring the adoption of binding 'rules' which limit government room for manoeuvre. Throughout Europe this is clearly seen in the preference for the fixed exchange rate management system the centre-piece of which is the ERM and the convergence rules governing the move to Stage 3 of European Monetary Union. In Britain in late 1989, membership of the ERM was advocated as the best possible means of securing low inflation whilst shielding the government from the impact of recession. Major and Lawson agreed with the Bank of England in early 1990 that Britain would reap substantial benefits from joining the ERM. In particular by ruling out periodic exchange rate realignments both sides of industry, in Major's view, would be forced to face the long-standing problem of inflationary wage settlements. Thatcher's remedy for the 1980s, that policy should focus on the control of monetary aggregates (the Medium-Term Financial Strategy), weakened as the government found increasing difficulty in controlling the money supply, and as different measures of money contradicted each other (Bonefeld, 1993a, pp. 162–7; Grant, 1993, p. 56). The prerequisite for sustained ERM membership was a reduction in unit labour costs through lower wages and the intensification of work. The Bank of England made this quite clear: 'The Governor has emphasised that henceforth companies can have no grounds for expecting a lower exchange rate to validate any failure to control costs. The greater stability which ERM membership offers sterling against other European currencies should in itself be welcome to business as it will enable firms to plan and invest with greater certainty. If companies recognize that they are now operating under a changed regime, the benefits of lower inflation will accrue sooner, and at a lower cost in terms of lost output, than could otherwise be expected. But if they fail to recognize the constraints under which they now operate the outcome will prove painful to them' (D. Smith, 1992, p. 187). With inflation rising, the ERM offered the government the opportunity to have monetary discipline 'implemented from without' (Sandholtz, 1993, p. 38). Clearly, the Major administration hoped it could be insulated from the unpalatable consequences of 'economic adjustment' by joining an international regime constructed on the basis of binding rules. ERM membership, the government hoped, would force employers to compensate for the high interest rate pressure on profits by confronting their labour force to secure lower wage rates and increase output per worker. A falling exchange rate would no longer compensate sluggish productivity, or enable wage negotiators, to agree 'unacceptably' high claims. In essence, the ERM replayed the episode of Britain's return to the Gold Standard in 1925. The 'politics of austerity' could now be legitimated in the language of globalization with 'rules' and 'external commitments' uppermost. In many respects, and from the viewpoint of the governors, ERM membership 'worked'. Inflation fell from 10.9 per cent in October 1990 to 3.7 per cent by September 1992. Lamont heralded the 'sea-change' in attitudes to inflation that occurred in Britain, particularly amongst trade union leaders, since joining the wide band in October 1990. But above all else, this act of depoliticization enabled Major to preside over the second worst recession since the Second World War and survive for a further term of office (Bonefeld, Brown *et al.*, 1995, pp. 74–112). In a wider context, the adoption of rules-based strategies is also evident in government support for new international institutions such as the World Trade Organisation and in particular the linchpin of the organization, its dispute settlement mechanism which seeks to integrate previously disparate settlement procedures and enforce the rules of the WTO (Marceau, 1997, pp. 25–81).

The argument of this section has been that by retaining a clear conceptualization of the internal and necessary relations between labour, state and capital, it is possible to avoid the vague generalizations about the future of the state, which abound in orthodox IPE. It is more productive, I have suggested, to analyse the politics of state management, which in the 1990s seem to be characterized by a number of depoliticization strategies.

Conclusion: what is 'political' about IPE?

If the central task of IPE is held to be the elucidation of the relationship between political authority and market power, then the sub-discipline must, to date, be judged a failure. In the late 1960s Ralph Miliband restated the centrality of methodological assumptions in social science arguing that political analysts must acknowledge that all studies are underpinned by a theory of the state (Miliband, 1969, p. 4). It appears that most practitioners of IPE have failed to heed Miliband's, albeit quite modest, methodological stricture. Lack of reflection on state theory not only diminishes IPE's claim to offer a 'political' as opposed to an 'economic' interpretation of events. It also has serious implications for its understanding of state–market relations. Although 'globalization' has become the leitmotif of the sub-discipline, IPE has failed to lay bare the dynamics of the process primarily because IPE theorists deny the need to conceptualize the relations between labour, state and capital. Moreover not only are labour markets generally ignored but the category of labour itself recedes from view and is treated as external to state–market restructuring.

In order to 'repoliticise' the sub-discipline in a meaningful fashion, IPE analysts face a choice. Either accept the conservative implications of the methodological pluralism of Max Weber which gives all variables that comprise a social order (such as the economy, the polity and civil society) real autonomy, or reconstruct the discipline on the basis of a 'totalising' theory rooted in an organizing principle (marxism, feminism, ethnicity, radical environmentalism). I have indicated above how a particular reading of Marx allows us to approach the social formation as an interacting set of processes historically specified and inserted in such a way that all relations are subsumed under the capital relation as the basis of the valorization process. The notion of class is therefore analytically prior to the distribution process forming the basis of production relations on which accumulation is constituted, whilst the apparent separation of the state from the economy cannot be taken at face value but is rather seen as a historically specific form taken by the social relations of production. This approach identifies the internal and necessary unity of state and market in capitalism. Space is thereby opened up to view new developments in the global political economy in terms of the reorganization (rather than bypassing) of states. Moreover, this recomposition is undertaken actively by states as part of a broader attempt to restructure, and respond to crisis (rooted in labour–capital conflict) in capitalist society. From the viewpoint of state managers, 'politicised' forms of labour management and inflation control involving voluntary restraint, incomes policies and the machinery of tripartism have for the moment given way to 'depoliticised' forms of management which marketize aspects of state activity and reassign responsibility publicly for management onto 'external' regimes and independent organizations. In this way, depoliticization strategies aim to capitalize on recent changes in the global system to the advantage of national governments.

The technicalities of new currency bands, central bank independence, the re-regulation of financial markets and single currencies can be understood politically as part of a wider process of depoliticization designed to achieve the subordination of labour to capitalist command. 'Globalization' is therefore as much a state strategy as it is a market one (Panitch, 1994, p. 63; G. Strange, 1997; Wolf, 1997, p. 20). Although individual governments may be bucked by markets, market-based solutions offer governments opportunities to recast labour–capital relations (often in the guise of controlling inflation) without resorting to the overtly 'politicised management' of the 1960s and 1970s. In short and in contrast to much IPE theory, it is too simplistic to see 'globalization' as transferring 'power' from states to markets. The task for radical political economy is to retain a clear conceptualization of labour–state–capital relations and plausibly explain changing global processes in terms of the recomposition of relations of domination and struggle. This, in essence, is a political explanation.

Notes

1. On heterodox international political economy see Murphy and Tooze (1991). The classic popular liberal view of the state in the era of globalization is Ohmae (1990, 1996).
2. For an extended treatment see Burnham (1995a, pp. 135–59) and Burnham (1995b, pp. 92–115).
3. This is pursued in more detail in Chapter 3.
4. For an extended discussion of the limits of 'fractionalist' approaches to policymaking see Clarke (1978).
5. Although Cox sees some 'social forces' benefitting from globalization, he adopts the standard IPE view that powerful globalizing trends opened up national economies and weakened the 'protective response' of national governments. In short, 'global finance limits drastically the capacity of states to conduct autonomous economic and social policies for the protection of their populations' (see Cox with Sinclair, 1996, pp. 515–16). For an excellent critique of orthodoxy in international relations see Rosenberg (1994).
6. For much greater elaboration see Holloway and Picciotto (1977), Clarke (1988), Barker (1978/1991), Burnham (1990, pp. 180–8), and Bonefeld, Brown *et al.* (1995, pp. 6–33).
7. *PRO T267/12* 'Policy to Control the Level of Demand 1953–58' (UK Treasury, Treasury Historical Memoranda No. 8, July 1965).
8. This was a plan to make sterling convertible on a floating rate in 1952. For details see Cairncross (1985, pp. 234–71) and Procter (1993, pp. 24–43).
9. *PRO T236/3242* 'Setting the Pound Free' Memo Cherwell to Churchill, 18 March 1952. Cherwell, an opponent of the plan, used this argument to persuade the Cabinet that Robot was a risky strategy for the Conservative government given their slender overall majority. He nevertheless accurately represented the argument of Robot's advocates.
10. The term 're-regulation' is preferred to 'deregulation' since in the last 20 years we have seen a complex process of the drafting of new regulations (often new market-oriented rules) rather than a simple lifting of regulations (see Cerny, 1993b, pp. 51–85). Also see Helleiner (1994) and H. Thompson (1994).
11. For an overview of literature on rules versus discretion see Keech (1992, pp. 259–78), or Kydland and Prescott (1977, pp. 473–91). Also see the useful discussions of 'new constitutionalism' by Gill (1995a) and Gill (1998).
12. For a good overview of the impact of legislation see McIlroy (1997).
13. This section draws on Fairbrother (1994) and Fairbrother (1998).

7
Structural Change and Neo-liberalism in Mexico
'Passive Revolution' in the Global Political Economy
Adam David Morton

Introduction

Nowhere did the 'silent revolution' of neo-liberalism become more embraced and contested than in Latin America. Equally, it can be argued that the case of Mexico stands out in the region because of the state's pivotal position in 1982 in announcing it could no longer service its debt obligations. The ensuing era of first generation neo-liberal reforms throughout the 1980s and 1990s also exceeded in many ways the transformations envisaged by the so-called Washington Consensus. Moreover, as Harry Browne (1994, p. 17) noted at the time, 'the evolving free trade relationship between the United States and Mexico foreshadows the future of North–South relations in general'. This chapter therefore develops a critical analysis of these significant and pivotal processes in Mexico commonly understood under the rubric of globalization. Linking directly with the theoretical framework detailed throughout the book (see Chapters 2 and 9), it will do so by tracing the rise of certain social class forces, shaped by a restructuring of social relations of production within the form of state in Mexico, to suggest that a shift occurred in the 1970s, which began the move towards a neo-liberal strategy of capitalist accumulation. This shift not only heralded an end to the phase of Import Substitution Industrialization (ISI) growth, or *'desarollo estabilizador'*, but also fundamentally altered and unravelled the social basis of the hegemony of the once-ruling Institutional Revolutionary Party (PRI). It was this dwindling class hegemony that was finally ended by the victory of Vicente Fox Quesada on the 2 July 2000 elections in Mexico. Yet this electoral change raises questions about whether a second-generation of neo-liberal capitalist development is underway in Mexico, heralding an underlying continuity in policy, regardless of recent debate on the 'post-Washington consensus' (Broad and Cavanagh, 1999; Charnock, 2006; Fine, *et al.*, 2001; see Morton, 2005a; Naím, 2000).

To tackle these issues the chapter will elaborate upon an enduring context of passive revolution in the history of Mexico. This refers, in Antonio Gramsci's idiom, to conditions of socio-economic modernization so that changes in production relations are accommodated within existing social and institutional forms but without fundamentally challenging the established political order (Gramsci, 1971, pp. 106–7). It is a theory of the survival and reorganization of capitalism through periods of crisis, when crucial aspects of capitalist social relations are not overcome but reproduced in new forms, leading to the furtherance of state power and an institutional framework consonant with capitalist property relations. The main benefit of this recourse to the notion of passive revolution is that it leads one to analyse prevalent *consensual* aspects within conditions of hegemony. To put it in Hugues Portelli's (1973, p. 30) apt words, 'There is no social system where consensus serves as the sole basis of hegemony nor a state where the same [*mismo*] social group can durably maintain its domination on the basis of pure coercion.'[1] In contrast to earlier debates on bureaucratic-authoritarianism and state corporatism in Mexico and Latin America, as well as more recent analyses of hegemony that develop similar conclusions, the following argument does not conflate hegemony with dominance or coercion, nor does it presume that conditions of class hegemony are here one day and are gone the next.[2] Instead, the argument draws attention to the variations in, and the gradual erosion of, conditions of hegemony as well as the mix of consensual and coercive elements that have constituted these conditions within the making of modern Mexico.

To promote this analysis the argument is structured into two main sections. The first section will briefly outline the centrality of a theory of passive revolution and class hegemony in understanding the making of modern Mexico. This builds on the conceptual vocabulary introduced in other parts of the book (Chapters 2 and 9). Second, the analysis will concentrate on a context of passive revolution in the history of Mexico by developing an account of structural change to the political economy since the 1970s. This will proceed by, first, examining the accumulation strategy of neo-liberalism and, second, how this impacted on the hegemonic project of the PRI. Whilst neo-liberalism was to gain ascendancy as the chief accumulation strategy in Mexico through the 1980s and 1990s this section draws initial attention to the context of the 1970s in order to account for contingent processes of struggle between social forces that provided the background for subsequent developments. Key developments in this period, linked to the restructuring of production relations, promoted cleavages between social class forces in Mexico that would lead to a shift from the accumulation strategy of ISI to the eventual agenda of neo-liberalism.

It will be clear that the promotion of neo-liberalism and the consequent struggle between social class forces proceeded in a particular way in Mexico more attuned to specific socio-political conditions. Neo-liberalism did not involve the rollback of the state in Mexico but was rooted in the restructuring of state–civil society relations that included a constant renegotiation of state–business–labour relations and the promotion of interventionist projects designed to harness social mobilization. This is important because it becomes possible to show how social class forces within the state in Mexico *authored* the globalization of neo-liberal restructuring within specific structural constraints, thus taking on board one of the main challenges to studies on globalization raised in Chapters 2 and 9 (Panitch, 1994). Put differently, from a neo-Gramscian perspective, the agency of particular social class forces in constituting and reproducing the globalization of neo-liberalism is realized. It will thus be clear how the overall discussion is linked through the notion of passive revolution by considering *both* the restructuring of capitalism, or the 'counter-attack of capital', organized by ruling social class forces through neo-liberal restructuring *and* the articulation of 'anti-passive revolution' strategies of resistance by progressive forces in Mexico (Buci-Glucksmann, 1979, pp. 223, 232).

Understanding Gramsci, hegemony and passive revolution

In recent debates in International Political Economy (IPE) the concept of passive revolution has gained currency within a series of similar but diverse neo-Gramscian perspectives, to address historical processes of state formation in the industrializing world. Whilst a focus is generally drawn to processes of capitalist expansion in 'developmentalist states', within which the state mediates between classes acting as an arbiter of social conflict, very little attention is granted to specific conditions *within* states confronted by an impasse in social development (Cox, 1983, 1987, pp. 218, 230–44; van der Pijl, 1998, pp. 105–6). Rarely is there an effort to focus on the arrangements within particular forms of state that lead to the incorporation of fundamental economic, social, political and ideological changes in conformity with changes in capitalism on a world scale (exceptions would be Augelli and Murphy, 1988; Davies, 1999; van der Pijl, 1993; Sassoon, 2001). In short, very little study has addressed the imperatives of class struggle brought about by the expansion of capital and the *internalization* of class interests within historically determined forms of state (Poulantzas, 1975, pp. 73–6). At the same time, scepticism has also been raised about the lack of direct engagement with the thought and practice of the main exponent of the notion of passive revolution, namely the Italian Marxist Antonio Gramsci (see Germain and Kenny, 1998 and my immanent critique in Morton, 2003a). Hence a turn, first, to the specific writings of Antonio Gramsci to outline in more detail the notion of passive revolution before, subsequently, considering how these conditions inhere within the specific circumstances of class struggle within the state in Mexico.

The Risorgimento, the movement for Italian national liberation that culminated in the political unification of the country in 1860–61, and a whole series of other historical phenomena throughout nineteenth-century Europe were described by Gramsci as 'passive revolutions' (see Morton, 2005b). The concept, rooted in his writings analysing the crisis of the liberal state in Italy, was linked to the rise of so-called 'bourgeois revolutions' with the history of Europe in the nineteenth century seen as a struggle of passive revolution (see Gramsci, 1994a, pp. 230–3, 1995, pp. 330, 348–50). According to Gramsci, the French Revolution (1789) eventually established a 'bourgeois' state on the basis of popular support and the elimination of old feudal classes yet, across Europe, the institution of political forms suitable to the expansion of capitalism occurred differently in a more reformist manner (Gramsci, 1971, pp. 119). Following the post-Napoleonic restoration (1815–1848), the tendency to establish bourgeois social and political order was regarded as something of a universal principle but not in an absolute or fixed sense (Gramsci, 1994a, pp. 20–1). 'All history from 1815 onwards', wrote Gramsci, 'shows the efforts of the traditional classes to prevent the formation of a collective will … and to maintain "economic-corporate" power in an international system of passive equilibrium' (Gramsci, 1971, p. 132). As Eric Hobsbawm (1975, pp. 73, 166) has elaborated, this was indicative of mid-nineteenth-century European national unifications during which people became ancillaries of change organized from above based on elite-led projects. A process that in underdeveloped parts of the world was mimetic as 'countries seeking to break through modernity are normally derivative and unoriginal in their ideas, though necessarily not so in their practices'. A 'passive revolution', therefore, *was* a revolution, marked by violent social upheaval, but it involved a relatively small elite giving a decidedly capitalist imprint to the changes leading to the creation of state power and an institutional framework consonant with capitalist property relations.[3] Moreover, such transformations are linked to processes of uneven development, meaning that the international expansion of capitalism is given important causal significance through the notion of passive revolution in shaping productive development, social prestige and ideology (Gramsci, 1971, pp. 116–17).

The 'passive' aspect refers to the way challenges may be thwarted so that changes in production relations are accommodated within the current social formation. This might not be done in a 'passive' way but refers to the attempt at 'revolution' through state intervention or the inclusion of new social groups within the hegemony of a political order but without an expansion of mass control over politics (Sassoon, 1987, p. 210). A passive revolution may therefore unfold due to popular demands and entail a 'progressive' element or fundamental change in the organization of a political order. Yet it was more likely to result in a dialectical combination of progressive and reactionary elements described as 'revolution-restoration' or 'revolution without revolution' (Gramsci, 1992, p. 137). Whilst the ruling classes might garner real political support among the wider population, a passive revolution tends to indicate a highly restricted form of class hegemony (Sassoon, 2000, p. 72). Within conditions of passive revolution 'the important thing is to analyse more profoundly ... the fact that a state replaces the local social groups in leading a struggle of renewal' (Gramsci, 1971, pp. 105–6). This unfolds when the ruling class is unable to fully integrate the people through conditions of hegemony, or when 'they were aiming at the creation of a modern state ... [but] in fact produced a bastard' (Gramsci, 1971, p. 90). It is one of those cases when a situation of 'domination without that of "leadership": dictatorship without hegemony' prevails because it is possible for the state to dominate civil society which is 'shapeless and chaotic' as it is in 'a sporadic, localised form, without any national nexus' (Gramsci, 1971, pp. 105–6, 1992, pp. 214–15). However, there is also an intrinsic weakness within the state, which is 'lacking effective autonomy' linked to both 'internal as well as international relations', because of the narrow and debilitating interests of 'a sceptical and cowardly ruling stratum' (Gramsci, 1971, p. 90, 1992, p. 151). Hence, through the expansion of state intervention, a partial or relatively fragile form of class hegemony may only prevail, limited to a narrow social group rather than the whole of society. This may have various 'path-dependent' (determined but not deterministic) effects that shape and define the nature and purpose of state actions during particular phases of development and the distinctive institutional configurations of capitalism (Jessop, 2002, pp. 40–2, 58).

The conditions of passive revolution therefore differ from 'the real exercise of hegemony over the whole of society which alone permits a certain *organic equilibrium*' (Gramsci, 1971, p. 396, emphasis added). This expression of class hegemony is based on the development of a ' "diffused" and capillary form of indirect pressure' relying on the organic development of a relationship between leaders and led, rulers and ruled, where real predominance is concealed behind a veil of consent (Gramsci, 1971, pp. 110, 188). In such cases, opposition elements are assimilated through 'capillary articulations' transmitted via channels of public opinion, albeit still with difficulty, friction and loss of energy (Gramsci, 1985, p. 384).

> The 'normal' exercise of hegemony ... is characterised by a combination of force and consent which balance each other so that force does not overwhelm consent but rather appears to be backed by the consent of the majority, expressed by the so-called organs of public opinion. (Gramsci, 1992, pp. 155–6)

A situation of passive revolution contrastingly expresses a condition in which social class forces are in conflict, without any prevailing in the struggle to constitute (or reconstitute) an organic equilibrium based on relations of hegemony. The equilibrium of a passive revolution is therefore unstable and contains within itself the danger of disintegrating into a *catastrophic equilibrium* (Gramsci, 1971, pp. 219–23). Within these structural conditions, 'events that go under the specific name of "crisis" have then burst onto the scene' (Gramsci, 1971, pp. 220–1).

Finally, the concept of passive revolution was also used to describe similar but discrete situations characterized by the expansion of capital and the emergence of the modern state. 'The concept of passive revolution, it seems to me', declared Gramsci, 'applies not only to Italy but also to those countries that modernise the state through a series of reforms ... without undergoing a political revolution of a radical Jacobin-type' (Gramsci, 1996, p. 232). The following section therefore poses particular questions about conditions of passive revolution in relation to a period of structural change in the history of Mexico within which the rise of a strategy of neo-liberal capitalist accumulation can be situated.

Structural change in the form of state in Mexico

One way of examining the social constitution of neo-liberalism in Mexico and the social bases of the state, meaning the specific configuration of class forces that supports the basic structure of state–civil society relations, is to distinguish *analytically* between an accumulation strategy and a hegemonic project. An accumulation strategy defines a specific economic 'growth model' including the various extra-economic preconditions and general strategies appropriate for its realization. The success of a particular accumulation strategy relies upon the complex relations among different fractions of capital as well as the balance of forces between dominant and subordinate classes, hence the importance of a hegemonic project. This involves the mobilization of support behind a concrete programme that brings about a unison of different interests (Jessop, 1990, pp. 198–9, 207–8). An *accumulation strategy* is primarily oriented at the relations of production and thus to the balance of class forces, whilst *hegemonic projects* are typically oriented to broader issues grounded not only in the economy but the whole sphere of state–civil society relations. These are not to be regarded as separate realms but two aspects of political action grounded in the same social relations of production (see Chapters 2 and 9). As Bob Jessop (1990, p. 201) highlights, 'the crucial factor in the success of accumulation strategies remains the integration of the circuit of capital and hence the consolidation of support within the dominant fractions and classes', that is the struggle over hegemony. My argument is that the rise of neo-liberalism in Mexico can be understood within these terms. The conflicts of interest that eventually culminated in the accumulation strategy of neo-liberalism, reflected especially in the Presidency of Carlos Salinas de Gortari (1988–94), were pursued whilst reconfiguring the hegemonic project of the PRI. This resulted in fragmentation leading to a contemporary crisis of authority in Mexico. It now remains to give an account of the context within which the conflicts of interest between class forces took place that led to changes in the form of state in Mexico before considering more contemporary circumstances.

The rise of a neo-liberal accumulation strategy in Mexico

In order to account for the period that Mexicans refer to as the 'tragic dozen' (1970–82), the determinant factor for the transition from an ISI strategy of accumulation to that commonly referred to as the neo-liberal strategy of *salinismo* has been seen as a set of institutional changes *within the organization of the state* (Centeno, 1994, p. 41). The crucial phase that laid the basis for this shift in accumulation strategy in Mexico was the period in the 1970s that set the stage for subsequent developments (Peters, 2000, p. 45).

By the 1970s, during the *sexenio* (six-year term) of Luis Echeverría (1970–76), the government needed to revive its deteriorating legitimacy and responded with a neo-populist programme of political and social reforms. Hence the Echeverría administration embarked on a macroeconomic strategy of 'shared development' within a supposed *apertura democráta* (democratic opening) to forge a populist coalition between national industrialists, peasants, urban marginals, disillusioned labour sectors, students and the middle classes. Yet, faced by pressure from internationally linked industrialists, Echeverría was unable to implement sufficient tax increases in order to support public spending directed towards national industry and the working- and middle-class sectors. Unable to implement tax increases on internationally linked capital, foreign borrowing therefore became the major source of financing for development policies (Davis, 1993, p. 55). Also, due to expanded state intervention in the economy and the increasingly anti-private sector rhetoric, the government began to lose the support of significant sectors of capital. Such state intervention increasingly alienated the private sector and as a result, 'the alliance that ha[d] existed between state and national capital was severely strained' (Centeno, 1994, p. 69). An indication of this was the rise of the private sector in vocally articulating its opposition, notably with the founding of the Business Coordinating Council (CCE) in 1975, that proposed economic policies for the first time in opposition to the government following the impact of the oil crisis of 1973 on Mexico's economic performance. It is important to note that whilst neo-liberalism *had not* taken hold at this time crucial cleavages within the organization of the state were developing that would lead to shifts in capitalist accumulation.

Pivotal in preparing the conditions for such changes was the Mexican financial crisis of 1976. As James Cockcroft (1983, p. 259) has put it, 'capital flight, noncompetitiveness of Mexican products, dollarisation of the economy, and IMF pressures forced a nearly 100 per cent devaluation of the peso in late 1976, almost doubling the real foreign debt ... as well as the real costs of imported capital goods – to the detriment of nonmonopoly firms and the advantage of the TNCs.' Yet the financial crisis can be seen to be as much related to the expansionary public sector expenditure policies driven by the crisis of the PRI as the macroeconomic disequilibria driven by structural change in the globalizing political economy linked to US inflation. Whilst the IMF certainly imposed austerity measures and surveillance mechanisms on Mexico it has been argued that these were less violatory than feared, although they did have a strong impact in altering the internal distribution of power between social classes in Mexico (Whitehead, 1980, pp. 846–7, 851).

At almost the same time, large oil reserves were also discovered which, by 1982, were estimated at 72 billion barrels with probable reserves at 90–150 billion and potential reserves at 250 billion, amounting to the sixth largest reserves in the world (Cockcroft, 1983, p. 261). Hence the political economy of Mexico became dependent on petroleum-fuelled development under the administration of José López Portillo (1976–82) whilst attempts were made to balance the tensions between competing social classes. However, a coherent course, capable of satisfying the interests of national and internationally linked capital in Mexico, was not set. By the time world oil prices dropped in 1981, leading to reduced oil revenues, accelerating debt obligations and a surge in capital flight, Mexico faced another financial crisis that initially led to the nationalization of the banks on 1 September 1982. This was a 'last-ditch effort' to recoup revenues for the public sector and reassert some form of state autonomy but it resulted in reinforcing private sector opposition, capital flight, inflation and balance of payments problems (Davis, 1993, p. 61).

Similar to the earlier crisis, the result of the 1982 debt crisis was a combination of mutually reinforcing factors both within the globalizing political economy and the form of state in Mexico.

> The crisis was precipitated by the world oil glut, a world economic recession, and rising interest rates in the United States, but its root causes were domestic: excessively expansionary monetary and social policies, persistent overvaulation of the peso, over-dependence of the public sector on a single source of revenue (oil exports), a stagnant agriculture sector (at least that part which produced basic foodstuffs for domestic consumption), an inefficient and globally uncompetitive industrial plant, excessive labour force growth ... , a capital-intensive development model that made it impossible to create an adequate employment base, endemic corruption in government, and resistance by entrenched economic and political interests to structural reforms. (Cornelius, 1985, pp. 87–8).

This resulted in another IMF austerity programme – involving reductions in government subsidies for foodstuffs and basic consumer items, increases in taxes on consumption, and tight wage controls targeted to control inflation – that the Mexican administration implemented by exceeding planned targets. Therefore, the crisis arose as a result of a conjunction of factors that also included the rise of technocrats – underway throughout the 1970s – which led to the ascendancy of the accumulation strategy of neo-liberalism. Crucial at this time was the institutional career paths of the elite which began to alter so that ministries associated with banking and finance planning provided the career experience likely to lead to the upper echelons of government. Consistent with the argument in other chapters (see Chapters 2 and 9), what eventually unfolded in Mexico were specific transnational fractions of capital that would come to fuse the concerns of state managers, sectors of the business elite, large conglomerates tied to the export sector such as the *maquila* (in-bond) strategy of export-led industrialization, and sectoral reform of agriculture that integrated farmers into a transnational system of agricultural production. Notably this was the context within which the Ministry of Programming and Budget (SPP) came to rise to institutional predominance as a pivotal *camarilla* (clique) within the organization of the state.

The SPP was created in 1976 and culminated the process of taking economic policymaking away from the Ministry of the Treasury and Public Credit (SHCP). Overall, not only was direct control over the most important resources of information for plans and projects in the bureaucracy secured, but competing factions within the PRI could also be circumvented. Significantly, up to president Ernesto Zedillo (1994–2000), the previous three presidents all originated from agencies related to these changes with López Portillo (1976–82) heralding from SHCP and Miguel de la Madrid (1982–88) and Carlos Salinas (1988–94) from SPP. By 1983 almost 60 per cent of all cabinet-level appointees had started their careers in these sectors and over 80 per cent had some experience within them whilst in the Salinas cabinet 33 per cent had experience in SHCP and 50 per cent had worked in SPP (Centeno and Maxfield, 1992, p. 74). The rise of such technocrats, consistent with the thesis on the internationalization of the state outlined in Chapter 2, ensured that precedence was accorded to ministries of finance like SPP that would subordinate other ministries and prioritize policies more attuned to transnational economic processes. The growing influence of neo-liberal ideas can therefore be linked to the existence of a transnational capitalist class connecting IMF analysts, private investors, and bank officials as well as government technocrats in and beyond the PRI in Mexico. This is how the internationalization of the state proceeded in Mexico. To cite Gramsci, it was a process whereby, 'in the political party the elements of an economic social group get beyond that moment of their historical development and become agents of more general activities of a national and international character' (Gramsci, 1971, p. 16).

A pivotal factor in the formation of this transnational capitalist class in Mexico was the move during the Echeverría presidency after the oil boom of 1975–76 to expand scholarships to foreign universities as a method of integrating dissidents radicalized by the massacre of students at Tlatelolco on 2 October 1968 (Berins Collier, 1992, p. 66). Thus, throughout the 1970s, not only was there a dramatic increase in the educational budget *within* Mexico, leading to a 290 per cent increase in university students between 1970 and 1976, but the number of scholarships for study *abroad* increased even more dramatically (Centeno, 1994, p. 152n.25). It can therefore be argued that the dissemination of foreign ideas in Mexico increased as a direct result of the oil boom. This led to many *tecnócratas* adopting a more conservative ideology whilst becoming dependent on the president for their subsequent governmental position. Hence the crucial rise of *camarillas* that shifted institutional loyalty from a particular ministry or subgroup within the bureaucracy to close political and personal links with the president. It was this technocratic elite that took for granted the exhaustion of the previous ISI development strategy and engendered a degree of social conformism favouring the adoption of an accumulation strategy of neo-liberalism. Yet it was hardly questioned to what extent such structural problems were not just intrinsic to ISI but related also to a series of exogenous shocks, such as the oil crisis, combined with erroneous decisions made in the 1970s following the oil boom. Overall, though, the overriding significance of the above changes was that the rise of *tecnócratas* (or the 'cult of technocracy') in Mexico was advanced by links with transnational capital during a period of structural change in the 1970s (Cockcroft, 1983, p. 217).

For example, during this period of structural change or the 'reformation of capitalism' in Mexico, fractions of a transnational capitalist class became influential in shaping the *maquila* (in-bond) strategy of export-led industrialization fuelled by foreign investment, technology and transnational capital (Sklair, 1993, pp. 13–14). Whilst the *maquila* industry has its roots in the Border Industrialisation Programme (BIP), introduced in 1965 after the United States ended the bracero programme (which provided a legal basis for labour migration from Mexico to the United States), it was not until the 1970s that economic promotion committees began to bring to fruition the earlier visions of border industrialization. Particularly under the auspices of the Secretariat of Commerce and Industrial Development (SECOFI), the industry ministry, within de la Madrid's administration. Between 1979 and 1985 *maquilas* increased by 40 per cent and employees almost doubled (Sklair, 1993, p. 70).

At an early stage in this transformation the interests of private capital were represented by organizations within the National Chamber of Manufacturing Industries (CANACINTRA). Along with other capitalist groups – such as the Confederation of Chambers of Industry (CON-CAMIN), the Confederation of National Chambers of Commerce, Services and Tourism (CONCANACO) and the Employers' Confederation of the Republic of Mexico (COPARMEX) – the major fractions of large- and medium-sized manufacturers co-ordinated and consolidated capital's influence over the state. This influence proceeded further when such capitalist organizations regrouped through the CCE, in 1975, to represent the interests of large-scale monopoly capital within the state. The *maquila* industry was thus promoted, nurtured and supervised by fractions of a transnational capitalist class in Mexico through processes of carefully managed state–labour–business relations that developed into a full-blown export-led strategy of industrialization (Sklair, 1993, p. 227). However, the interests of transnational capital also reached beyond the *maquila* industry to gradually secure the integration of Mexico into the global political economy. Hence, 'the official agricultural policies of the Díaz Ordaz and Echeverría periods [also] promoted transformations which deepened the integration of local farmers into a transnational system of agricultural production' (Gledhill, 1996, p. 183). One consequence of this effort to reproduce the accumulation strategy of neo-liberalism in Mexico was the 1992 reform of collective *ejido* land-holdings enshrined in Article 27 to the Mexican Constitution, undertaken as a prelude to entry into NAFTA in 1994 (Craske and Bulmer-Thomas, 1994). This led to the increased capitalization of land – involving changing property relations and shifts from rank-based social ties and communal commitments of civil-religious hierarchies to cash derived from wage labour – that would impact on forms of resistance such as the *Ejército Zapatista de Liberación Nacional* (EZLN) (see Morton, 2002, 2006b).

An additional feature that also became crucial in the struggle over the neo-liberal accumulation strategy was the introduction of the Economic Solidarity Pact (PSE) in 1987. The PSE was initially a mixed or 'heterodox' programme that aimed to tame the current account deficit and inflation based on a commitment to fiscal discipline, a fixed exchange rate and concerted wage and price controls. It has been heralded as instrumental in achieving a successful renegotiation of external debt following the debt crisis of 1982, in line with the Baker (1985) and Brady (1989) Plans, and further radicalizing the import liberalization programme following Mexico's entry into the General Agreement on Tariffs and Trade (GATT) (Urquidi, 1994, p. 58).

Overall, three components of the PSE were crucial: the government's pledge in favour of the acceleration of privatization and de-regulation; the centrality awarded to the CCE; and the use of large retailers' market power to discipline private firms and further ensure the participation of business elites (Heredia, 1996, p. 138). The CCE – itself formed from a forerunner of big business private sector groups within the capitalist class known as the Mexican Businessmen's Council (CMHN) – became pivotal in initiating and implementing the PSE (Whitehead, 1989, p. 210). As indicated earlier, the class interests of the CCE became centred on a 'transnationalised' segment of national capital including direct shareholders of large conglomerates tied to the export sector with experience in elite business organizations (Luna, 1995, p. 83). Subsequently, many of the CCE leaders became more closely linked with the PRI via committees and employers' associations to increase interest representation within the state. Little wonder, therefore, that the class interests represented by the CCE had a huge impact on the policies implemented by the PRI, including increased privatization (Ugalde, 1994, p. 230). One commentator has gone as far to argue that the relationship between the private sector and the political class became part of a narrow clique exercising a 'private hegemony' so that, 'it would be no exaggeration to say that this alliance was based on a carefully thought-out strategy to bring public policy in line with private sector demands, to effect a global reform of the relationship between the state and society, and hence to redesign Mexico's insertion into the emerging neoliberal global order' (Ugalde, 1996, p. 42).

As a consequence, there was a shift in the PSE from a commitment to state–labour corporatist relations to a disarticulation, but not severing, of the state–labour alliance in favour of the overriding interests of capital. This has been variously recognized as a form of 'new unionism' or neo-corporatism, 'an arrangement involving the reduction of centralised labour power and the participation of labour in increasing productivity' (Teichman, 1996, p. 257). The privatization of the Mexican Telephone Company (TELMEX) in 1990, one of the pinnacles of the privatization programme, particularly reflected the strategy of 'new unionism'. This not only involved manipulation of the Mexican Telephone Workers' Union (STRM), one of the key labour organizations used to secure privatization. It also entailed Salinas permitting the leader of STRM, Hernández Juárez, to create an alternative labour federation, the Federation of Goods and Services Unions (FESEBES), to further facilitate privatization. Hence labour became more dependent on the PRI during the privatization of TELMEX, which generated new resources for corruption and clientelism and lessened union democracy within STRM (Clifton, 2000). What is important here, then, is that the accumulation strategy associated with neo-liberalism did not involve a wholesale retreat of the state nor did the state act as a simple conduit or 'transmission belt' for neo-liberal globalization (see Chapters 2 and 9 on this controversy). As Centeno (1994, p. 195) has commented, 'the pacto [PSE] demonstrated that the *técnocratas* were not generic neoliberals who applied monetarist policies indiscriminately but were willing to utilise a variety of mechanisms to establish control over the economy.' What the case of Mexico does exhibit, though, is precisely the internalization of certain transnational class interests conducive to a specific reorganization of production relations and changes in the form of state (as argued in Chapters 2 and 9). The analysis now turns from discussing the details of how the neo-liberal strategy of accumulation privileged particular social relations of production in Mexico to address how the interlinked hegemonic project of the PRI was also altered and undermined.

The changing circumstances of PRI hegemony

Intrinsically linked to changes in the social relations of production stemming from the 1970s was an increase in the sources of political instability in Mexico. 'Political struggles over national economic policy began in the early 1970s when problems associated with import-substituting industrialization began to mount' (Cook *et al.*, 1994, p. 18). These struggles were manifest in the *sexenios* of Echeverría (1970–76) and López Portillo (1976–82) to the extent that the PRI faced problems involving an erosion of political legitimacy following the Tlatelolco massacre in 1968, a discontented urban middle class, disaffection with the ISI accumulation strategy, the emergence of new opposition movements outside the officially recognized party system, the additional emergence of urban and rural guerrilla movements and the declining ability of the PRI to compete with registered opposition parties (Middlebrook, 1993).

For instance, the National Co-ordinating Committee of Educational Workers (CNTE), founded in 1979, came to challenge, particularly in the peasant communities of Chiapas, the state-imposed and privileged position of the National Education Workers' Union (SNTE), established in 1943 (Foweraker, 1993). This was also the period when independent unions articulated a so-called *insurgencia obrera* (labour insurgency) to question the lack of autonomy and democracy of official unions and to articulate demands across a variety of sectors beyond purely economic concerns (Carr, 1991, pp. 136–9). Yet, as a harbinger of reforms under the neo-liberal accumulation strategy, the López Portillo administration

coercively suppressed many of these opposition movements and implemented economic reforms in favour of the private sector as a prelude to
introducing the Law on Political Organisations and Electoral Processes
(LOPPE) in 1977. Between 1976 and 1979 the dynamism of the
insurgencia obrera faded and became dominated by the themes of economic crisis and austerity (Carr, 1991, p. 137). At the same time, the
LOPPE became an attempt to manage political liberalization within
the current of the *apertura democráta* (democratic opening) by enlarging
the arena for party competition and integrating leftist political organizations whilst inducing them to renounce extra-legal forms of action.
The measures, for example, involved the Mexican Communist Party
(PCM) obtaining its *official* registration as a political party that led
to its first legal participation, since 1949, in the elections of 1979.
Subsequently, in 1981, the PCM merged with four other left-wing parties
to establish the Unified Socialist Party of Mexico (PSUM) (Carr, 1985).
Thus the PCM, the oldest communist party in Latin America at that
time, effectively dissolved itself whilst attempting to electorally compete
within the parameters of the LOPPE reform (Cockcroft, 1998, p. 265).
The reform, therefore, was more than a simple co-optation measure. It
was designed to frame and condition the very institutional context of
opposition movements and constituted the construction of a specific
legal and institutional terrain that was capable of containing popular
demands by defining the terms and fixing the boundaries of representation and social struggle (Foweraker, 1993, pp. 11–12). It thus epitomized
the structures of passive revolution: an attempt to introduce aspects of
change through the state as arbiter of social conflict. In the words of
Echeverría the political reform strived to 'incorporate the majority
of the citizens and social forces into the *institutional* political process'
(as cited by Pansters, 1999, p. 241 original emphasis). As Kevin
Middlebrook (1995, pp. 223–4) has argued, this was a limited political
opening that was essential at a time of severe social and political tension
in order to balance stringent economic austerity measures with policies
designed to diffuse widespread discontent. The capacity of labour to
articulate an alternative vision for Mexican economic and social development through either official or independent unions, evident in the
1970s, thus declined throughout the 1980s to become scarcely evident a
decade later (Cook, 1995, pp. 77–94).

What was evolving in the social formation at this time in Mexico,
therefore, within the context of structural change in the global political
economy, was a shift in the hegemonic influence of the PRI. More accurately the attempt at political reform in the 1970s was an indication of

the ailing class hegemony of the PRI. No longer capable of representing class-transcending interests, the PRI began to re-orient the social relations of production towards a new hierarchy in favour of particular class forces. As a result it is possible to perceive the fraying and unravelling of PRI hegemony in the 1970s. The LOPPE political reform was a clear indication of an attempt to balance the competing demands of subaltern classes with those of the private sector and transnational capital in Mexico. It was a response to the erosion of support for the basic structure of the political system.

Yet it is not easily explained as the exercise of 'normal' hegemony as outlined earlier. Hegemony in this sense relies on the organic equilibrium of a relationship between leaders and led, rulers and ruled, based more on consent. Instead, the PRI became increasingly unable to conceal its real predominance and relied on more coercive measures. 'Between consent and coercion', Gramsci (1971, p. 80n.49) notes, 'stands corruption/fraud (which is characteristic of certain situations when it is hard to exercise the hegemonic function, and when the use of force is too risky).' This is a situation when the party turns, 'into a narrow clique which tends to perpetuate its selfish privileges by controlling or even stifling opposition forces' (Gramsci, 1971, p. 189). It can then entail a shift in the threshold of power from consensual to coercive means indicative of state crisis and the disintegrative elements of catastrophic equilibrium. As a counterpart to the neo-liberal accumulation strategy, the PRI began to increasingly reflect these traits of passive revolution throughout the 1980s.

For example, during the Salinas *sexenio* attempts were particularly made to reconstruct history in order to naturalize radical neo-liberal changes to the political economy (Salinas, 2002). As a result, neo-liberalism came to represent a 'hegemonic shift' in the attempt to dismantle the nationalism of the Mexican Revolution linked to ISI and displace its political symbolism as a focal point of national consciousness (Powell, 1996, p. 40). Yet, the government's ideological use of the legacy of the Mexican Revolution was not merely a straightforward foil for neo-liberalism but, instead, was adapted to specific conditions in Mexico. This fundamental reconstruction of the hegemony of the PRI and transformation of state–civil society relations within Mexico was particularly exhibited through projects like the National Solidarity Programme (PRONASOL).

Following the continued crisis of representation facing the PRI and the tenuous electoral majority Salinas received from the electorate in 1988, a significant attempt was made to try and maintain hegemony.

A notable feature in this effort was PRONASOL, a poverty alleviation programme combining government financial support and citizen involvement to design and implement community development and public works projects. As the PRI had moved away from an inclusive party designed to cover all segments of society to an exclusive one in which only some sectors were represented, PRONASOL was emblematic of the attempt to shore up the loss of hegemonic acquiescence (Centeno, 1994, p. 224). It combined material and institutional aspects focusing on social services, infrastructure provision, and poverty alleviation in order to rearrange state–civil society relations and the coalitional support of the PRI (Cornelius *et al.*, 1994, p. 3). There were three main objectives of PRONASOL. First, it attempted to adapt the state's traditional social role to new economic constraints and redefine the limits of its intervention in the context of a neo-liberal strategy of accumulation. Second, it attempted to diffuse potential social discontent through selective subsidies, accommodate social mobilization through 'co-participation', and undermine the strength of left-wing opposition movements. Third, it attempted to restructure local and regional PRI elites under centralized control (Dresser, 1991, pp. 1–2). Clearly PRONASOL was therefore a targeted attempt to buttress both the accumulation strategy of neo-liberalism and the hegemony of the PRI that was under threat from those very changes.

Emanating from the Salinas *camarilla* that had dominated the SPP, PRONASOL was officially described as an attempt to modernize, pluralize, and democratize state–civil society relations in Mexico as part of the doctrine of 'social liberalism': 'a mode of governance that ostensibly seeks to avoid the worst excesses of both unfettered, free market capitalism and heavy-handed state interventionism, by steering a careful middle course between these "failed" extremes' (Carlos Salinas as cited by Cornelius *et al.*, 1994, p. 4). Usurping the language and mobilizing role of grassroots organizations, PRONASOL was itself portrayed as a 'new grassroots movement', empowering citizens through 'an experience of direct democracy', whilst also redefining members of traditional corporatist organizations as 'consumers' of electricity, improved infrastructure and educational scholarships (Carlos Salinas as cited by Cornelius *et al.*, 1994, pp. 6–7). This new style of thinking amongst state officials, 'was reinforced by ideas recommending the involvement of the poor and NGOs in anti-poverty projects promoted by many international actors, including international financial institutions such as the World Bank and the Inter-American Development Bank, the United Nations, and international donors and development specialists' (Piester, 1997, p. 473).

Between 1989–93, the World Bank directly lent PRONASOL US$350 million to improve rural service provision and to support regional development in four of Mexico's poorest states – Oaxaca, Guerrero, Hidalgo and Chiapas – whilst the Bank also supported a health and nutrition pilot project (Cornelius *et al.*, 1994, p. 16).

Despite the rhetoric, though, PRONASOL preserved and even reinforced presidential rule and complemented the established bureaucracy. As Denise Dresser (1991, p. 2) states, 'the politics of PRONASOL sheds light on why hegemonic parties like the PRI can survive even when threatened by powerful alternative organisations, and why the party has apparently been able to revive after a period of crisis and decline.' Essentially PRONASOL was crucial to maintaining the lagging effect of the PRI's hegemony because it provided the political conditions for sustaining the neo-liberal accumulation strategy notably through a modernization of populism and traditional clientelist and corporatist forms of co-optation. This was carried out through a process of *concertación*, understood as the negotiation of co-operative agreements between social movements and the state involving division and demobilization. The *concertación* strategies espoused by PRONASOL represented a convergence of interests between those of the popular organizations and the technocratic sectors within the PRI and the government (Dresser, 1991, p. 32). Thus, whilst the Salinas administration presented neo-liberalism as a hegemonic project in Mexico, it used PRONASOL to create a sense of inclusion and a durable base of support within civil society. This objective was also fulfilled through PRONASOL by denying the existence of class antagonisms whilst at the same time claiming to transcend class differences (Dresser, 1994, p. 147).

By the time PRONASOL became institutionalized within the Ministry of Social Development (SEDESOL), in 1996, it was clear that the programme had been successful in sustaining the passive revolution of neo-liberalism (Soederberg, 2001). Meaning that it was intrinsic in changing the correlation of class forces in Mexico – to supervise the 'counterattack of capital' through passive revolution – within which there was a transformation of the elite from arbiter of class conflict to ruling in its own interests (Hodges and Gandy, 2002, p. 246). PRONASOL incorporated potentially threatening leaders, alternative programmes and ideas by nullifying substantive differences. Hence, despite the neo-liberal accumulation strategy making it increasingly difficult to conceal the real predominance of its narrow basis of interest representation, the PRI still managed to exert some form of dwindling hegemony albeit relying more on coercion rather than true leadership. The increasing prevalence of coercion throughout the late 1980s and 1990s, particularly reflected in impunity towards human rights violations evident by the rise in the number and profile of political assassinations and kidnappings, bears this out. As Wil Pansters (1999, p. 256 original emphasis) puts it, 'the combined result of neoliberal economic adjustment, institutional malfunctioning and the decomposition of personalistic networks and loyalties [w]as ... an increase in violence *at all* societal levels.'

Hence the view that there was a worsening crisis of hegemony throughout the phase of neo-liberal restructuring in the 1980s and 1990s in Mexico. It was a situation when, 'the ruling class has lost its consensus, i.e. is no longer "leading" but only dominant, exercising coercive force alone', it means, 'precisely that the great masses have become detached from their traditional ideologies, and no longer believe what they used to believe previously' (Gramsci, 1971, pp. 275–6). As the prominent intellectual Carlos Fuentes expressed it at the time: 'It is as though the PRI has gone out to kill itself, to commit suicide. There are Priístas killing Priístas. ... What we see is the internal decomposition of a party, which has, in effect, completed its historic purpose' (*Mexico & NAFTA Report*, 8 December 1994).[4] The PRI, to summarize, became a party that increasingly existed as 'a simple, unthinking executor ... a policing organism, and its name of "political party" [became] simply a metaphor of a mythological character' (Gramsci, 1971, p. 155). Social order was increasingly regressive, to the extent that the party was 'a fetter on the vital forces of history' so that it had, 'no unity but a stagnant swamp ... and no federation but a "sack of potatoes", i.e. a mechanical juxtaposition of single units without any connection between them' (Gramsci, 1971, pp. 155, 190).

As a result, the changes inaugurated in Mexico that led to the promotion of neo-liberalism can be understood as an expression of passive revolution. Neo-liberalism continued to reflect the incomplete process of state and class formation in Mexico that was never truly settled after the Mexican Revolution. It represented a furtherance of particular path-dependent responses to forms of crisis and thus a strategy developed by the ruling classes to signify the restructuring of capitalism, or the 'counter-attack of capital', in order to ensure the expansion of capital and the introduction of 'more or less far-reaching modifications ... into the economic structure of the country' (Gramsci, 1995, p. 350). Neoliberalism, therefore, can be summarized as less 'tightly linked to a vast local economic development, but ... instead the reflection of international developments which transmit their ideological currents to the periphery' (Gramsci, 1971, p. 116). In Mexico, hegemony became limited to privileged groups and was based on a central core of elite and exclusionary decision making that enacted rhetorically 'revolutionary' changes in the social relations of production, through the neo-liberal accumulation strategy, alongside engineered social and political reform. Needless to say, as the contradictions of neo-liberalism become more apparent, the 'path-dependent legacies of neoliberal errors' will also need to be addressed (Jessop, 2002, p. 169).

However, it should not be presumed on the basis of the above argument that both the accumulation strategy and the hegemonic project of neo-liberalism entailed the erosion of state power. Neo-liberalism in Mexico did not involve the dismantling, or retreat, of the state, but the rearrangement of social relations into a new hierarchy. As Dresser (1994, p. 155) has commented,

> Even though neoliberal policy currents underscore the importance of reducing the economic power of the state, the Mexican case reveals that the imperatives of political survival will often dictate the need for continued state intervention through discretionary compensation policies.

The modernization, rather than dismantling, of the state through PRONASOL was thus based on a 'neo-corporatist' arrangement that was pivotal in bolstering the accumulation strategy *and* hegemonic project of neo-liberalism (Craske, 1994).

Conclusion: the shifting sands of hegemony

The central contention of this chapter is that the process of historically specific interest representation and class struggle in Mexico, reflected in the transition from ISI to neo-liberal capitalist accumulation, began in the 1970s due to structural changes in the nature of capitalism that contains within itself contradictions. By focusing on these features from a neo-Gramscian perspective it was possible to emphasize how the agenda of neo-liberalism was constituted, or *authored*, by particular social forces in Mexico linked to processes of transnational class agency.

It was argued that the accumulation strategy of neo-liberalism, especially reflected in the era of *salinismo*, seriously eroded the historical basis of PRI hegemony in Mexico. This bears out the view that granting priority to the accumulation function of the state can undermine its legitimation function and thus weaken hegemony (Cox, 1982, p. 54). The demise of ISI and the rise of neo-liberalism were accompanied by the exhaustion of PRI hegemony. Since the phase of structural change in the 1970s, the historical and social basis of PRI hegemony began to alter and seriously erode. Throughout the 1980s and 1990s, the PRI increasingly resorted to forms of dominance and coercion, reflecting an increasingly dwindling form of class hegemony. It is within this era of structural change that a crisis of hegemony unfolded.

> In every country the process is different, although the content is the same. And the content is the crisis of the ruling class's hegemony. ... [Hence] a 'crisis of authority' is spoken of: this is precisely the crisis of hegemony, or general crisis of the state. (Gramsci, 1971, p. 210)

By thus tracing these shifting sands of hegemony it was argued that the PRI was only hegemonic in a very narrow sense and it continued to lose a large degree of internal coherence and legitimacy from the 1970s onwards. Whilst the lagging effects of such class hegemony were evident during the restructuring of state–civil society relations within the accumulation strategy of neo-liberalism, the historic purpose of the PRI was ended by the victory of Vicente Fox on 2 July 2000. It is beyond the scope of this chapter to determine whether a cohesive form of hegemony can be refashioned under the National Action Party (PAN) or whether the PRI will be able to revive its historic role. Yet it was possible in this account to emphasize variations or lags in hegemony and how forms of hegemony were discernible but recessive over the period under consideration since the 1970s. This helps to avoid either assuming that hegemony is switched on and off like a light switch or indulging in crude dichotomies between coercion and consent in understanding the role and influence of the PRI within the conditions of passive revolution and recurring crisis.

More generally the above analysis of neo-liberalism in Mexico also highlighted how social forces engendered common perspectives on the importance of fiscal discipline and market-oriented reforms between technocratic elites of a common social background. Put differently, building on the framework established in Chapters 2 and 9, attention was drawn to an unfolding process of class struggle brought about by the expansion of capital and the *internalization* of class interests between various fractions of classes within state–civil society relations. This involved focusing on how social relations within the form of state in Mexico were actively and passively implicated in transnational structures of the global political economy. The discussion of the PSE and

PRONASOL, two coexisting measures both introduced to offset political instability resulting from the neo-liberal accumulation strategy and the reconfigured hegemonic project of the PRI, exemplify this process of struggle.

A further point that the argument has raised is that the case of Mexico does not signify the straightforward reproduction of a uniform 'model' of neo-liberalism. Instead, the dissemination and acceptance of neo-liberal values in Mexico has meant an adaptation of social relations to culturally specific conditions. To be sure, this may result in resemblances with similar processes elsewhere in the global political economy but, as the development of policies in Mexico display, there is a certain peculiarity to local tendencies in response to changes in world order. It would be inappropriate to assume therefore that the social constitution of neo-liberalism in Mexico was brought about in a manner that matched the metaphorical view of the state as a simple 'transmission belt' for global restructuring purposes.

Notes

I would like to thank Marcus Taylor for his critical feedback and, importantly, his friendly spirit of intellectual engagement that grew out of a continual exchange of ideas linked to this chapter. Whether the arguments that are proposed are persuasive in overcoming his concerns remains an issue for future debate.

1. I am grateful to Bob Jessop for bringing this *aperçu* to my attention.
2. On bureaucratic-authoritarianism see Collier (1979), O'Donnell (1973, 1978), Malloy (1977), or Reyna and Weinhart (1977). The conflation of hegemony and coercion is *still* a tendency prevalent in more recent studies that beclouds the contribution this notion can make to the study of the Mexican state, see Berins Collier (1992), Collier (1995), Cornelius (1996), Dresser (1996).
3. It is worth noting that the concept of passive revolution was developed as an explicit elaboration of Marx's 'Preface' to *A Contribution to the Critique of Political* Economy, see Marx (1987b, pp. 261–5).
4. For a more detailed examination of this intellectual's role in Mexico, see Morton (2003b).

8
Human Progress and Capitalist Development

Werner Bonefeld

Introduction

A central theme of this book is the relationship between the national state and the global political economy. According to neo-Gramscian approaches, this relationship has undergone a fundamental change that necessitates analyses of current developments in terms of a transition to a new capitalist epoch. According to this view, 'the nation-state phase of capitalism' has been eroded and its Fordist mode of regulation is superseded by globalization – an 'open-ended process of transition' towards new capitalist structures (Robinson, 2004, pp. 42, 43). The crisis-ridden development of capitalism is thus not conceptualized as a crisis of capitalism but is understood as a crisis of a mode of regulation, and neo-liberalism is seen by implication as a capitalist strategy appropriate to transition to the new capitalist epoch of globalization. Globalization thus means that 'the power of capital attains a hegemonic status' (Gill, 2003, p. 105). However, although neo-liberalism is conceived as a means of transition from one mode of regulation to another, the precise result of transition is contested by human agency (cf. Rupert, 2000) at the national and global level. Politically, the demand is either for the '*democratisation of global society*' (Robinson, 2004, p. 178) or the 'transformation of the state' in favour of labour (Panich, 1994, p. 87).

Periodization of capitalist development will necessarily elevate certain capitalist characteristics to defining qualities of this or that mode of regulation. This procedure tends not only to distract from enduring capitalist features but, also, disconnect us from the lessons of history (cf. Bonefeld, 1987/1991). Against the background of world wars and the industrialized slaughter of millions, Gill's (2003, pp. xii) verdict that 'capital is now perhaps more destructive than creative' does indicate the danger inherent in an analytical perspective that seeks to validate the 'novelty' of social structures on the basis of an imagined and at times idealized past. In contrast to the neo-Gramscian perspective, the global economy and the national state belonged together since the inception of capitalism, and the contradiction between the two is therefore not new (Clarke, 1988). Their contradictory relationship comes to the fore more strongly in times of crises, when the going gets tough and competition intensifies. Thus, rather than seeing capitalist crises as crises of a mode of regulation, and thus as means of transition from one mode of regulation to another, crises express the contradictory form of capitalist accumulation. As was argued in Chapter 4, an important feature of the crisis of capitalist accumulation is the dissociation between monetary accumulation and production accumulation.

I

Since the early 1970s, monetary accumulation has expanded much more rapidly than productive accumulation. The growing gap between monetary accumulation and productive accumulation has led the cycle of capitalist accumulation to look more and more like an upside down pyramid. As was argued in Chapter 4, the more money accumulates dissociated from productive accumulation, the less it is validated by the production of surplus value and the more claims on the future exploitation of labour accumulate in an increasingly speculative and potentially fictitious dimension. While money asserts itself as the source of its own wealth – M ... M' – its validity exists in and through the harnessing of labour as the variable component of capital accumulation. Dissociated from productive accumulation, money capital continues to function as capital in the form of credit, sustaining capitalist reproduction by mortgaging its future. Financial crises, then, indicate the precarious foundation of this speculative gamble. Whether this gamble will lead to a full-blown crisis or whether it can be contained on a permanent basis, with a progressive deterioration of conditions, increase in poverty, violence, famine, ecological destruction, and local, regional or world wars, depends on the outcome of class struggle. There is no certainty.

The resolution to monetary crisis relates to the relationship between necessary labour and surplus labour that is, the parts of the working day that constitute the class relation. However, this resolution is necessarily destructive of the environment and violent in relation to labour or, in Schumpeter's (1992) much friendlier caption, it amounts to a process of creative destruction. For Schumpeter, 'creatively' handled destruction belongs to the 'normality' of capitalist reproduction. Crisis is a means of renewal or, in neo-Gramscian terms, of transition from one mode of regulation to another. The contemporary terms that describe this 'creative' renewal quâ destruction are flexibilization, deregulation, downward wage pressure, the opening-up of new markets, the discovery of new commodities and forms of market socialization, a longer and more intense working day, a longer working life, and a worldwide increase in the number of marginal, that is, redundant labour.

The political economy of time is thus of central importance. In Marx's (1976b, p. 127) phrase, capitalism entails existence of the worker as *'time's carcase'*, and as was argued in Chapter 4, in the capitalist production process the employment of living labour achieves validity only as a vanishing moment of the global equalization of the rate of profit. On the one hand, there is thus the speculative gamble on the future development of value extraction. On the other hand, the validity of this gamble depends on the conquest of additional atoms of labour time in the present. Richard Sennett (2000) has rightly argued that this conquest through means of greater labour flexibility 'corrodes the character'. The flexible worker is the adaptable worker who, released form the 'welfare state prison' (cf. Giddens, 1998), is empowered as a self-reliant and self-responsible employer of his or her labour power or, in the words of Beck (1998) the new worker is a 'labour-force-employer'. Thus, the projection of the new worker as a 'just-in-time' worker – ever ready to be called upon, ever ready to be made redundant, and ever more mobile to go where required and to do what is told in the shortest possible time. In other words, the flexible worker is a worker without time – a worker that can be switched on and off like a machine and who can perform a multitude of functions as a self-responsible object of the world of things. Time is money, and money is time. 'The economy of time: to this all economy ultimately reduces itself' (Marx, 1973, p. 173).

The chapter charts the process of 'creative destruction' and examines the condition of the democratic personality. The democratic personality and the corrosion of character belong to two different worlds. How, then, might Schumpeter's creative destruction be inverted into one that is creative of the democratic personality? The chapter focuses first on the divorce of monetary accumulation from productive accumulation, and then analyses its social consequences. The conclusion suggests that the democratization of social relations is key to development as human progress.

II

Currency instability and speculative runs on currencies have been described as a new form of foreign policy crisis (see Benson, 1995; Cockburn and Silverstein, 1995; Holloway 2000). This does not mean that old-style foreign policy crises – aggression between states, movements of troops, the threat of nuclear war and bombing of populations – have been replaced by potential national bankruptcy and the threat of global financial collapse. The former continues to exist in deadly form; and the potential of global financial collapse has been part of the history of capitalism since its inception. Nevertheless, the accumulation of potentially fictitious wealth in the form of money, M ... M', and the coercive control of populations belong together, then and now. 'We know how rapidly an epoch of global prosperity, underpinning prospects of world peace and international harmony, can become an epoch of global confrontation, culminating in war. If such a prospect seems unlikely now, it seemed equally unlikely a century ago' (Clarke, 2001, p. 91), and the slide into global war seems more likely today than only yesterday. And then there is terrorism. The events of September 11 demonstrated with brutal force the impotence of sense, significance, and thus reason and truth. The denial of human quality and difference was absolute. Their death was total – not even their corpses survived. And the response? It confirmed that state terrorism and terrorism are two sides of the same coin. They feed on each other, depend on each other, encourage each other, and recognize each other in their totalitarian world views: them and us. Between them, nothing is allowed to survive. Doubt in the veracity of the action is eliminated by the authoritarian decision to bomb and maim, to search and destroy.

In the context of a global economy plagued by debt and threatened by the collapse of debt, Martin Wolf has argued that the realization of globalization's wealth-creating potential requires better and that is, stronger states. As he put it in relation to the so-called Third World, 'what is needed is not pious aspirations but an honest and organized coercive force' (Wolf, 2001). And the developed world? The dynamic of the new economy was sustained by an enormous increase in consumer debt, especially in the United States, a huge transfer of resources in the form of interest payments from debtor countries to Western banks, especially to US banks, and military Keynesianism – increased war spending – that subsidized the military-industrial complex and sustained the credit-based booms of the 1980s and 1990s (cf. Veltmeyer, 2004). On the other side, then, of Wolf's neo-imperialist demand for action is a world economy that is dependent upon, and overshadowed by, a mountain of debt. Debt entails a politics of debt, and Wolf's insistence that the free economy and the strong state belong together is therefore apt. Terrorism, as Soros (2003) reports, provided not only the ideal legitimation but also the ideal enemy for the unfettered coercive protection of debt-ridden free market relations 'because it is invisible and never disappears'. The premise of a politics of debt is the ongoing accumulation of 'human machines' on the pyramids of accumulation.

The history of the last decades suggests that capital has found it increasingly difficult to adjust monetary accumulation to productive accumulation. Certainly, rates of productivity have increased. Yet, there is no surer indication than the ballooning of bad debt that capital has not succeeded in imposing a recomposition of the relations of exploitation adequate to the accumulated claims upon surplus value. The fictitious dimension of capitalist accumulation has, like a cancer, ingrained itself into capitalist reproduction since the breakdown of the Bretton Woods system in the early 1970s. This breakdown showed that the relationship between the monetary system and the rate of productivity growth was not just precarious but that it had in fact ruptured. Already in the late 1960s, depressed rates of profits and sluggish economic growth indicated that the post-war boom had come to an end.[1] Capital responded by financializing profits and by moving labour-intensive production to so-called developing countries where labour costs were seen to provide competitive advantages, and where emerging dictatorships guaranteed a more docile labour-force and thus a more reliable human factor of production (cf. Bonnet, 2002). Yet, despite this worldwide search for compliance, the dissociation between monetary accumulation and productive accumulation continued unabated. Indeed, in the early 1970s credit-sustained expansion postponed economic recession until shortly after the official abandonment of the Bretton Woods system in 1971–73. Following upon the quadrupling of oil prices at the end of 1973, which in its effect coincided with the downturn of accumulation, wealth started to be accumulated in the money form without a corresponding increase in the extraction of value.

After the breakdown of the Bretton Woods system, capital movements within the international economy began to dominate balance of payments and exchange rate considerations. Under conditions of little economy growth and intense competition, the spectrum of economic activity about which decisions have to be made shifted to a much quicker and more unstable regime, led by the exchange rates. The breakdown of Bretton Woods involved the abandonment of currency relations in a fixed relation to the dollar and the deregulation of currency relations. This deregulation is referred to as the floating of exchange rates. The integration of the world market through floating exchange rates established not only a market for currency speculation. It established also means of monetary discipline. Floating exchange rates allow speculative capital to operate like an international police force. As the *Financial Times* (9 September 1993) explained against the background of the European currency crises of 1992 and 1993, 'governments know that if policy ceases to be credible, international markets will simply switch off the financial tap'. If states have difficulties in imposing austerity upon social relations, capital flight and speculative runs on currency would reinforce financial crisis.

Monetarism's call for a capitalism of 'value for money', formulated first under the Carter and Callaghan administrations in the United States and the United Kingdom, promised monetary tightness and a leaner and fitter economy. Rather than allowing for deficits and an accumulation of potentially worthless debt, it sought to strengthen the link between money and exploitation by adjusting working class consumption to productivity growth. By the early 1980s under Thatcher and Reagan, the doctrine of the free economy and the strong state became the rallying cry in the formidable attempt of attacking entrenched class relations. Like any other commodity, the price of labour power was to be determined by the operations of the 'price mechanism'. As von Mises (1949, p. 591) put it, 'as far as there are wages, labour is dealt with like any material factor of production and bought and sold on the market'. Thus, social labour power in excess to labour market demand is deemed redundant, like any other commodity that cannot be sold at prevailing prices. Instead of income guarantees, labour was asked to price itself into jobs, instead of full-employment guarantees, unemployment was seen as 'natural', instead of welfare guarantees, the welfare state was seen to inhibit the employability of labour and thus its freedom to respond flexibly to labour market developments; instead of discretionary policy-making that always entails an element of compromise and thus decommodifying concessions to labour in the form of welfare guarantees, the conduct of policymaking was to be shifted to a rule-based system, restraining the democratic character of the liberal-democratic state to its liberal foundation.[2]

Initially, monetarist policies focused on the control of the money supply as a means of effecting economic adjustment (see Bonefeld, 1993a). The idea was that by making credit expensive, mainly through high real interest rates, producers would be forced to 'reassert' their right to manage, while labour confronted with the reality of mass unemployment would work harder for less. Unemployment was thus seen as a useful disciplinary force. As the board member of Toyota, Mr Shiramizu, helpfully explained recently, 'in France there are many unemployed people and so [those with jobs] tend to work harder' (*Financial Times*, 3 March 2003). However, the attempt to effect adjustment through the control of the money supply was short-lived. The deep recession of the early 1980s brought to the fore the contradictions of credit-sustained accumulation. When the crisis struck, costly and scarce money reinforced mass insolvency and liquidation of productive capacities as well as mass unemployment. Companies faced intense financial pressure because the introduction of new methods of production at the end of the 1970s was largely by credit. By clamping down on credit, the anticipated profitability of these new investments fell below the rate of interest, so permitting a continued transfer of earned profits into money markets. Upon credit default, banks invested new recycling credits (see Mandel, 1987, pp. 210–11). The spillover of capital into speculative channels, rather than being halted, continued, precipitated by high interest rates and a lack of profitable opportunities in productive investment. Although high interest rates prevented banks from defaulting in the early 1980s, the default of productive companies threatened financial stability because of the overextension of credit. Yet, at the same time as functioning capital went into receivership, slashed investment and devalued productive capacity, the money supply, far from contracting, exploded as companies borrowed heavily from global credit markets to maintain solvency and cash flow. In addition, the pro-cyclical fiscal policy stance of the monetarists of the New Right failed to reduce public deficits. Instead of cutting back on public deficits, government borrowing increased as the tax base deteriorated and unemployment rose (Clarke, 1988).

Finally, the tightening of the money supply substantially raised the cost of debt service. During the 1970s, when real interest rates had been negative because inflation rates had been higher than nominal interest rates, the future debtor countries did not have to dip into their reserves to meet their obligations. However, when interest rates began to rise rapidly, their ability to turn credit into means of payment deteriorated. When Mexico came within a hairbreadth of default in 1982, the danger to the international financial system was averted by a huge reflation package, led by a sharp reduction in US interest rates, that in its effect restored pseudovalidation on a global scale. As Mandel (1988) argued, the most committed value for money monetarists became the most ardent Keynesians. In addition to cuts in interest rates, governments led by the United States deregulated the financial system further, providing financial markets with new investment opportunities. Also, privatization came to the fore as a means of public policy. It allowed the balancing of budgets and offered the 'debt-hit' financial system new profitable investment opportunities. Privatization and financial deregulation unleashed the money-for-nothing bonanza of the 1980s. In the course of this development, the United States transformed into the world's biggest debtor. Its average budget deficit for 'the six years 1982–87 was $184billion' (Friedman, 1989, p. 19). By 1986 the United States had accumulated over $250 billion debt: 'This $250 billion is only the foreign debt: as of 1986, the US government owed an additional $1750 billion to American purchasers of government securities, so its total public debt was actually $2 trillion' (George, 1988, p. 25). The transfer of debt to the United States stabilized the financial system for a time and it did so by reasserting credit-expansion as a central means of capitalist rule in times of crisis (cf. Holloway, 1996).

The dollar's pre-eminent role was sustained by an inflow of speculative capital and debt bondage forced upon the world's working classes. Between 1982 and 1985, the net transfer from Latin American countries alone was $106 billion (George, 1988, p. 63). At the same time, 'embarrassed' creditors, like the big banks, were refinanced upon their gambling losses, received tax relief on 'bad debt' and sold 'bad debt' to public institutions (Mandel, 1987). As George (1992, p. 106) put it, 'during the 1980s, the only thing that was socialised rather than privatised was debt itself'. Thus the expansionary response to Mexico 1982 did not mean that monetarism was simply abandoned. In fact, monetarist policies continued. The other side of the politics of monetary expansionism was the attempt to strengthen the link between consumption and work through the attack on that part of public expenditure that put money into the hands of workers, anti-union policies, privatization of public companies, unemployment, deregulation of wage-protection, segmentation of labour markets and the use of the welfare state as a means of making people work for their benefits (Bonefeld, 1993a).

Growing investment into the fantastic world of monetary self-expansion recomposed the global relations of exploitation and struggle. The world market became a market in money (see Walter, 1993). Rather than indicating transition to a new capitalist formation, the attempt to make money out of money created a much more fragile capitalism on a world scale. Without the global search for profit in money it would have been unthinkable for the Mexican crisis of 1982 to have had such an immediate knock-on effect on 'western' banks and through them the global circuit of capital. Mexico 1982 indicated that the formidable attempt at containing social relations through a policy of tight money associated with monetarism had reached an impasse. The 'crisis of 1982' indicated a tremendous recomposition of class relations. Seemingly 'marginal' pockets of resistance to the politics of austerity threatened to transform the attempt to make money out of poverty into a severe global financial crisis. After 1982 monetarist policies developed thus in two ways: credit-sustained accumulation and the unrestricted expansion of credit on the one hand, and the socialization of debt through a politics of austerity, on the other. In contrast to the anti-cyclical dimension of credit-expansion associated with Keynesianism, the military Keynesianism of the New Right was pro-cyclical. It supported the boom through deficit-demand financing. It also provided the coercive means for adjustment. Neo-liberalism's policy of market freedom rested on a systematic exercise of state power that attacked what Anthony Giddens later rejected as the 'welfare state prison' – and it did so with the cruel conviction that 'poverty is not unfreedom' (Joseph and Sumption, 1979, p. 47). The Keynesianism of the New Right, then, sustained the boom through a pro-cyclical credit expansion, and sought to strengthen the link between money and value by making workers work harder for less. The shift from the monetarist attempt of controlling the money supply to neo-liberalism's direct attack on conditions (Clarke, 1987) recognized that the safeguarding of credit-expansion required a forceful attack on entrenched class relations to bring about the much hoped for 'supply side revolution' in the form of cheaper and flexible workers.

Yet, the boom of the 1980s was not based on an increase in labour productivity adequate to the monetary claims on value extraction already committed in the form of credit. Rather, the boom of the 1980s was a boom in money – it was credit based. Despite downward pressures on wages, mass unemployment, and the intensification of work, monetary accumulation by far outstripped productive accumulation. The deregulation of finance that provided the financial system with new investment opportunities at a time when it was 'bogged' down by the effects of the debtor crisis, fuelled the takeover mania of the 1980s, and the global property bubbles, and led to the invention of esoteric means of speculation – all this because of the tremendous opportunities that these investments offered. However, these investments represented a considerable avoidance of real investment, an aversion to precisely the supply-side launching of accumulation that the deficit financing of demand had tried to induce.

The crash of 1987 revealed the fictitious dimension of the boom of the 1980s. Like in 1982, the response to the crash in 1987 was a Keynesian one. Interest rates were lowered, banks and other financial institutions received financial support, and, especially in Europe, remaining exchange rate and capital controls were deregulated further.[3] Samuel Brittan's advice was well followed: 'When a slump is threatening, we need helicopters dropping currency notes from the sky. This means easier bank lending policies and, if that is not enough, some mixture of lower taxes and higher government spending' (quoted in Harman, 1993, p. 15). This reflationary response helped to sustain the illusion of prosperity until the end of the decade.

When the recession struck in 1990, investors began to run for the exits. The life-blood of the boom, that is credit, changed into a forcible collection of unpaid debt, which is the backbone of a policy of state austerity. The irony of the Keynesianism of the New Right was that, when the recession came in 1990, there was no leeway for a Keynesian anti-cyclical policy of deficit spending as currency speculation intensified in a desperate gamble on capitalism's future. Labour unit costs had accelerated by the late 1980s (*Financial Times*, 4 October 1999) and corporate indebtedness increased dramatically during the 1980s from about 8 per cent of capital stock in 1980–81 to around 20 per cent in the late 1980s (Smith, 1992). By 1990, manufacturing investment fell sharply and profits dipped seriously (ibid.). In the face of corporate failures and personal bankruptcies, including the property market, the banking system was again on the 'brink of collapse' (ibid., p. 244). During the last decade we have seen the deep recession of the early 1990s, the European currency crises in 1992 and 1993, the plunge of the Mexican peso in December 1994 which rocked financial markets around the world, the Asian crisis of 1997, the Brazilian crisis of 1999, the Argentinean crisis of 2001. Japan teeters on the edge of depression, the European economies are in dire straigts, the trade deficits of both the United States und the United Kingdom are at record level, and debt fed on to itself (cf. Solomon, 1999, Bootle, 2003).

It was against the background of the deep recession of the early 1990s that the term globalization came to the fore. Its sudden rise to prominence made it appear as if capitalism had transformed itself. The 'new world order' and the 'new economy' conjured up the idea of a new beginning and globalization appeared as the term that summarized its irresistible force. The *Financial Times* praised globalization as 'the most effective wealth-creating system ever devised by mankind'. However, it also acknowledged that globalization was incomplete since 'about two-thirds of the world's population have gained little or no substantive advantage from rapid economic growth. In the "developed world" the lowest quartile of income earners has witnessed a trickle-up rather than a trickle-down' (*Financial Times*, 24 December 1993). This one-quarter has since expanded to include about half the population.

And the so-called 'developing' world? Where did it stand in 1993 and where does it stand now? Figures on poverty and deprivation suggest its expanded consolidation into a 'global' slum (see Chossdovsky, 1997). Since 2000/01, the World Bank defines poverty as income below $2 a day and extreme poverty as below $1 a day. Even on this measure, poverty affects 40 per cent of the population in Latin America (Petras and Veltmeyer, 2004, p. 29). Using data from national accounts of 39 of the poorest countries, UNCTAD (2002, p. 59) estimated an increase in the number of people in these countries living on less than $1 a day from 125 million to 278.8 million between 1965–69 and 1995–99. According to UNDP (2000) one-quarter of the world's population are earning under $1 per day, and 100 million children living or working on streets. According to Martin Wolf, a proponent of a more effective form of globalization, the gap in the average living standards between the richest and poorest countries has increased from a ratio of about 10 to 1 a century ago to 75 to 1 and under existing conditions of globalization 'it could easily be 150 to one' in half a century (Wolf, 2004). The World Bank stated in 1997 that '44 low-income countries did not have the money to pay for basic minimum health services' and UNDP stated that '21 million children's lives could be saved if the money used for debt service was put into health and education' (cited in WHO, 2005).

And its wealth-creating potential? It appears to have run out of steam.[4] The New Economy was sustained by credit-expansion. There was no breakthrough in productivity growth. Indeed, according to Robert Gordon (1999), during the last century, the lowest increase in productivity growth occurred between 1988 and 1996 – Gordon estimates a 0.5 per cent growth in productivity. For all the hype about the new economy boom, its prosperity was more apparent then real. Overall daily trading in international financial markets amounts to about $1 trillion. Only a small portion of this trading is connected with real economic exchanges, from the selling and buying of commodities to capital investment. Much of this trade is speculative (see World Bank 2000, p. 24). At the same time, the United States supported the boom through an enormous trade deficit that, by 2000, had grown to $437 billion. This deficit, as James Petras (2003, p. 29) put it, 'was covered only because of the flows of foreign capital, much of it from Japan but also from dirty money from the Third World'. The flow of this dirty money showed that Marx's insight according to which 'a great deal of capital, which appears today in the United States without certificate of birth, was yesterday, in England, the capitalized blood of children' (Marx, 1983, p. 707), remains a powerful judgement of contemporary conditions. Today it is the capitalized blood of the poor and miserable across the globe, especially in Latin America and Africa. Debt bondage of the so-called Third World entailed that US banks received 'over $329 billion in interest payments, while the total debt [of the Third World] grew from $476 billion to $698 billion, debt payments amounting to about 30 percent of total exports' (Petras and Veltmeyer, 2004, p. 28). The mirror image of fictitious wealth accumulation was the spread of poverty and misery.

The *Financial Times* had already reported in 1993 (27 September) that the 'IMF privately fears that the debt threat is moving north. These days it is the build-up of First-World debt, not Africa's lingering crisis, that haunts the sleep of the IMF official', appears to have been borne out. The New Economy was sustained by credit, including especially consumer credit. In addition to the growth of the Federal budget deficit to 2.3 per cent in early 2000, the trade deficit stood at a record $435 billion in 2001, and the current account deficit at $400 billion (Monthly Review, 2003, p. 8), 'US families increased their personal indebtedness beyond anything ever experienced in any other place or time. ... US consumer debt rose from $1.4 trillion in 1980 to $6.5 trillion in 2000' (Wolff, 2002, p. 121). The Economic Policy Institute (2002) noted that 'by 2001, total household debt exceeded total household income by an all-time high of nearly 10 percent. Much of the run-up in debt occurred over the economic boom, as the ratio of debt to personal income rose from 87.7 per cent in 1992 to 109.0 per cent in 2002'. Writing in the context of the United States, Magdoff *et al.* (2002) argue that, by 2002, outstanding private debt is two and one quarter times GDP, while total outstanding debt – private plus government – approaches three times the GDP. The economy, they conclude, is now completely dependent upon a mountain of debt.

III

The meaning of debt and its coercive enforcement upon populations through a politics of debt is all-too evident in the so-called debtor countries, and remains hidden under the cloak of apparent prosperity in the so-called First World. The Argentinean meltdown of 2001 is an obvious case. In a country of 35 million, 19 million are classified as poor as of

June 2002, 'with earnings of less than $190 a month, 8.4 million are considered destitute, with monthly incomes below $83' (Auge, 2002). This presents a poverty rate of 54 per cent of the population whereas in 1993, according to the World Bank, the poverty rate was a 'mere' 17.6 per cent (World Bank, 2000). Argentina is far from an anomaly. Mexico's poverty rate hovers around 40 per cent (Cypher, 2001). In the great city of Sao Paulo, of its 14 million inhabitants, about 5.5 million live in the so-called favelas in conditions of unspeakable poverty and desperation. And the United States?

For many, the United States is the example of a successfully globalized economy that, by the late 1990s, achieved full-employment. Given these achievements, one would be tempted to conclude that Clinton's war on poverty was successful. However, when looking at conditions in the United States, the declared war on poverty looks more like a war on the poor (Wacquant, 2000). Vulliamy (2002) reports that 33 million people are living below the poverty line. Estimates suggest that about 15 per cent of the poor in the United States live in conditions of abject deprivation (cf. Negt, 2001, p. 269). According to Vulliamy (2002), one in eleven families, one in nine Americans, and one in six children are officially poor. The scale of poverty that persists amid US affluence has led to the most unequal distribution of income among developed countries (Madrick, 1995; Negt, 2001). And the much praised job-creating potential of the New Economy? Most of these jobs were created in the service industry, where work is precarious and badly paid. Full-time employment declined and by late 2000 over 500,000 manufacturing jobs had been shed (Petras, 2003, p. 71).

According to Wacquant (2000) one of the main public policy concerns over the last decade was the recruitment, training and employment of prison wardens to operate the 213 new prisons that have been built between 1993 and 1998. In 1997, 600 out of 100,000 people were incarcerated compared with 60–80 out of 100,000 people in the EU. In addition, there are about 5.4 million people under juridical supervision. Over the last 15 years, the prison population has increased three-fold. The huge increase in the prison population has offered not only profitable opportunities for companies specializing in the building, running and securing of prisons. It has also created a big pool of cheap labour in an expanding prison-industry. Prisoners deemed employable are 'contracted out' to nearby companies, such as IBM and Microsoft. Suffice to say that prisoners disappear from the labour market and prison labour is stripped of all rights: they are set to work as prisoners (cf. Wacquant, 2000).

William Robertson (1890, p. 104) rightly argued that 'in every inquiry concerning the operation of men when united together in society, the first object of attention should be their mode of subsistence'. Poverty and misery are not the result of a lack of desire for development but a direct consequence of a 'mode of subsistence' in which humanity exists as a mere economic resource. Given contemporary conditions of misery, what would a fully, capitalistically developed world look like? How many planets would be needed to 'serve as mines and waste dumps' (Sachs, 1999, p. 2)? Sachs rightly insists that 'it is not the failure of development which has to be feared, but its success' (ibid., p. 4). Dalla Costa (2003, p. 147) makes a similar point when she argues that in discussions on sustainable development, 'there is usually no mention of the *unsustainability* for humankind and the environment'.

The Economist reported in 1986 that it is a generally held belief in investment circles that no development can occur in a country until the land question is settled and land property is privatized (quoted in Caffentzis, 1995, p. 27; see also Petras and Veltmeyer, 2004). From the perspective of capitalist value, the privatization of land property is crucial. It is the basis for development as capitalist freedom. Capital, as Marx noted, 'is the separation of the conditions of production from the labourer' (1972, p. 422) and this separation 'forms [*bildet*] the conception [*Begriff*] of capital' (Marx, 1966, p. 246). Capitalist freedom depends on the separation of social labour from its means; it is capital's constitutive force. What, however, happens to those populations who have been rendered independent from their conditions and who are now 'free to collide with one another and to engage in exchange within this freedom'? (Marx, 1973, pp. 163–4). Development as capitalist freedom will allow some to find jobs as wage labourers. This, however, will be, as Dalla Costa (2003) shows, the fate of only a small minority, that is, those who can find employment in the rapidly expanding sweatshops of the Third World, or the inhospitable countries to which they emigrate. Then there is the proliferation of child labour, cheap to hire and easy to fire, many crippled before they reach adulthood, if indeed they do (Seabrook, 2001). According to estimates of the International Labour Organization (ILO) the overall number of children under 15 who were 'economically active' was around 50 million at the beginning of the 1980s. Today, it reports, there are 'more than 200 million child labourers worldwide, some 180 million are now suspected to be toiling in the "worst forms" of child labour' (ILO, 2002, p. 1). Nevertheless, they are not shot as so many are in Latin America, they have not been killed after birth because of their gender, and they have not been forced into prostitution.

What however happens to those who fail to find work? Erich Fromm once argued that no psychology is needed to explain why a hungry person steals food. Psychology, and ultimately mass psychology is needed, he argued, to explain why those who are starving do not steal bread. Altvater (2002) suggests that the informal economy has grown as a result of rising unemployment, with, for example, the percentages of informal labour in total employment ranging from 30 per cent in Chile to 84 per cent in Uganda. Poverty and misery is a great laboratory for the invention of new forms of wage labour and for the re-discovery of old forms of 'human capital' utilization.

Over the last decade there has been an increase in the trafficking of women and children, who are literally 'stolen', under the pretence of a wage contract in the North, into prostitution. Global human smuggling has grown into a multi-million dollar business spanning the entire globe (cf. Kyle and Koslowski, 2001, Phinnes, 2005). Then there is the commercialization of body parts and hence the income-generating sale of these parts. Dalla Costa (1998) reports that in the last few years, the sale of human organs has become a desperate means of earning money particularly for people from the Third World. What is the price of a kidney? There are no reliable data. Claire Nullis-Kapp (2004) estimates that donors 'may receive as little as US$ 1000 for a kidney although the going price is more likely to be about US$ 5000'. Once, however, a kidney has been sold what further dissections are possible to generate income?

Now, as then, mass prostitution continues to generate profits for one of the most flourishing industries at the world market level, the sex industry. Sex tourism is one example and the trafficking of women to work as prostitutes in slave-like condition is another (Kempadoo and Doezema, 1998). Trafficking of women is rampant (*Observer Magazine*, 23 February 03). These women, many as young as 14 or 15, if that, are held in conditions akin to slavery. Modern slavery was raised as a significant problem in the 1993 meetings of the Non-Governmental Organizations in Vienna and of the UN's World Conference on Human Rights. According to *The Economist* (6 January 1990) over 20 million people worked in conditions of slavery. This figure has since then increased – Bales (2000) suggests a figure of 27 million – because of the continued expansion of child labour working in slave-like conditions in the sweat shops of the world and because of the vast increase in the trafficking of women that followed the implosion of the former Eastern Bloc. Besides, for many women, prostitution has become the only means of generating means of subsistence.

The ongoing conversion of human beings into human capital, into a resourceful utility, cash and product, is founded on the negation of human values. This negation celebrates its triumphs in the transformation of the individual owner of redundant or, in any case, superfluous labour-power into a bodily thing that can be hired out or dissected into saleable parts. The 'logic of separation', which as Marx insists, is constitutive of capital, 'begins with primitive accumulation, appears as a permanent process in the accumulation and concentration of capital, and expresses itself finally as centralisation of existing capitals in a few hands and a deprivation of many of their capital (to which expropriation is now changed)' (Marx, 1966, p. 246). It now passes through labour as a carrier of human capital – development as capitalist freedom where humanity is 'turned topsy turvey, vivisectioned, and made a commodity' (Dalla Costa, 1995, p. 12). Marx's notion of the doubly free wage labourer appears to have been transformed. The doubly free wage labourer has indeed become, at least for a growing part of humanity, more than just a labouring commodity. It has also become a carrier of body substances that, like any other commodity, can be sold on the market at prevailing prices.

IV

Marx's critical insight that bourgeois society overcomes crises 'by enforced destruction of a mass of productive forces' and 'by the conquest of new markets, and by the more thorough exploitation of the old ones' (Marx and Engels, 1997, p. 19) appears to have been borne out by developments. Nevertheless, in spite of all the poverty and misery, neoliberalism's aim of 'adjustment' has not been successful however painful the results of its attempt. The fact that 'investment is not lifting off ... is perhaps testimony to the radicality of the challenge to capitalist power, and of the fear that followed from it that every upturn in the economy would reactivate conflict. A testimony, in short, that the dismantling and restructuring of all parts of the capitalist valorization process is still in full motion' (Bellofiore, 1997, p. 49). Although, as Nariarosa Dalla Costa (1995, p. 7) puts it, 'social "misery" or "unhappiness" which Marx considered to be the "goal of the political economy" has largely been realised everywhere', the dissociation of monetary accumulation from productive accumulation has not been redeemed. Far from stimulating investment, employment and output, the result of credit expansion in a context of austerity was the deterioration of conditions, plunder, enforced destruction of a mass of productive forces, conquests of new markets and new atoms of labour-time, and the discovery of new areas of exploitation. There was, however, no breakthrough in productive investment relative to the accumulated claims on surplus value still to be pumped out of labour.

The experience of the last decades suggests that the transformation of money into truly productive capital is both essential and impossible. The crises since the 1990s indicate that there seems to be no way forward, for capital or for labour. Yet this is not the first time. Writing in 1934, that is after the first global imperialist war and in the face of Fascist/Fordist attempts of disciplining labour (cf. Gambino, 2003), Paul Mattick suggested that capitalism had entered an age of permanent crisis: The periodicity of crisis is in practice nothing other than the recurrent reorganization of the process of accumulation on a new level of value and price which again secures the accumulation of capital. If that is not possible, then neither is it possible to confirm accumulation; the same crisis that up to now had presented itself chaotically and could be overcome becomes permanent crisis. In contrast to previous crises of capitalism, which had always led to a restructuring of capital and to a renewed period of accumulation, the crisis of the 1930s appeared to be so profound and prolonged as to be incapable of solution. Crisis, Mattick suggested, had ceased to be a periodically recurring phenomenon and had become an endemic feature of capitalism.

Mattick's suggestion, pessimistic though it was, turned out to be far too optimistic. The crisis was resolved, in blood. Capital was restructured and the basis created for a new period of accumulation. Post-war capitalism is now a memory, as is the blood-letting through war and gas. Once again it would seem that we are in a situation of permanent crisis. It is possible that the crisis will be permanent, with a progressive deterioration of conditions. It is possible too that the crisis will not be permanent, that it will in fact be resolved: what the resolution of 'permanent crisis' can mean stands behind us as a warning of a possibly nightmarish future (cf. Bonefeld and Holloway, 1996).

V

In the misery of our time, I would suggest to orient development on a completely different entelechy of human progress – on the society of the free and equal. Taken, as Johannes Agnoli (2000, p. 203) has argued, 'as a basic orientation of our social practice, this orientation can lead us forward to humanisation. Our entire behaviour, from the mundane to the highest expressions of the intellect, would look different, friendlier, more human, if we allow ourselves to be led not by the existing reality of profit, power, the seizure and pursuit of power, and the preservation of power; but instead by this utopian ideal of the society of the free and equal'. The democratic personality is not an abstract individual. Nor is it a 'new form of political agency whose defining myths are associated with the quest to ensure human and intergenerational security on and for the planet, as well as democratic human development and human rights' (Gill, 2003, p. 211). In distinction to Gill's equation of democratic values with myth, the democratic personality is a figure of critical reason (cf. Psychopedis, 2000) that walks upright in dignity (cf. Bloch, 1986). Human dignity has no price, nor can it be bestowed upon individuals through the good offices of the state, as the theoretician of the autonomy of the state, Thomas Hobbes (1996), argued that it can. Human beings have either a price or a dignity (cf. Kant, 1974, p. 87). Agents or agencies can have no dignity. Dignity belongs to subjects.

In the misery of our time, how might one conceive of progress as development of human freedom? Wage levels and income guarantees – be it in terms of money, goods or services – have to be defended and improved conditions have to be demanded. Pressure needs to be used to liberate millions of people from conditions of poverty and deprivation. However, the concept of welfare is not enough. The demand is for human dignity. This demand formulates a conception of development that opens up the satisfaction of the basic human 'needs on whose suppression capital was born and has grown' (Dalla Costa, 1995, p. 14). Dignity entails the human need for time, as against a life consisting solely of labour-time. Dignity entails the need of relations of human integrity, as against the reduction of human existence to a mere resource. Dignity entails the need for collectivity and solidarity, against the isolation of and indifference between individuals seeking to make ends meet as personifications of economic categories. Dignity entails the need for public space, as against enclosure, privatization and communicative systems driven by development as capitalist freedom. Dignity entails the need for education, pleasure, human significance and mutual recognition. Dignity, in short, entails the equality of individual human needs for food, shelter, clothing, love, affection, knowledge and human significance. It entails the mutual recognition of Man as the highest being for Man.

The anti-globalization conception of cosmopolitan democratic renewals or the anti-capitalist call for the intensification of economic struggle and building on that struggle, and the intensification of political struggle to achieve a shift in the balance of class forces reduce the struggle for democracy to a struggle for political power. The realism of these conceptions lacks emancipatory contents and is, in fact, much more removed from social reality than the concept of humanity that embraces Kant's categorical imperative: act in such a way that you recognize humanity in your person and in all other persons always as a purpose, never as a means.[5] 'It is Man, who, as a single individual, as a group, or as a mass, understands himself as subject and who defends himself against merely objective existence' (Agnoli, 1996, p. 29). Democracy, if taken seriously, entails this conception of humanity in action. It does not belong to coercive institutions. It belongs to subjects. The struggle for democracy subverts the economic existence of Man as a resource. Subversion is 'a truly human phenomenon' (ibid.). Instead of myth, it espouses critical reason.

Development as human freedom has thus to mean the complete democratization of all social relations, including its prerequisite, that is, the democratization of social time, transforming it from its reduction to product and cash into human social time (cf. Wilding, 1995). Time as measure of social wealth and time as human social self-determination belong to different worlds (cf. Tischler, 2005). The first is the time of Man as a mere agent of economic categories, the second is the time of Man as a democratic being. Anti-globalization demands for humanization qua democratization have to be taken seriously. This democratization has however to be a democratization from below (cf. Fracchia, 2005).

The struggle for the democratic organization of relations of economic necessity and the struggle for the 'shortening of the working day' belong together. This shortening is the 'basic prerequisite' of human emancipation (Marx, 1966, p. 820). Negt (2001) is therefore right when he charges many left critics of globalization for their failure to offer any views on how socially necessary labour might be organized to liberate millions and millions of people, not only in the 'developing' societies but in the centres of wealth too, from conditions of misery and poverty. The capitalist form of wealth restricts the potential of society (cf. Marx, 1973, p. 421) as every crisis shows and as is also shown by every commodity that cannot be sold for profit in the face of want. How much labour time was needed in 2005 to produce the same amount of commodities that was produced in 1995? Twenty per cent? Forty per cent or fifty per cent? Whatever the percentage might be, what is certain is that labour time has not decreased. It has increased. What is certain too is that the distribution of wealth is as unequal as never before. And how does world market society of capital cope with the expansion of 'redundant populations', on the one hand, and, on the other, the overaccumulation of abstract wealth in the form of a potentially irredeemable mortgage on the future value extraction? The contradiction between the forces and relations of production does seek resolution: destruction of productive forces, scrapping of labour through war and generalized poverty and misery, and all this against the background of an unprecedented accumulation of wealth.

Struggle for the democratic self-organization of society entails the politicization of social relations, and therewith the cancellation of the concentration of the political in the form of the state. Discussion of this issue is beyond the remit of this chapter. Suffice to say that such politicization does entail social conflict, which might succeed or bring to power 'well-meaning dictators ... genuinely anxious to restore' the limited character of democracy (Hayek, cited in Cristi, 1998, p. 168). There is no certainty. Against the background of the contemporary transformation of the indebted citizen into a security risk, the democratic personality is a scandal and is thus treated as a subversive element – and rightly so.

Notes

1. See Clarke (1988). For documentation, see Armstrong *et al.*, (1984) and Mandel (1975).
2. On this, see Bonefeld (2001c, 2005a) and Burnham (2000, and Chapter 6). Gill's (2001) 'new constitutionalism' looks at the same issue from a neo-Gramscian perspective, arguing that neo-liberalism amounts to a process of de-democratization. For a systematic account on the connection between democracy and the rule of law, see Agnoli (2000). On Gill's concept, see also Bieler, Chapter 5.
3. On the Single European Act, its provision for the free movement of capital, and its swift implementation after the crash, see Grahl and Teague (1990).
4. For documentation, see Brenner (2002).
5. On this see Bonefeld and Psychopedis (2005).

Part III

Global Restructuring: Contesting Neo-Gramscian Perspectives

9
Globalization, the State and Class Struggle
A 'Critical Economy' Engagement with Open Marxism

Andreas Bieler and Adam David Morton

Introduction: a sonorous silence within critical international theory?

Theorizing the capitalist state has for some time been an abiding concern of the approach of Open Marxism, as clearly outlined in the preceding chapters throughout the book. This approach is constituted by a diverse but nevertheless distinct group of scholars committed to the dialectic of subject–object and theory–practice and the (re)constitution of categories in and through the development of a crisis-ridden social world in the analysis of the state as an aspect of the *social relations of production* (Bonefeld, Gunn and Psychopedis, 1992a, p. xi).[1] By extension, the intention *inter alia* of scholars such as Peter Burnham and Werner Bonefeld is to focus on the social class antagonism between capital and labour. By theoretically calling into question the separation of subject from object, or struggle from structure, and practically engaging with social action within which aspects of class struggle obtain and unfold, they affirm a commitment to emancipation within the social world. Ultimately, then, Open Marxism is a *critical theory* that interrogates theoretical and practical categories – it is reflexive about the constitution of the social world – in a spirit of opposition and resistance to capitalist relations of exploitation (also see Backhaus, 1992; Bonefeld, 1995; Gunn, 1992). Hence the significance of Open Marxism lies in its *critical theoretical* questioning of taken-for-granted assumptions about the social world and the practical conditions of dominance and subordination in capitalism; thereby criticizing directly liberal institutionalist and neo-realist, as well as structural

Marxist, approaches in International Relations (IR) and International Political Economy (IPE).

Yet, despite these issues having striking importance to similar concerns within critical theory debates in IR and IPE, there has been very little, if any, direct engagement with the contentions of Open Marxism. Indeed, there has been what we term a sonorous silence within the debates of critical international theory on the contributions of Open Marxism and its concern with class struggle. This neglect has manifested itself throughout early defining debates within critical international theory (Linklater, 1990a and 1990b). It has been present within state-of-the-art reviews of Marxism and International Relations theory (Burchill and Linklater, 2001; Hobden and Wyn Jones, 2001; H. Smith, 1994); overviews on theories of the state within IR and historical sociology (Hobden, 1998; Hobden and Hobson, 2002; Hobson, 1997 and 2000; Shaw, 2000); constructivist theorizing on the state system (Wendt 1999); and in wider and more recent discussions of critical theory, security and world politics (Wyn Jones, 1999 and 2000; Booth, 2005). This is despite the admission that the Marxist critique of ideology and radical political economy (Marxian) approaches more generally were a 'conduit by which critical theories of society began to make their mark felt on the study of world politics' (Linklater, 1998, p. 20 and 2000, p. 10). It is therefore reasonable to suggest that this sonorous silence has been enduringly present within the self-image, or foundational myths, of IR as a discipline in many recent post-positivist debates (S. Smith, 1995 and 2000; S. Smith *et al.*, 1996).

The purpose of this book in general as well as this chapter in particular is to engage with the critical theory of Open Marxism in an attempt to overcome the above noted silences. In doing so, the argument in this chapter is structured into two main sections. The first section develops a critical outline of Open Marxism by focusing on three principal aspects of its critique of political economy: (1) a critique of the separation of state and civil society and of politics and economics; (2) a focus on the social class antagonism of capital and labour as a relation in and against domination and exploitation; and (3) a theory of the state as an aspect of the social relations of production embedded within globalization which is cognisant of the relationship between structure and struggle and thus the constitution of national states within global capitalist accumulation. While highlighting the positive contributions of Open Marxism, several criticisms are also raised. These include tendencies within Open Marxism to obscure how class struggle is mediated through specific material social practices; to prioritize the dominant reproduction of capitalism over resistance; to refuse distinguishing between different forms of state whilst also frequently indulging in state-centric analysis; and to succumb to an overly theoretical and abstract style of discussion. In the second section of this chapter, the neo-Gramscian alternative to Open Marxism, introduced in Chapter 2, will be further developed by drawing extensively from the writings of Antonio Gramsci and his previously neglected 'Critical Economy' conceptualization of the state as well as the work of Nicos Poulantzas. It is argued that drawing from these authorities provides the intellectual resources with which to develop a theory of the state as well as issues of resistance in the context of globalization, which can incorporate the positive aspects of Open Marxism while overcoming its limitations at the same time. The conclusion will examine what the previous neglect of Open Marxism has to say about the wider development of critical theory within IR and IPE. Thereby leaving open several questions about the project of critical theory itself that can be taken up in future debate.

A critical outline of Open Marxism

The emergence of Open Marxism can be situated within a reaction to abstract and ahistorical currents within historical materialism, particularly the 'structural Marxism' of Louis Althusser, and the perceived shortcomings of mainstream neo-realism and neo-liberal institutionalism in IR/IPE (see Keohane, 1984; Waltz, 1979). The 'scientific' character of knowledge was customarily asserted within 'structural Marxism' in order to reveal the inner essence of the universe (Althusser, 1969 and 1970, p. 132). Yet the structuralist approach failed to explain social action and resulted in 'the repression of the processes through which the conditions of social life are constituted', as well as 'the human values affirmed/revoked through those conditions' (Psychopedis, 1991 and 2000, p. 76). This resulted in the fetishisation of social reality and the related separation between politics and economics (Bonefeld, 1992, p. 114). Similarly, neo-realist and neo-liberal institutionalist IR approaches take for granted 'state' and 'market', in the form of two separate entities, as their starting-point of investigation (see, for example, Gilpin, 1987, pp. 9–10 and 2000, p. 13). Yet this inner connection between state and market cannot be problematised. 'Instead "the state" is fetishised whilst "the market" is dehistoricised and viewed as a technical arena in which the "external" state "intervenes" ' (Burnham, 1995a, p. 136). In contrast to structural Marxism and mainstream IR approaches alike, Open Marxism suggests taking the social relations of production as a starting-point. It is particularly affirmed that a return to Marx on the relation between capital, the state and labour would reveal the separation between state and market as illusory; thereby opening up theorizing to consider state-civil society relations as differentiated but connected forms of capitalist social relations of production (Burnham, 1995a, p. 146 and 2000, p. 10).

According to Marx, the state has a set of presuppositions in civil society in terms of religion, the judiciary, private property and the family and under capitalist social relations these become divided into separate spheres. Therefore a scission of 'state' from 'civil society' unfolds as discrete forms of expression of social relations under capitalism. This induces a mystification of the powers of the state to the extent that collective identities become separated into individual elements. The public and private spheres are shorn, so that individual freedom forms the foundation of civil society and class exploitation is set aside to give decisive status to abstract citizenship (Marx, 1843b/1975, pp. 143–4, 147). Civil society therefore becomes equated with individual rights and private interests and 'appears as a framework extraneous to the individuals, as a limitation of their original independence' (1843c/1975, p. 230). The individual is presented as an 'isolated monad' to the extent that the state 'regards civil society, the world of needs, of labour, of private interests and of civil law, as the *foundation of its existence*, as a *presupposition* which needs no further grounding, and therefore as its *natural basis*' (ibid., pp. 229, 234 original emphases). Accordingly, concepts such as security become predicated on the protection of individual freedoms and private interests within civil society separate from state 'intervention'. Yet, declares Marx, 'the *real person* reappears everywhere as the essence of the state – for people make the state' and the very social existence of people within the state constitutes their participation and relation to the state. 'Not only do they share in the state, but the state is *their* share' (1843b/1975, pp. 83, 187 original emphasis).

Within Open Marxism such reflections on the separation of the state (politics) and civil society (economics) are further developed in order to dissolve the state as an institutional category and to understand it, not as a thing in itself, but as a form of social relations. Once the unquestioned category of the state is problematized in this way it then becomes possible to ask what is peculiar about the social relations of production under capitalism that gives rise to the separation and constitution of the economic and political as distinct moments within the same social relations (Holloway and Picciotto, 1978b, p. 18; Holloway, 1995, pp. 120–1). As highlighted in Chapter 2, understanding how the relations of production are presented in their political aspect within capitalism provides an answer to this query. In contrast to pre-capitalist forms, characterized by the extra-economic direct political enforcement of exploitation and surplus extraction, surplus appropriation and exploitation within capitalism is indirectly conducted through a contractual relation between those who maintain the power of appropriation, as owners of the means of production, over those who only have their labour to sell, as expropriated producers. Capitalist exploitation is therefore conducted within the 'private' economic realm of civil society between appropriators and expropriated, capital and labour, which is presented as separate from the 'public' sphere linked to the coercive political realm of the state (Holloway and Picciotto, 1977, p. 79; see also Wood, 1995, pp. 31–6). Nevertheless the latter ultimately secures such processes through the guarantee of private property, the contractual relationship between employer and employee and the process of commodity exchange (Burnham, 1995a, p. 145). Hence, the political dimension is intrinsic to capitalist relations of production. It is this understanding that is therefore cognisant of the relation between the state (politics) and civil society (economics) as discrete but related forms of the expression of social relations under capitalism. The state is conceived as a form of capitalist social relations, as an aspect of the social relations of production, predicated upon the reproduction of antagonisms and exploitation within the crisis-ridden development of capitalist society.

For Open Marxism, a crucial consequence of the separation of the economic and the political is the obscuring of the social class antagonism between capital and labour. The relation between capital and labour is assumed to be an antagonistic one that asserts itself in the form of class struggle. 'Class struggle is ... the daily resistance of the labouring class to the imposition of work – a permanent feature of human society above primitive levels' (Burnham, 1994, p. 225). Therefore, the capitalist state is determined by the social form of the class antagonism between capital and labour and thus by the historical process of class struggle in and against exploitation (Bonefeld, 1992 and 1995). Yet class is not related to a static structural location – a form of stratification – but instead is conceived as a social phenomenon within which conflict obtains (Bonefeld, Gunn and Psychopedis, 1992b, p. xiii). Class antagonism is thus regarded as a primary social relationship within which structures are instantiated and internally related to struggle (Bonefeld, 1992, pp. 113–14). Class struggle is by definition also seen as open-ended which promotes enquiry beyond the economic determinism of base–superstructure explanations (Burnham, 1994, p. 225).

Further, it is argued that the separation of politics and economics distorts the relationship between the state and globalization in mainstream

IR/IPE approaches. Approaches to globalization commonly succumb to this misconception by counterpoising state and market as two opposed forms of social organization. Hence arguments that posit the loss of 'state sovereignty' or 'autonomy' in an exterior relationship to 'globalization', which supposedly results in 'the retreat of state' (*inter alia* Burnham, 1994, 1997 and 2000). External linkages are therefore sought between the state and globalization rather than appreciating that 'national' states exist as moments *within* the global flow of capitalist social relations. By contrast, Open Marxism regards a change in the form of the global existence of capital as characteristic of the current epoch, which has to be understood through an examination of the changing contradictions between capital, the state and labour. After all, states have to be inserted within the global character of capitalist accumulation because 'the state itself is a form of the class relation which constitutes global capitalist relations' (Burnham, 1995a, p. 149).

> Sovereign states via the exchange rate mechanism, are interlocked internationally into a hierarchy of price systems ... national states therefore founded on the rule of money and law are at the same time confined within limits imposed by the accumulation of capital on a world scale – the most obvious and important manifestation of which is their subordination to world money. (Burnham, 1995a, p. 148)

In other words, global class relations are nationally processed. 'It is for this reason that the struggle of the proletariat with the bourgeoisie is not in substance, but only in form, a national struggle' (Burnham, 1995a, p. 152). Overall, then, Open Marxism argues that 'a return to classical Marxist ideas on the relation between class, capital and the state in a global context', can offer, 'a more productive approach for mapping recent industrial, political and economic change' (Burnham, 2000, p. 10). It is in this sense that Open Marxism strikes an important and resonant chord against conventional mainstream neo-realist and neo-liberal institutionalist approaches within IR and IPE. By emphasizing the historical specificity of capitalism it promotes reflection about the potential for transformation beyond the prevalent social conditions.

Several criticisms, however, can be levelled against the overall approach of Open Marxism. First, there is a clear ambition to project a 'totalising' theory, rooted in central organizing principles, capable of accounting for the myriad contradictory forms of relations between capital, the state and labour (Burnham, 1999). Yet it is unclear as to whether this totalizing approach collapses into a variant of 'Theological Marxism' that views the relationship of capital and class not as hypotheses but as absolute knowledge (Cox, 1992/1996, p. 176). It is noteworthy that an aversion to the 'religious fervour' was long noted within the Open Marxist theorizing of capitalism and the states-system (Solomons, 1979, p.146). For example, in asserting that all 'social phenomena have to be seen as forms assumed by class struggle, as forms in and against which social conflict obtains' (Bonefeld, Gunn and Psychopedis, 1992b, p. xiii), there is a tendency to uphold a vision of class struggle as an undifferentiated mass that obscures the varied and specific forms assumed by social class, which are rarely given concrete reference or historical analysis. Generalizations within Open Marxism thus reduce the social antagonism between capital and labour to the unmediated effect of class struggle. Exploitation, domination and class struggle appear in this view as antagonisms that are unmediated in and through social forms or specific material social practices, institutions and norms of conduct.[2] The specificities of class and class-relevant struggles within particular historical conjunctures, or the consideration of distinctive struggles over hegemony, are therefore lost by reducing everything to an objective developmental logic of capital (Jessop, 1988/1991, pp. 72–3 and 1990, pp. 258–9). Mantras such as 'capital *is* class struggle' (Holloway, 1988/1991, p. 100 original emphasis), propagated by Open Marxism, simply elide how the historical development of capital accumulation is mediated by the institutional forms of the social relations of production and how the state itself is one aspect of this (cf. Jessop, 1991; Holloway, 1991a).[3] There is also a tendency to eschew a direct focus on the social class antagonism between capital and labour to prioritize instead the reproduction of capitalism, or the governing strategies of *depoliticization*, which results in occluding the creative resistance of actual historical struggles (see Chapter 6 of this book). Even Holloway (1988/1991, p. 99, emphasis added) confesses that 'the working class is *not* the focus of analysis, but all the time it is present as the implicit subject of the analysis, as constant counterpoint, as threat.' There is thus a danger of upholding a somewhat heroic vision of class struggle that collapses into an essentialist 'workerist' interpellation of identities and interests divorced from everyday lived experience (Jessop, 1991, p. 165).

Separately, there is a rejection throughout the Open Marxism literature of distinguishing between different forms of state (how the functions of different forms of state are revised and recomposed by the capital relation) or of developing a periodization of the capitalist mode of production (Clarke, 1992 and 2001). Instead, Bonefeld (1992, p. 120) comments that, 'the coercive character of the state exists as presupposition, premise and result of the social reproduction of the class antagonism and not as an exceptional form of the state or as a qualitatively new period of capitalist development'. Yet not only does this view neglect other forms of social power beyond coercive aspects of the state, but it also inadequately conceptualizes changes within capitalist social relations of production. The question left begging is whether this results in an ahistorical conception of capitalism so that capitalism, is capitalism, is capitalism, without due regard for the changing modalities of capitalist exploitation and social organization.

Furthermore, despite the aspiration to situate the state dialectically within global capitalist relations, a state-centrism can nevertheless be detected within Open Marxism. Whilst the social antagonism between capital and labour is considered to be global in substance as noted above, the form of this at the global level is assumed to be state interaction. For example, Holloway argues that 'the competitive struggle between national states is ... to attract and/or retain a share of world capital (and hence a share of global surplus value)' (Holloway, 1995, p. 127). Similarly, according to Burnham (1995a, p. 149):

> the dilemma facing national states is that, whilst participation in multilateral trade rounds and financial summits is necessary to enhance the accumulation of capital on the global level, such participation is also a potential source of disadvantage which can seriously undermine a particular national state's economic strategy. The history of the modern international system is the history of the playing out of this tension.

One is painfully reminded here of the intra-mural debate in IR between neo-realists and neo-liberal institutionalists over absolute and relative gains and the possibilities of conflict or co-operation between states as rational actors (Baldwin, 1993; Grieco, 1988). Elsewhere, Burnham classically states that, 'growing competition among the bourgeoisie indicates that conflict and collaboration is the norm in the global system and is manifested in *national terms as a struggle between states*'. As he continues, 'based on this reading ... international relations is defined as the study of the *national processing* of global class relations' (Burnham, 1998, pp. 196, 199 emphases added). Whilst other important voices are beginning to develop criticisms of such theorizing of the system of capitalist states (Lacher, 2003; Callinicos, 2004; Teschke, 2005), in the words of Gramsci (1978, p. 244) it is argued here that 'the construction of a national state is only made possible ... by the exploitation of factors of international politics'.[4] For the present purposes of this chapter, we tend to accord with Colin Barker's insight in relation to 'Open Marxism' that 'in a capitalist world, it becomes ever more the case that "forgetting" the international dimension of the capitalist state system puts the theorist in the position of a one-handed violinist' (Barker, 1978/1991, p. 120). It is to such issues of critical state theory that we turn to in full in the next section. For the moment, it is reasonable to suggest that much conjecture within Open Marxism leans towards an overly theoretical and abstract style. This charge of abstraction does not simply derive from a lack of familiarity with the method of historical materialism (Clarke, 1977/1991, p. 85). It is levelled because of the difficulty in plausibly explaining the structuring of social power by the 'capital relation' and in thus providing a coherent account of how the 'capital relation' encompasses once and for all the role of the state (Jessop, 1990, p. 101).

As it has been indicated in Chapter 2, neo-Gramscian perspectives can incorporate the positive aspects of Open Marxism. A neo-Gramscian analysis starts by investigating the social relations of production and understands that the state and the market are two different forms expressing the same configuration of class forces. Hence, the artificial separation of state and market is overcome and their inner connection can be comprehended. Second, again similar to Open Marxism, a focus on class struggle is the heuristic approach to explaining structural change in the global order. At the same time, neo-Gramscian perspectives can go beyond Open Marxism's state-centric assumptions. By drawing the analysis of the social relations to their full conclusion, neo-Gramscian perspectives appreciate that the transnationalization of production has led to new, transnational social forces of capital and labour. Hence, class struggle may take place at the global level not only in substance, as Open Marxists would argue, but also in form.

Nevertheless, similar to the objections raised by Baker (1999) and Panitch (1994) (see Chapter 2), Open Marxism is severely critical of the notion of the internationalization of the state and the idea that the state functions as a 'transmission belt' between the requirements of the global and national economy (see Cox, 1992, p. 31). At the centre of this argument is, once again, the disaggregation of politics and economics so that 'class relations (and by implication, struggle) are viewed as external to the process of [global] restructuring, and labour and the state itself are depicted as powerless' (Burnham, 2000, p. 14). This leads to the identification of external linkages between the state and globalization while the 'social constitution' of globalization within and by states is omitted, since the relationship between capital and labour is viewed as external to the process of global restructuring (see Chapter 4 on this aspect of social constitution and Holloway, 1995). Most significantly the overall charge is that there is a 'failure to develop a coherent theory of the state and its relationship to class' (Burnham, 2000, p. 14).

In specific response to this criticism, it was outlined in Chapter 2 how, by asking what modes of social relations of production within capitalism have been prevalent in particular historical circumstances, the state is not treated as an unquestioned category. Indeed, rather closer to positions within Open Marxism than hitherto admitted, the state is treated as an aspect of the social relations of production so that questions about the *apparent* separation of politics and economics or states and markets within capitalism are promoted. Nevertheless, a theory of the state and how this relates to the restructuring of different forms of state within the global political economy is not fully developed by neo-Gramscian perspectives. This may be related to the way the rather problematic notion of the internationalization of the state has been received. Whilst, across neo-Gramscian perspectives, there clearly exists a set of at least implicit assumptions about the state as a form of social relations through which capitalist hegemony is expressed, this needs to be more clearly elaborated. In the next section, therefore, we turn to the 'Critical Economy' conception of the state proferred by Antonio Gramsci and subsequently extended by Nicos Poulantzas in order to demonstrate how this aspect can be more fully developed from within a neo-Gramscian perspective in an engagement with Open Marxism.

A 'Critical Economy' conception of the state

Whilst previously neglected, it is clear that Antonio Gramsci advanced a conception of the state within a broader Marxist approach to political economy that he referred to as 'Critical Economy'.[5] For Gramsci, a 'Critical Economy' approach was distinguished from the 'Classical Economy' of Adam Smith and David Ricardo in that it did not seek to construct abstract hypotheses based on generalized, historically indeterminate conditions of a generic 'homo oeconomicus' (Gramsci, 1995, pp. 166–7). The whole conception of 'Critical Economy' was historicist in the sense that categories were always situated within historical circumstances and assessed within the particular context in which they derived, rather than assuming a universal 'homo oeconomicus' (ibid., pp. 171–3, 176–9). Moreover, the importance of a theory of value was acknowledged to the extent that 'in economics the unitary centre [of analysis] is value, alias the relationship between the worker and the industrial productive forces' (Gramsci, 1971, pp. 402–3). Therefore,

> one must take as one's starting point the labour of all working people
> to arrive at definitions both of their role in economic production and
> of the abstract, scientific concept of value and surplus value, as well
> as ... the role of all capitalists *considered as an ensemble*. (Gramsci,
> 1995, p. 168, emphasis added)

This distancing from liberal ideology was then continued in Gramsci's
direct reflections on the state. According to Gramsci, the conception of
the state developed by dominant classes within capitalist social relations
derived from a separation of politics and economics. 'The state', as represented by the intellectual class supportive of dominant social forces, 'is
conceived as a thing in itself, as a rational absolute' (Gramsci, 1992,
p. 229). Additionally, in those situations when individuals view a collective entity such as the state to be extraneous to them, then the relation
is a reified or fetishistic one. It is fetishistic when individuals consider
the state as a thing and expect it to act and,

> are led to think that in actual fact there exists above them a phantom
> entity, the abstraction of the collective organism, a species of
> autonomous divinity that thinks, not with the head of a specific
> being, yet nevertheless thinks, that moves, not with the real legs of a
> person, yet still moves. (Gramsci, 1995, p. 15)

In contrast, a 'Critical Economy' approach understands the state not
simply as an institution limited to the 'government of the functionaries'
or the 'top political leaders and personalities with direct governmental
responsibilities'. The tendency to solely concentrate on such features –
common in much mainstream debate in IR – was pejoratively referred to
as 'statolatry': it entailed viewing the state as a perpetual entity limited
to actions within political society (Gramsci, 1971, pp. 178, 268). Instead,
the state presents itself in a different way, beyond the political society of
public figures and top leaders, so that 'the state is the *entire complex of
practical and theoretical activities* with which the ruling class not only justifies and maintains its dominance, but manages to win the active consent of those over whom it rules' (ibid., p. 244, emphasis added). This
different aspect of the state is referred to as civil society. The realms of
political and civil society within modern states were inseparable so that,
taken together, they combine to produce a notion of the integral state
(ibid., p. 12, cf. Gramsci, 1994b, p. 67).

Within this extended or integral conception of the state there is a fusion between political and civil society within which ruling classes organize the political and cultural struggle for hegemony, to the extent that distinctions between them become 'merely methodological' (Gramsci, 1971, pp. 160, 258, 271). The state was thus understood not just as the apparatus of government operating within the 'public' sphere (government, political parties, military) but also as part of the 'private' sphere of civil society (church, media, education) through which hegemony functions (ibid., p. 261). Accordingly, civil society 'operates without "sanctions" or compulsory "obligations" but nevertheless exerts a collective pressure and obtains objective results in the form of an evolution of customs, ways of thinking and acting, morality etc.' (Gramsci, 1971, p. 242). In these circumstances 'one cannot speak of the power of the state but only of the camouflaging of power' (Gramsci, 1995, p. 217).

Once again, the notion of integral state was developed in opposition to the separation of powers embedded in a liberal conception of politics. Hence a rejection of the notion of the state as a 'nightwatchman', only intervening in the course of safeguarding public order, because '*laissez-faire* too is a form of state "regulation", introduced and maintained by legislative and coercive means' (Gramsci, 1971, pp. 160, 245–6, 260–3). The state is not therefore agnostic and the ensemble of classes that constitute it have a formative activity in civil society to the extent that the bourgeoisie governs itself through banks and 'great capitalist consortia' reflecting the combined and unified interests of a particular class. As a result, Gramsci maintained, 'the bourgeois class no longer governs its vital interests through Parliament'. Instead, government, or political society in the narrow sense, would rest on coalitions of class interests with such institutions reduced to police activity and the maintenance of social order within an attenuated form of democracy (Gramsci, 1977, pp. 167–72, 174–5).[6]

Thus it can be argued that the state in this conception is understood as a social relation. The state is not unquestioningly taken as a distinct institutional category, or thing in itself, but conceived as a form of social relations through which capitalism is expressed. It is a view that reappraises different modes of cultural struggle within 'a critique of capitalist civilisation' that goes beyond a 'theory of the state-as-force' (ibid., pp. 10–13; Gramsci, 1995, pp. 343–6, 357). It does so by introducing the 'theoretical-practical principle of hegemony' that takes on an 'epistemological significance'. This means that the struggle over hegemony revolves around shaping intersubjective forms of consciousness in civil society – 'the trench-systems of modern warfare' which have to be targeted 'even before the rise to power' – rather than focusing on gaining control of the coercive state apparatus (Gramsci, 1971, pp. 59, 235, 365). It is through state–civil society relations, then, that particular social classes may establish hegemony over contending social forces. By constituting a 'historical bloc', that represents more than just a political alliance but indicates the integration of a variety of different class interests, hegemony may be propagated throughout society, 'bringing about not only a unison of economic and political aims, but also intellectual and moral unity ... on a "universal" plane' (ibid., pp. 181–2).

The granting of concessions beyond the 'economic-corporate' level, within a 'compromise equilibrium', connotes this struggle for hegemony (ibid., p. 161). Hegemony is attained by a fundamental social class but it is presented as 'the motor force of a universal expansion, of a development of all the "national" energies' to become identified with the interests of subordinate social classes (ibid., p. 182). An unstable equilibrium of compromises, characteristic of the struggle for hegemony within 'the life of the state', also entails relating the economic realm to that of the political and cultural spheres more broadly. This is essential as ' "civil society" has become a very complex structure and one which is resistant to the catastrophic "incursions" of the immediate economic element (crises, depressions, etc.)' (ibid., p. 235). As indicated elsewhere, the social function of the intellectual, 'whether in the field of production, or in that of culture, or in that of political administration', becomes pivotal in overcoming the impact of such crises (ibid., p. 97; Morton, 2003b).

Yet this conception of the state and concern with the struggle over hegemony was not simply confined to understanding domestic 'national' experiences. For Gramsci was a fastidious student of the 'international' circumstances of hegemony and argued that whilst the 'national' sphere remained the starting point to eliminate class exploitation and private property, capitalism was a world historical phenomenon within uneven development (Gramsci, 1977, pp. 69–72). This was combined with an acute awareness of the ramifications of world capitalist production and the 'global politico-economic system' of 'Anglo-Saxon world hegemony' that was manifest within a focus on aspects of 'Americanism and Fordism' concerning the expansion of mass-production techniques and scientific management processes on a world scale (ibid., pp. 79–82, 89–93). Forms of 'American global hegemony' (Gramsci, 1996, p. 275) were therefore recognized, with the United States described as the supreme 'arbiter of world finance' (Gramsci, 1992, p. 261) that was trying to 'impose a network of organisations and movements under its leadership' (Gramsci, 1996, p. 11).

Forms of regional and international economic integration, within which 'hegemonic states' may organize national and 'international (interstate) markets', were also discussed (Gramsci, 1992, pp. 285–7, 350–1). As a result, the historical fact cannot have strictly defined 'national' boundaries because 'history is always "world history" and ... particular histories exist only within the frame of world history' (Gramsci, 1985, p. 181). Hence '*relations within society*' – involving the development of productive forces, the level of coercion, or relations between political parties – that constitute '*hegemonic systems within the state*', were dealt with by the same concepts as '*relations between international forces*' – involving the requisites of great powers, sovereignty and independence – that constitute '*the combinations of states in hegemonic systems*' (Gramsci, 1971, p. 176).

The implication of all of this is the need to appreciate the specific meaning attributed to the 'national' point of departure. One can begin analysing the originality and uniqueness of national specificities and historical differences whilst still displaying a dialectical awareness of how relations within a state react both passively and actively to the mediations of international trends (Gramsci, 1971, p. 176). A focus on the 'national' point of departure therefore affords analysis of the concrete development of the social relations of production and the relationship between politics and economics which is inscribed in the struggle over hegemony within a state, whilst remaining aware that 'the perspective is international and cannot be otherwise' (ibid., p. 240; cf. Sassoon, 2001). The next question is, then, how to combine this emphasis on the 'national' point of departure with a focus on emerging transnational social forces but without lapsing into a one-sided view of the internationalization of the state. Here, we turn to the work of Nicos Poulantzas and his understanding of the internalization within the state of different configurations of national and transnational class interests.

Nicos Poulantzas and the internalization of class interests within the state

One way of expanding this 'Critical Economy' approach in light of changing circumstances is evident in the work of Nicos Poulantzas.[7] Poulantzas explicitly warned against emptying the state of class struggle as 'this leads directly to the ideology of "globalization", in other words that of an abstract process whose uneven development would be simply the "dross" of its concretisation into social formations' (Poulantzas, 1975, p. 49). Instead, he emphasized that class bias is inscribed within the very institutional ensemble of the state as a social relation of production which not only permits a radical critique of liberal ideology but also promotes interest in the class pertinency and practices of the state as a strategic site of struggle (Poulantzas, 1973, pp. 63–4). Social classes do not therefore exist in isolation from, or in some exterior relation to, the state. The state is present in the very constitution and reproduction of the social relations of production and is thus founded on the perpetuation of class contradictions. 'The state is the condensation of a relationship of forces between classes and class fractions ... *within the state itself* (Poulantzas, 1978, p. 132, original emphasis). Social classes are therefore defined principally, but not exclusively, by the production process and related to the political, ideological and economic social practices of the state. Hence 'the structural determination of every social class involves its place both in the relations of production and in the ideological and political relations' of the institutional ensemble of the state (Poulantzas, 1975, p. 207). Yet, again, this should not be taken as economic reductionism as 'the economic includes not only production, but also the whole cycle of production-consumption-distribution, the "moments" of this appearing, in their unity, as those of the production process' (ibid., pp. 18, 200–01). This leads to enquiry about the institutional materiality of the state or the various class interests that support the economic, political and ideological dimensions of capitalist social relations.

The state is not a simple class instrument that directly represents the interests of dominant classes. Dominant classes consist of several class fractions that constitute the state, which thereby enjoys a *relative autonomy* with respect to classes and fractions of classes (Poulantzas, 1975, p. 97 and 1978, p. 127). Yet, lest the meaning of this phrase is misunderstood, it should be made clear that relative autonomy *does not* mean a distancing from the social relations of production but solely that the state experiences relative autonomy *vis-à-vis* the classes and fractions of classes that support it (Poulantzas, 1973, p. 256). Within the unstable equilibrium of compromises, discussed above, the state organizes hegemony by imposing certain concessions and sacrifices on the dominant classes in order to reproduce long-term domination (Poulantzas, 1978, p. 184; see also Gramsci, 1971, pp. 161, 245, 254–7).

It also means that relations between different fractions of capital and labour distinguish the struggle over hegemony. The different forms assumed by capital – commercial, industrial, financial – can shape class fractions that share common orientations and interests linked through concrete industrial and financial firms (Poulantzas, 1973, pp. 233–4). These interests can become formulated to represent the general interest through the struggle over hegemony by 'which a class or fraction manages to present itself as incarnating the general interest of the people-nation' to thereby condition relations of domination and subordination (ibid., p. 221). Once a hegemonic relationship is established, distinct class fractions can constitute themselves as a social force that expand their horizons beyond distinct interests. Particular economic-corporate interests are transcended to bind and cohere the diverse aspirations and interests – or 'fringe limits' – of various social classes and class fractions into a historical bloc (ibid., pp. 85, 111–12).

Finally, capital is not simply represented as an autonomous force beyond the power of the state but is represented by classes or fractions of classes *within* the very constitution of the state. There are contradictory and heterogeneous relations internal to the state, which are induced by class antagonisms between different fractions of (nationally- or transnationally-based) capital. Hence 'foreign' capital, represented by transnational corporations or 'footloose' investment, does not simply drain 'state power' (Poulantzas, 1975, p. 170). Instead, stemming from a new phase in imperialism related to the expansion of US hegemony and the *internationalization* of American capital in the 1970s, Poulantzas argued that, through a process of *internalization*, there was an 'induced reproduction' of capital within different states. This means that the internationalization, or transnationalization, of production and finance capital does not represent the expansion of different capitals outside the state but signifies a process of internalization within which interests are translated between various fractions of classes within states (ibid., pp. 73–6). 'The international reproduction of capital under the domination of American capital is supported by the various national states, each state attempting in its own way to latch onto one or other aspect of this process' (ibid., p. 73). The phenomenon now referred to as globalization therefore represents the transnational organization of production relations which are internalized *within* states to lead to a modified restructuring (but not retreat) of the state in everyday life.

In short, these specific issues concerning the changing role of the state are ultimately related to capitalist reproduction on a *global* scale, that is 'global relations of production' (ibid., pp. 63, 83). After all 'imperialism is consubstantial with the modern nation in the sense that it cannot be other than *inter*nationalization or rather *trans*nationalization of the processes of capital and labour.' Capital is located within an *inter*national spatial matrix in order to reproduce itself through *trans*nationalization, 'however deterritorialised and a-national its various forms may appear to be' (Poulantzas, 1978, p. 106). Hence sustaining a dialectical awareness of the mediation of relations between the 'national' and 'international' dimensions, which is the very essence of capitalism, 'contrary to the belief upheld by various ideologies of "globalization" ' (Poulantzas, 1975, p. 78).

To come full circle, it is now the task to incorporate a 'Critical Economy' conception of the state, that includes a conceptualization of the internalization of production relations within the state, in order to overcome the problems with the notion of the internationalization of the state evident within neo-Gramscian perspectives. To start with, it should be highlighted that Cox's framework does include a focus on different forms of state, which are principally distinguished by 'the characteristics of their historic[al] blocs, i.e. the configurations of social forces upon which state power ultimately rests. A particular configuration of social forces defines in practice the limits or parameters of state purposes, and the modus operandi of state action, defines, in other words, the *raison d'état* for a particular state' (Cox, 1987, p. 105). In short, by considering different forms of state, defined in terms of the historical bloc or class configuration that determines its *raison d'état* (Cox, 1989, p. 41), it becomes possible to analyse the social basis of the state or to conceive of the historical 'content' of different states. Attention is thus given to social forces and how these relate to the development of states, including states in alternative conditions of development (Bilgin and Morton, 2002). Further, the state also obtains a relative form of autonomy *vis-à-vis* social classes stemming from the formal separation of economic and political power created by its *raison d'état* (Cox, 1987, pp. 399–400; Holman, 1993, pp. 227–8, 231–2). The 'relative autonomy' of the state therefore regulates dominant class interests in a manner consistent with the economic project of the class as a whole, without yielding to the particular interests of fractions of this class (Cox, 1987, p. 149).

It is this definition of the form of state that is entirely consistent with the 'Critical Economy' perspective outlined above. It allows us to treat the state as more than a narrow apparatus by prompting analysis of the interaction of social forces within political and civil society, that is the integral state, in their struggle for the determination of state purpose. Analysing different forms of state, as an expression of the social relations of production, along this line also overcomes the separation of state and civil society, of economics and politics, and thus one of the main methodological demands of Open Marxism. A dialectical cognizance is also demonstrated of the 'national' and 'international' dimensions, or the set of 'inter-linking hegemonies' (Gills, 1993, p. 117), that make up the global political economy. Seen in this way, globalization and the related emergence of new transnational social forces of capital and labour has not led to a retreat of the state. Instead, there has unfolded a restructuring of different forms of state through an internalization within the state itself of new configurations of social forces expressed by class struggle between different (national and transnational) fractions of capital and labour. This stress on the internalization of class interests through the transnational expansion of social relations is different from assuming that various forms of state have become simple 'transmission belts' from the global to the national level (Cox, 1992).[8] At issue, instead, is the aim of establishing through empirical inquiry how concrete different forms of state have internalized the conflicting interests between national and transnational class fractions (e.g. van der Pijl, 1998; Overbeek, 1990 and 1993). In some instances, the state may indeed function as a 'transmission belt', adapting the national economy to the requirements of the global economy. In others, however, a redefined state purpose could equally well imply a protection of the national economy against global competition. In sum, the internalization of global class relations in concrete forms of state has to be established empirically for each different state form. As should be clear, we have developed such accounts related to the internalization of class interests in different forms of state throughout the book (see Chapters 5 and 7). We feel that the framework developed dovetails well with other arguments within the Open Marxist canon on the internationalization of capital and changes in the capitalist states-system so that, in Sol Picciotto's words, 'changes in the international system involve a contradictory and conflictual process of internationalisation *both* of capital *and* of the state; and the crisis of international capital is also a crisis of the international state system' (Picciotto, 1991b, p. 216, original emphasis).

Conclusion: on 'world class contradictions'

It is argued that an adequate approach to a theory of the state and political economy within critical international theory is not possible without engaging with Open Marxism, although such an approach on its own is not enough. The argument has therefore focused on 'world class contradictions' in a double sense. First, some of the contradictions within Open Marxism itself have been highlighted that are of major (i.e. 'world class') importance in adequately understanding the modalities of power in the context of globalization. Second, we have aimed to stress the importance of remaining engaged with the state as a site of class (-relevant) struggle and strategic selectivity whilst maintaining awareness of the wider dimension of 'world class' (i.e. global) contradictions. As Poulantzas (1975, p. 78, emphasis added) reminds us,

> The task of the state is to maintain the unity and cohesion of a social formation divided into classes, and it focuses and epitomises the class contradictions of the whole social formation in such a way as to sanction and legitimise the interests of the dominant classes and fractions as against the other classes of the formation, *in a context of world class contradictions*.

The 'Critical Economy' conception of the state – based on arguments derived from shared methodological and ontological assumptions – prompts an interest in these very 'world class contradictions'. It does so by not only viewing the state as a *social relation of production* but by also situating the state within the dialectical interplay of structure and agency (or structure and struggle) in the context of globalization. This is the principal merit of a 'Critical Economy' approach to globalization and the state within which a premium is placed on understanding globalization *as* class struggle in its mediation through the institutional forms of capitalism. As a result, the contestation of globalization through class struggle is given centre stage combining a focus on the internal relation of hegemony and resistance (Bieler and Morton, 2001a and 2004; Morton, 2002).

In turn, it is this political economy approach to globalization, the state and class struggle that potentially might open up new critical avenues of inquiry by further revealing the 'neo-Smithian' disposition underpinning wider 'critical' approaches in IR/IPE (Brenner, 1977). This means raising questions about whether other 'critical' approaches are ultimately founded on an understanding of capitalism that is based on the functional expansion and development of market relations rather than the exploitative accumulation of capital and historically specific class struggle. Contrastingly, at present, it seems that there is little place for the subject of class within much recent 'critical' international theory. An enduring sonorous silence on the subject of class, we maintain, is particularly reflected within the milieu of identity politics in international theory. As Andrew Linklater (1999, p. 174) opines, however unfashionable and controversial it may be, 'the swing from class politics to identity politics has gone too far'.

This neglect cannot just be blamed on the blinkers imposed by an American social science disciplining of IR theory. Nor, due to the existence of such a silence on the subject of class, can claims to greater openness within British IR theory be celebrated (S. Smith, 2000, p. 376). Critical international theory is seemingly a set of diverse propositions in search of a subject. Whilst there is clearly no transcendental universal subject, class (-relevant) characters have nevertheless been ostensibly written out of the plot and are no longer materially recognized within the script of critical international theory. A starting point is, therefore, to signal this neglect.

Beyond this recognition, it might be worth questioning whether such neglect reflects a deeper collective bias towards more palatable forms of critical international theory and away from a historical materialistic problematic. A theory of historical materialism grants primacy to the 'decisive nucleus of economic activity' but without upholding an attachment to universal truths that can result in a philosophical position similar to medieval theologism: making an 'unknown god' of the economic structure (Gramsci, 1971, p. 161 and 1994a, p. 365). After all, *contra* Open Marxism, Karl Marx is not some 'shepherd wielding a crook', or 'some Messiah who left us a string of parables laden with categorical imperatives and absolute, unchallengeable norms, lying outside the categories of time and space' (Gramsci, 1994c, pp. 54–8). It has to be shown how historical materialism can progress as a practical canon of historical study rather than as a total conception of the world based on the refinement of dogma (Gramsci, 1994a, p. 311). This is the merit of a historicist approach that 'does not envisage any general or universally valid laws which can be explained by the development of appropriate generally applicable theories' (Cox, 1985/1996, p. 53). It is the purpose of a critical theory that 'is conscious of its own relativity but through this consciousness can achieve a broader time perspective and become less relative' (Cox, 1981, p. 135). A question that can thus be taken up in further debate is whether critical international theory, due to the growing neglect of historical materialism and class struggle, might itself become simply another follower of fashion within bourgeois social science. Hence the importance of remaining critical about the preconditions of critical theory itself.

Notes

1. The wider literature linked to Open Marxism, many aspects of which will be discussed in the ensuing argument, is indeed considerable. For overviews see Bonefeld (1993a and 2001c), Bonefeld, Brown *et al.* (1995), Bonefeld, Gunn and Psychopedis (1992a and 1992b), Bonefeld, Gunn, Holloway *et al.* (1995),

Bonefeld and Holloway (1988/1991 and 1995), Bonefeld and Psychopedis (2000), Burnham (1990), Clarke (1988 and 1991b), Holloway and Picciotto (1978b). These concerns of Open Marxism were especially influential within the early founding and flourishing of the Conference of Socialist Economists (CSE) in Britain (see Conley *et al.*, 2001; F.S. Lee, 2001). Importantly, the Open Marxism presently under discussion should not be confused with entirely different appropriations of the same term (see Drainville 1994). Although we would note, with a touch of irony, that Gramsci's own approach has been called 'open Marxism' as 'the economic base sets, in a strict manner, the range of possible outcomes, but free political and ideological activity is ultimately decisive in determining which alternative prevails' (Marzani, 1957; Femia, 1975: 38).

2. See the similar point by John Michael Roberts who criticizes Open Marxism for reducing 'discrete social forms of life to the main contradiction between capital and labour within the capitalist mode of production'. In order to understand social forms beyond the capitalist mode of production, it is argued that one has to conceptualize how 'social form is refracted through both a mode of production and social relations' (Roberts, 2002, pp. 88, 102).

3. Also see the debate between Bonefeld (1994/2001) and Hay (1994/2001). The importance of considering the political and ideological mediation of state and economic failure is also evident in Hay (1999, pp. 335–6).

4. See also Morton (2005b) on issues of capitalist expansion, modernity, and the international states-system.

5. This does not imply reading Gramsci at face value. Whilst the contemporary use of his concepts is not unproblematic, it is nevertheless maintained that ideas can be understood both within and beyond their original context (see Morton, 2003a).

6. Civil society here should not be understood as a mere reflection of the state. Rather, civil and political society are two tightly inter-linked terrains of struggle, struggle within one realm having an impact on the power configuration of the other.

7. Poulantzas' work is often controversial because of a link to Althusserian 'structural–functionalism' (e.g. Jessop, 1990, p. 87; Foster-Carter, 1978, p. 56n.39). Whether these criticisms are justified or not cannot be discussed here. It would, however, be improvident to dismiss the wider richness of Poulantzas' theory of the state (Jessop, 1990, p. 69). For a broader critical engagement with Poulantzas' Marxist theory and political strategy see Jessop (1985). The classic Poulantzas–Miliband debate highlights some of the controversies on theorizing the capitalist state; see Poulantzas (1969 and 1976) and Miliband (1970 and 1973).

8. Again, it is noteworthy that this metaphor of a 'transmission belt' has been dropped from more recent work (see Cox, 2002, p. 33).

10
Social Constitution and Critical Economy

Werner Bonefeld

I

In Chapter 9, Andreas Bieler and Adam Morton charge so-called 'Open Marxism' with state centrism. This is a strange charge. Usually Marxism is associated with a critique of the state, and not with an affirmative political theory (cf. Bonefeld, 2003). In fact, state-centrism is generally levelled against neo-Gramscian accounts (cf. Clarke, 1991b). In this perspective, it was not only the state that was national in the past but also capitalist 'accumulation', 'capitals' (big national companies), the economic process was 'nationally controlled', and the phase before globalization was the 'nation-state phase of capitalism' (W.I. Robinson, 2004, pp. 75, 102, 107, 42). This focus on the state as the structurally determinant force is now said to be inappropriate because the new capitalist epoch is defined by the *'global economy* as the structurally determinant' force (ibid., p. 10). However, even here the state remains central. The national state continues to govern over the labour force (Hirsch, 1997; Robinson, 2004) and it is the only organization capable of providing the cultural, political and social conditions that capital, however global, requires for its reproduction. As Robinson (2004, p. 87) argues 'there must be some agency whose task is to produce these conditions or to regulate capital's access to them. This institution is the capitalist state'. The notion of the transformation of the national state into a transnational state entails the state not only as a strong state, but also as a capable and decisive organizer of the conditions that allow capital to function (Cox, 2002; Gill, 2003; Robinson, 2004). Further, although the global economy is seen to be structurally determinant, it was the 'transnational state cadre' – in Chapter 7, Adam Morton speaks about the transnational nucleus – that acted as globalization's midwife (Robinson, 2004, p. 101).

A central weakness of the neo-Gramscian approach is its conception of the relationship between the political and the economic: depending on historical circumstances, the economy is either run by the state or the state is run by the economy. Since globalization is said to be an epoch in which capital has attained hegemony (cf. Gill, 2003), the implication is that prior to globalization, the national state was in charge of capitalism and governed in favour on non-capitalist interests. The transition, then, is one from 'welfare to neo-liberal national states' (cf. Robinson, 2004, p. 121). In contrast to its previous incarnation as a welfare state, the state has now become an 'instrument that advances the agenda of global capitalism' (ibid., p. 109). The transition from the welfare state to the capitalist state is seen to be structurally determined.

The neo-Gramscian notion that capitalism hops from mode of regulation to mode of regulation in structurally determined ways, is surprising. Gramsci's work is usually seen as a philosophy of praxis. Gill (2003, p. 16) retains this insight – 'the social world is a human creation' – but then argues that 'society is a totality or system which is regulated or conditioned by structural relations'. Structures, as he puts it, 'are the fundamental unit of analysis' (ibid., pp. 23, 24). This dualism between 'structural determination' and 'human creation' leads to the often-invoked dialectics of structure and human agency. In this 'dialectic', human practice is devoid of creative qualities. In fact, it is deemed to operate within the framework of objective conditions and is thus framed by something outside of itself. Thus, human practice is not only disarticulated from its own social world – human agency mediates what is already structurally determined – it is itself also already and always presupposed as a structural derivate – a sort of living agent of structural properties.

Neo-Gramscian accounts see 'agency', 'social forces', or class struggle as means of mediation: within a structurally determined framework of capitalist development, their 'actions' mediate developments in concrete historical settings. That is, structures impose themselves 'objectively' on the backs of the protagonists and set in motion the decisive conditions of class struggle. Social forces derive from presupposed generic structures, work in and through historically contingent opportunity structures, and mediate the transition of historically specific epochs of capitalism, from the nation state form of capitalism to the global form of capitalism. In short, the approach argues that the rise to a '*global economy* [is] structurally determined' and its development offers opportunity structures to certain interests, such as the '*transnational state cadre*' who act as 'midwives' of the new capitalist world, and the opportunities created by these cadres are then taken up by the 'global ruling class' that seeks to establish its 'authority within a '*transnationally extended state*' (Robinson, 2004, pp. 10, 101, 128). Instead of a critical theory of social constitution, its analysis of social action within pre-determined structures transposes what economics posit as rational market behaviour, to the behaviour of social forces seeking to exploit 'opportunity structures' to further their competing interests.

Open Marxism derived its name from a book by Ernest Mandel and Johannes Agnoli (1980), in which the two protagonists debated the meaning of Marx's 'critique' and, connected with it, whether Marxist economics is a contradiction in terms. Mandel argued that it is not and Agnoli argued that Marx primarily negated the world of capital by revealing its human social content. The critique of social forms, in this view, amounts to a critique of economic categories on a human basis and it does so by returning the constituted forms of the economic categories to 'relations between humans' (Marx 1972, p. 147). Adorno (1993) rightly saw this *reductio ad hominem*, which inspired the critical tradition of the Enlightenment, as the essential core of Marx's critique of political economy.

Helmut Reichelt's (2002, p. 143) argument, that economic categories report the objective delusion of society's alienation from itself, focuses the objective of the remainder of this chapter well. Human social relations appear contradictorily as relations between things. Their objective delusion is fostered by the capitalist exchange relations themselves. They suggest that rationally acting subjects meet on the market to realize their rational interests, whereas in fact they act as executives of abstract social laws which they themselves have generated historically and reproduce through their rational behaviour, and over which they have no control. The understanding that subjective rational behaviour subsists through a context of objective irrationality, that is, beyond the control of human reason, is often taken to mean that human social praxis moves within an objective framework of apparently extra-mundane structures. The critical task of social theory is, however, to uncover the social constitution of these structures so that poverty and misery achieve consciousness of and about themselves.

II

In Bieler and Morton's (2003, see also Chapter 9) 'Critical Economy' account, the 'critical' element points towards an assessment of economic categories in terms of their political significance. Their account goes beyond the crude base–superstructure idea where the economy is determining the political superstructure. In their view, this determination is not automatic but requires social struggle as an element of mediation. As Andreas Bieler and Adam Morton see it, social forces are engendered by economic development and derive from the relations of production. The social forces struggle over the spoils of the system and they do that by trying to exploit opportunity structures, and by doing so, they shape and determine state purpose. The struggles of social forces have, as they argue, a world significance and are concentrated politically in historically changing forms of state. 'Critical Economy' is seen as key for the analysis of the interrelation between the global economy, state and class struggle. Their discussion of 'Critical Economy' fails to show its meaning. In fact, a categorical understanding of the term is replaced by an abstract empiricism that is mirrored not only in the relativism of its logical claim but also in the circularity of their argument. Their account, I will argue, accepts economic categories uncritically and their analysis of the way in which social forces determine state purpose is thus based on unreflected presuppositions.

If economic categories are theorized, economics as a discipline reveals something other than it pretends, namely a historically specific form of human social relations (cf. Backhaus, 2005). This insight is hardly original. Classical political economy posed it without revealing its meaning. Marx's critique of political economy suggested that it can only be resolved negatively, that is by a critique of the economic standpoint. Max Weber (1989, p. 13) who was centrally involved in the marginalist debate in economics at the turn of the last century, retained an acute sense of the issue when he asked, 'how is it that one can buy something – sometimes more, sometimes less – with money? ... I would bet that even if there are economists in this room every one of them would provide a different answer to [this] question'. Max Weber seems to have had little trust in the ability of economists to comprehend the fundamental issues of social-economic reproduction. The neo-Gramscian account of Andreas Bieler and Adam Morton appears to have few if any doubts. 'Critical Economy' gives the answer. It is said to show how concrete state forms are the contingent result of a plurality of contesting social forces, each of which is engendered by the social relations of production, that is, the economic base.

III

The 'Critical Economy' approach 'understands the state not simply as an institution ... but as an 'integral state' (Bieler and Morton 2003, p. 482): it 'includes a concept of the internationalisation of production relations with the state'; 'allows us to treat the state as more than a narrow apparatus'; and prompts 'analysis of the interaction of social forces within political and civil society' (ibid., p. 488). This then is their conception of the integral state, where social forces 'struggle for the determination of state purpose' (ibid., p. 488). The form of the state is thus in itself indeterminate, a sort of black box whose historically concrete determination is contingent on the 'dialectic interplay of struggle and agency (or structure and struggle)' (ibid., p. 490). The 'Critical Economy' approach 'focuses on how social relations of production may give rise to certain social forces, how these social forces may become the basis of power in forms of state and how this might shape world order'. Social forces are the 'main collective actors engendered by the social relations of production' (ibid., p. 476). The social relations of production appear beyond reproach – they provide the objective conditions for the development of social forces. As they put it in Chapter 2, 'changes in the social relations give rise to new configurations of social forces'. Thus, social forces derive form changes in the social relations and move within an objective, structurally determined framework. Social reality appears to be pre-structured by extra-mundane social and political, and also economic, structures, comprising a sort of meta-form of social reality which operates like a systemic framework within which empirically concrete forms of state develop as a consequence of interacting social forces. That is, the action of social forces is structurally determined. Structures imposes themselves 'objectively' on the backs of the protagonists and set in motion the decisive conditions of class struggle. In other words, the generic structure of the social relations of production manifests itself in historical species capitalist forms, or formations, but remains, as the ideal-type of its concrete historical forms, separate from them as the meta-form of their structurally specific determinations. Thus, there cannot be a crisis of capitalism. Instead, there can only be a crisis of a mode of regulation, such as Fordism or Keynesianism, and crisis sets into motion transition to a new mode of regulation, such as Post-Fordism or neo-liberal globalization. In short, social forces derive from presupposed generic structures, work in historically contingent opportunity structures, and mediate the historically specific forms of capitalism, from the liberal international economy, through the era of rival imperialism, to *Pax Americana*, and its crisis (cf. ibid., p. 476, and Chapter 2).

Their 'Critical Economy' account suggests a resigned acceptance of society as a complex of intersubjective structures. They first argue critically against the hypothesization of ahistorical structures and then endorse them. As they put it, the ' "Critical Economy" approach was [for Gramsci] distinguished from the "Classical Economy" of Adam Smith and David Ricardo in that it did not seek to construct abstract hypotheses based on generalised, historically indeterminate conditions of generic homo oeconomicus'. They then propose 'Critical Economy' as a 'historicist conception' where 'categories were always situated within historical circumstances and assessed within the particular context from which they derived, rather than assuming a universal homo oeconomicus' (ibid., p. 481). Their methodological assumption of the 'primacy' of the 'decisive nucleus of economic activity' (ibid., p. 491) in every particular context appears to contradict their 'historicist conception' and, instead, suggests agreement with the criticized caricature of classical political economy. This is, however, not what they wish to endorse. Instead, they espouse Poulantzas' notion that proper science has to abandon the historical problematic of society which Marx understood as 'Man [*Mensch*] himself in his social relations' (Marx 1973, p. 600). Poulantzas' (1968, p. 65) espousal of an 'empirical-pragmatic conception of knowledge' entailed analysis of structural entities in concrete settings, contingent on social forces and indeterminate in terms of concrete state purposes. Poulantzas announced a programme of research that substituted society with the substance of assumed structural properties, denouncing as irrelevant metaphysics the insight that society consists of human social relations, and demanding that proper science had to abstract from them in order to render the analysis of structural elements decisive. Science had to analyse the ensemble of structures, including the structured capacity of social forces to mediate their historically concrete forms. Their reformulation of this so-called dialectic between structure and agency, of institutional development quâ class struggle, offers the classic resolution: one should not see the economic structure as an 'unknown God' although it is decisive in the last instance: the nucleus of economic activity is of primary importance (Bieler and Morton 2003, p. 491). Social forces are structurally determined (ibid., p. 486), and the social relations of production give rise to social forces (ibid., p. 476) whose struggles, as in Coser's (1956) functionalist conception of social conflict, mediate the concrete forms of institutional development, give dynamic to institutional change and develop complex social ensembles in concrete institutional forms (cf. Bonefeld, 1993b).

Andreas Bieler and Adam Morton are absolutely right to insist that economic structures should not be seen as an unknown God. The task of critical inquiry is indeed to show the social constitution of society, a task that attempts to dispel the myth of economic structures as extra-mundane entities endowed with the quality of an invisible but hard-hitting hand. Unfortunately, their approach is however one of avoidance. Their rejection of the unknown God of economics is merely abstract, and that is, the simple question of the social constitution of economic categories is not even posed as a task – it appears antiquated and ' "laden with categorical imperatives and absolute, unchallenged norms, lying outside the categories of space and time" ' (Bieler and Morton 2003, p. 491, citing Gramsci). Their rejection, then, of the unknown God of economic structures goes hand-in-hand with their endorsement of the social relations of production as the logical foundation and thus as the active ground of social forces. Their argument is constantly forced to posit what ostensibly it argues against. It appears haunted by the 'unknown God' of economic categories, as if they embody some sort of metaphysical transcendence.

Not once does their argument ask what the social relations of production are. Instead, they are presupposed 'as an unknown God' whom one should not take too seriously and who at the same time is presumed to be decisive. Social forces are thus structurally constrained and determined by the social relations of production. They give rise to social forces. At the same time, social forces determine state purpose. That is, there is a 'reciprocal relationship of structures and actors' (cf. Chapter 2). In their account, the life-practice of social forces appears as a class-based reformulation of the social action model that economic science calls its own and which reappears in Parson's sociology and pluralist conceptions of the state. The notion that historical development is contingent upon a plurality of social forces, each vying to determine state purpose, depends on assumed structural properties. It explains social development without offering conceptual understanding. If social forces make an impact then that is because social forces were able to exploit opportunity structures; if no impact is made, then the opportunity structure was either not present or it was not recognized as such and the opportunity to shape state purpose lost. The hypothesis of pre-existing structures engendering social forces is mirrored in the hypothetical speculation about developmental opportunity structures that connect social forces with the formal rationality of state action in concrete settings. Whatever the outcome, the explanation is presupposed in its definition and, thanks to its remarkable logic, the theoretical approach stands affirmed in every conceivable way. The argument moves in circles. Each element of the dialectic between structure and struggle points to the other; none is explained.

IV

The so-called Open Marxism approach asks about the social constitution of economic categories and attendant social structures. Hence its question: why does this content (human social relations) assume this form (the form of capital). Economic theory has unsuccessfully tried to answer this question. This has led to some quite remarkable admissions. For example, Myrdal wanted the Nobel Prize for Economics abolished because economics amounted in his view to an indeterminable soft science. Hayek was sceptical about economists' ability to make refutable predictions (Brittan, *Financial Times*, 19 December 2003). Kaldor argued that economic science is quite unable to determine its object matter with any satisfactory degree of certainty (cf. Backhaus, 1997). Daniel Bell concurred, pointing out that 'economic theory is a convenient fiction, an "as if", against which to measure the habitual, irrational, logical, egoistic, self-interested, bigoted, altruistic actions of individuals, firms, or governments – but it is not a model of reality. But even as a fictional ideal, it is inherently problematic' (Bell, 1981, p. 70).

Joan Robinson (1962) offered the hopeful view that it might still be possible to establish economics as a science and that this would entail the elimination of its hitherto metaphysically conceived foundational concepts. In accordance with his teacher Wicksel, Schumpeter argued early in his career that economics as a science has to view its categories as categories of natural laws (*Naturgesetze*) and that it therefore has to take care never to try to justify its social presuppositions. Later in his life, he appeared undecided whether economics could in fact be called a science – the question was still in the balance (Schumpeter, 1965, pp. 35, 37). Proudhon's mockery seems as relevant now as it was then: 'How might economics be a science? How can two economists look at each other without laughing? ... Economics has neither a principle nor a foundation ... it knows nothing; it explains nothing' (Proudhon, 1971, p. 106). The German magazine *Der Spiegel* (cited in Backhaus, 1997) echoed this view when, in 1984, it argued that 'economics is not a science but a philosophy playing with numbers'. Economics as a playful game of numbers is here equated with philosophy as a belief system or even a mere ideology. Philosophers might rightly feel offended. Yet, many serious economic thinkers, from Kenneth Galbraith to Joan Robinson, share this sentiment.

What is the social meaning of a number? Two and two is four, this is a determined structure. Four is however also the result of an infinite range of possibilities, and thus is the result of indeterminate equations. The issue thus is not to presuppose the explanation in the explanandum. Might Marx (1966, p. 818) therefore not be right when he argued that '"price of labour" is just as irrational as a yellow logarithm'? Yet, however yellow, it engenders social forces! The neo-Gramscian approach does well to follow Schumpeter's warning not to pose the question of the social constitution of economic categories. Better to keep the Pandora's box firmly closed. One then does not have to investigate the 'occult quality' of an 'economic' value that is unequal to itself. Then again, their theory of social action takes into account the determinate and the indeterminate and it looks at economics and politics in terms of these two modes. The force which integrates these modes in concrete institutional settings is the struggle of social forces which themselves carry these modes within their definition. In order to remove themselves from the crude bases–superstructure model, they add the adjective 'critical' to 'economics', putting good distance between the 'unknown economic God' and their view that the decisive economic nucleus should not be treated too seriously because concrete historical forms of society are the result of contesting social forces. Yet, these too are structurally determined! However one might judge the seriousness of the invisible, it remains invisible, and there enters, through the back door, an incomprehensible force that underpins and engenders social forces in the indeterminacy of their struggles. Critical economy dissolves political and economic structures into the practical purpose of contesting social forces and presupposes that the foundation of their social praxis rests on the metaphysical quality of unknown and invisible things – the often invoked but never conceptualized relations of production. Their assumption of these relations as a logical *a priori* whose presumed properties give rise to social forces that 'struggle' to shape the practical purpose of these relations in the real world presupposes what needs to be explained.

The core of Marx's critique of political economy is not some sort of determinist acceptance of the primacy of economic activity. This really is the domain of economic theory and its dogmatic opponents, from Leninism to neo-Gramscian-inspired conceptions of socialism, who wish to render the economy more effective, ostensibly in the name of labour. In contrast to these conceptions, the intention of Marx's critique was to reveal the human content of economic categories, that is, to decipher them as categories of human social relations. Instead of deriving class-divided forms of human social practice from hypothesized structural properties, his critique develops these forms from the way in which society organizes its exchange with nature. Classical political economy was in fact a first serious study of this kind, however flawed its labour theory of value (cf. Clarke, 1991a). William Robertson (1890, p. 104) posed its endeavour succinctly: 'in every inquiry concerning the operation of men when united together in society, the first object of attention should be their mode of subsistence'. Rather than pre-supposing the 'unknown God' in the 'nucleus of economic activity', Robertson's formulation hinted at Marx's later critique of economic categories as inverted forms of essentially human social relations.

Schumpeter's and Robinson's attempts to free economics from its metaphysical baggage amounted thus, as the late Joseph Schumpeter (1965) was well aware, to an impossible task. Crudely put, the metaphysical baggage is the social content of economic categories, which economics posits but cannot accept without calling itself into question as a science of economic quantities. Economics without the 'metaphysics' of human social relations leads to its definition as a science of numbers, or as a science of physical quantities; in the case of economics as an exact science that as Kunihiro Jojima (1985) sees it, deals with 'atoms' and 'molecules'. In both cases, economics is seen as some sort of second nature, independent from human social relations and yet structuring the actions of human beings who as agents of their own world struggle over the spoils of a system that appears to exist in abstraction from them, as if it were a person apart. Traditionally this 'indeterminacy within a determinate order' has been conceived in either of two ways. First, in terms of Say's infamous law of the real democracy of demand and supply, where social forces are seen to operate within the framework of a spontaneous order in which each social category is indeterminate in terms of its relative worth or position but where every single social category is obliged to all in the generality of their spontaneous intercourse. Or it has been conceived in terms of the tradition of thought represented by Andreas Bieler and Adam Morton, where presupposed structural properties give rise to class-divided social forces that contest state purposes and, in so doing, realize the forward march of instrumental rationality that pertains not only to 'things' but, also, to the social forces themselves as living embodiments of the iron cage of their structural determination.

V

Marx frequently refers to the forms of value as 'sensuous-supersensuous things', 'crazy objects', 'perverted forms', 'theological quirks', 'obscure things' and so on. These formulations are decisively 'uneconomic' and they suggest that his critique of political economy amounts to a theory of the social constitution of economic categories (cf. Bonefeld, 2001a). Economic theory is haunted by the spectre of social constitution. It views the human social reality of its subject matter as the 'metaphysical' baggage that has to be expelled from economics so that it can at last establish itself as a proper science. The approach represented by Andreas Bieler and Adam Morton seeks a similarly cleansed science of social forces, and it is this stance that characterizes the weakness of neo-Gramscian thought in general. Human social relations subsist indeed against themselves in mysterious economic forms. Yet, this mystery cannot be resolved by eliminating the question of their social constitution. In conclusion, 'all social life is essentially practical. All mysteries which lead theory to mysticism find their rational solution in human practice and in the comprehension of this practice' (Marx, *Theses on Feuerbach*).

11
Marx, Neo-Gramscianism and Globalization

Peter Burnham

The neo-Gramscian critique, as presented by Bieler and Morton, of the 'Open Marxist' approach amounts fundamentally to the claim that class struggle has moved from a 'national' to an 'international/transnational' plane. In the following chapter they claim, 'new, transnational social forces have emerged and class struggle is now taking place not only between capital and labour at a national level, but potentially also between national capital and labour and transnational capital and labour. It is this transnational form of class struggle which Open Marxists do not take into account' (this volume, 197). On this basis, Bieler and Morton suggest that the Open Marxist (or CSE) tradition is ahistorical, viewing class struggle in an outmoded fashion as a national phenomenon. In short, Open Marxism is criticized as 'unthinking materialism', shorn of any historical dimension. Neo-Gramscianism, it is claimed, by contrast is properly transnational and Bieler and Morton seek to demonstrate this primarily through a comparative analysis of trade union activity. Bieler and Morton clearly intend to remain within a framework of analysis informed more by Marx than Weber. However, their 'critique' sidesteps many of the complex methodological debates which have characterized Marxist analysis and in particular they show scant familiarity with the intricacies of the 'open' tradition itself. This chapter presents a brief review of the 'open' tradition before returning to some of the issues raised by Bieler and Morton in the conclusion.

Consistent with the 'open', critical tradition is the work produced by, amongst others, Luxemburg, Korsch, Bloch, Rubin, Pashukanis, Rosdolsky, the Italian tradition of 'autonomist' Marxism and the work of contributors to debates on value and the state held in the early years of the Conference of Socialist Economists (CSE).[1] The hallmark of the 'open', critical tradition fostered within CSE debates is the emphasis placed on recovering Marx's analysis of class, capital and the state as outlined in *Capital* and the *Grundrisse*. Class, in this view, is not to be understood in sociological fashion as a static, descriptive or geographical term applied to groups of individuals sharing common experiences or life-chances or workplace relations. Rather, it is recognized that the separation of labour from the means of production, and thereby the existence of private property, indicates that we are all born into a class society. The class relation between capital and labour is already present, already presupposed, the moment the possessor of money and the possessor of labour power confront each other as buyer and seller (Marx, 1978, p. 114). As Clarke (1978, p. 42), in a pivotal contribution, clarifies, it is the concept of class relations as being analytically prior to the political, economic and ideological forms taken by those relations (even though class relations have no existence independently of those forms) that makes it possible for a Marxist analysis to conceptualize the complexity of the relations between the economic and the political, and their interconnections as complementary forms of the fundamental class relation, without abandoning the theory for a pragmatic pluralism. Class relations, in this sense, are of course antagonistic relations. Class struggle therefore lies at the heart of Marx's account of accumulation as capital must not only extract surplus from labour daily in the production process but must also ensure the successful reproduction of the total social circuit of capital through its three principal forms. This calls for constant 'intervention' from state managers and for the establishment of various forms of international regimes and institutions. If the circuit of capital is understood in terms of struggle and potential crisis then determinism of all kinds is rejected. Struggle, as Holloway (1991b, p. 71) points out, by definition is uncertain and leaves outcomes open. In essence, this version of Marxism, based on an understanding of the complexities of the rotation of capital, focuses on resistance to the imposition of work and thereby points to the fragility of capitalism as a system of class domination.

Capital, as self-valorizing value, should be understood as 'movement', as a circulatory process, not as a static thing or structure (Marx, 1978, p. 185). Money capital and commodity capital do not, for instance, denote branches of business that are independent and separate from one another. Rather, they are simply particular functional forms of industrial capital, 'modes of existence of the various functional forms that industrial capital constantly assumes and discards within the circulation sphere' (Marx, 1978 p. 136). Accordingly, this tradition refuses to fetishize either the 'market' or the 'state'. Instead, focus is on the changing character of the form of the 'political' in relation to the circuit of capital. This presents a powerful alternative to deterministic base-superstructure images of Marxism. Monocausal economism is replaced with the dialectical notion that social relations of production only exist in the form of economic, legal and political relations. It is not simply a case of arguing in Weberian fashion that each of these relations exercise reciprocal and causative influence. Rather, Marx is at pains to stress that antagonistic class relations are always manifest in economic, political and legal forms. In this way 'economics' rests as firmly on 'politics' and 'law' as vice versa (Meiksins Wood, 1981). The fundamental error of determinist schools is that they understand the *social* relations of production in terms of *technical* economic relations, thereby replicating the fetishism that Marx's critique of classical political economy sought to dispel.

In opposition therefore to most international relations theory, the CSE tradition understands the 'state' as an aspect of a wider and more fundamental set of social relations based on the separation of labour from the conditions of production. The state should not be seen as 'autonomous' or as 'determined' by a supposed 'economic base'. Rather, the starting point is that provided by Evgeny Pashukanis (1978, p. 139) who poses the question, 'why does class rule not remain what it is, the factual subjugation of one section of the population by the other? Why does it assume the form of official state rule, or – which is the same thing – why does the machinery of state coercion not come into being as the private machinery of the ruling class?; why does it detach itself from the ruling class and take on the form of an impersonal apparatus of public power, separate from society?'. Similarly, in relation to the market, why do goods and services take the form of commodities? Why do the products of labour confront each other as commodities?

Marx indicates that our first task is to focus on the relationship between the direct producers and the owners of production to ascertain how the ruling class secures the extraction of surplus value. The particular form and mode in which the connection between workers and means of production is effected is what distinguishes the various economic epochs of the social structure (Marx, 1978, p. 120). On this basis, it is possible to introduce consideration of the state, since as Clarke (1983, p. 118) clarifies, 'the state does not *constitute* the social relations of production, it is essentially a *regulative* agency, whose analysis, therefore, presupposes the analysis of the social relations of which the state is regulative. The analysis of the capitalist state conceptually presupposes the analysis of capital and of the reproduction of capitalist relations of production, despite the fact that in reality, of course, the state is itself a moment of the process of reproduction'. The character of the capitalist state, and by implication the international state system, is therefore to be analysed against the background of the tensions and contradictions inherent in the development and reproduction of the capitalist mode of production.

Towards a critique of IPE

When turning to analyse global relations, a number of CSE theorists have argued that it is fundamental to switch our focus and level of abstraction from the 'state' (capitalist state form) to particular national states and more broadly to the political management of the global circuits of capital (Burnham 1995b; Holloway, 1995; Picciotto, 1991a). The fragmentation of the 'political' into national states, which from their very inception comprise an international system, has developed in an uneven fashion alongside the internationalization of capital. As Picciotto (1991a, p. 217) clarifies, the transition from the personal sovereign to an abstract sovereignty of public authorities over a defined territory was a key element in the development of the capitalist international system, since it provided a multifarious framework which permitted and facilitated the global circulation of commodities and capital. The 'capitalist state' thus originated in the context of an international system of states establishing a framework for the generalization of commodity production based (initially) on petty commodity production and a world market.

This view, which locates the development of the capitalist state in the establishment and maintenance of generalized commodity production, offers a distinctive way of understanding the emergence of the global political economy. Whereas 'World Systems-Analysis' theorists similarly emphasize the absolute dependence of the world economy on the state system, in taking a global perspective it is neither necessary nor helpful to start from the market. As Picciotto (1991a) again outlines, in Wallerstein's schema it is the world market and the consequent international division of labour that allocated a particular role to each region, from which flowed the relationship of exploitation and hence the form of the state. However, it was not trade that transformed production relations, but the contradictions of feudal and post-feudal production relations that led to transformations both of the world market and the form of the state (Brenner, 1977; Rosenberg, 1994). By viewing national states as political nodes in the global flow of capital, it is possible to avoid both the Smithian bias introduced by focusing uncritically on the market and the mistakes of orthodox IPE, which treat state and market as independent variables.

In this light, class relations do not impinge on the state; they do not exist in 'domestic' society and make their presence felt by influencing the state, which operates in the international realm. Rather, the state itself is a form of the class relation, which constitutes global capitalist relations. These relations appear, for example, as British relations on the world market. Yet, as Marx clarifies in *The Civil War in France*, struggles between states are to be understood, at a more abstract level, as struggles between capital and labour, which assume more and more the character of the national power of capital over labour. National states exist as political 'nodes' or 'moments' in the global flow of capital and their development is therefore part of the antagonistic and crisis-ridden development of capitalist society. The state itself cannot resolve the global crisis of capital. National states can, however, enhance their position in the hierarchy of the price system by increasing the efficiency of capitalist exploitation operating within their boundaries (Bonefeld, Brown *et al.*, 1995).

The CSE tradition thus suggests that the apparent solidity of the 'state' masks its existence as a contradictory form of social relationship. The 'state' is not only an institution but a form-process, an active process of forming social relations and therefore class struggles channelling them into non-class forms – citizens rights, international human rights – which promote the disorganization of labour (Holloway, 1991b, pp. 75–6). The key to comprehending capitalist society is that it is a global social system based on the imposition of work through the commodity-form (Cleaver, 1979, pp. 71–86). The reproduction of bourgeois social relations at all levels (from the overseer, to the managing director, state managers, international agencies and alliances between states) rests upon the ability of capital (in all its forms and guises) to harness and contain the power of labour within the bounds of the commodity-form. The struggles which ensue over the imposition of work, the regulation of consumption through the commodification of labour time as money and the confinement of the production of use values within the bounds of profitability produce constant instability and crisis. It is the everyday struggles in and against the dominance of the commodity-form, which are manifest as 'national' economic crises or balance of payments problems or speculative pressure on currency. This approach to international relations does not reject the 'state' as a category but rather sees relations between national states in terms of the antagonistic social relationships which constitute states as political moments of the global composition of class relations.[2]

Globalization and the political 'management' of global circuits of capital

A number of implications flow from the view that states should be conceptualized as political nodes in the global flow of capital. The first relates directly to current debates on whether capitalism has entered a new stage characterized by globalization. If we theorize the class relation as a global social relationship and national states as political nodes active in the reproduction of global circuits of capital, then 'globalization' loses some of its mystique. States are not to be thought of as 'thing-like' institutions losing power to the market. Rather, in a context characterized by the intensive and extensive development of the global circuits, state managers have been able to reorganize their core activities using market processes to 'depoliticise' the management of difficult aspects of public policy (see chapter). It should be no surprise that a global system resting on an antagonistic social relationship will be subject to dynamic change as both state and market actors seek to remove what they perceive to be 'blockages' in the flow of capital. In essence, state managers are above all circuit managers. 'Globalization' presents serious problems for approaches based on national conceptions of capitalism and for those frameworks which insist on regarding 'states' and 'markets' as fundamentally opposed forms of social organization. However, for this particular Marxist tradition, 'globalization' simply represents a deepening of existing circuits and a broadening of the 'political' as regulative agencies (both public and private) beyond the national state are drawn into the complex process of 'managing' the rotation of capital. To develop this point further, it is necessary to review aspects of Marx's discussion of the total circulation process of capital.

In *Capital Volume 1*, Marx introduces the 'general formula of capital'. Capital in its most general form is defined as value that expands itself, 'the value originally advanced, therefore, not only remains intact while in circulation, but increases its magnitude, adds to itself a surplus-value, or is valorised. And this movement converts it into capital' (Marx, 1976a, p. 252). Whilst passing through the sphere of circulation (as money-capital and commodity-capital) there can be a redistribution of value but its magnitude cannot be increased. Hence Marx identifies the commodity which when purchased can be used in production to create new value – labour power. In *Capital Volume 2* Marx continues this discussion emphasizing that capital, as self-valorizing value, is a movement, a circulatory process that passes through a sequence of transformations, a series of metamorphoses that form so many phases or stages of a total process

(Marx, 1978, p. 132). Two of the phases, or forms of capital, belong to the circulation sphere (money capital and commodity capital), one to the sphere of production (productive capital). As Marx summarizes, 'the capital that assumes these forms in the course of its total circuit, discards them again and fulfils in each of them its appropriate function, is *industrial capital* – industrial here in the sense that it encompasses any branch of production that is pursued on a capitalist basis' (ibid., p. 133).

Hence, Marx's basic representation of the circuit:

$$M - C(LP + MP) \cdots P \cdots C' - M'(M + m)$$

For our purposes, two important points emerge from this very brief overview of the circulation of capital. First, the determining purpose, the driving motive common to all three circuits is the valorization of value, the basis of which is the exploitation of labour power. Each particular circuit presupposes the others and although in reality each individual industrial capital is involved in all three at the same time, the circuit is a constant process of interruption as capital clothes itself in its different stages, alternately assuming them and casting them aside (Marx, 1978, p. 109). Hence, capital is simultaneously present and spatially coexistent in its various phases or modes of existence. If however a breakdown occurs in one part of the circuit, the whole process may be brought to a standstill. The cycle of accumulation therefore is fraught with the possibility of crisis at every stage. As Marx indicates, 'every delay in the succession brings the coexistence into disarray, every delay in one stage causes a greater or lesser delay in the entire circuit, not only that of the portion of the capital that is delayed, but also that of the entire individual capital' (ibid., p. 183). Since the circuitry of modern capitalism is both intensive and extensive (in terms of the interpenetration of capitals and the global domination of this mode of production) the potential for interruption and crisis is immense. Each of the three phases of the total circuit is prone to disruption (in a multitude of ways ranging from financial crisis to industrial unrest and lack of effective demand experienced as 'overproduction'). At the most basic level the circulation of capital is undermined by any process, which potentially reunites labour with the means of production and subsistence. This understanding of capitalism points to the permanence of crisis and the necessity for crisis management at both national and international levels. Every crisis in the international system of course has its own particular line of development. However, by focusing on the circuits of capital we are able to analyse the social form of crisis thereby relating the particular to the general. Second, this framework establishes a clear break with realist state-centrism and with crude Leninist 'state as capitalist trust' theories. As political nodes in the global flow of capital, states are essentially regulative agencies implicated in its reproduction but unable to control this reproduction or represent unambiguously the interests of 'national capital'. Rather, state managers seek to remove barriers to the capital which flows in and through their territories. The fundamental tasks of state managers (from welfare to the management of money, labour, trade, etc.) therefore relate directly to ensuring the successful rotation of capital both nationally and internationally. However, as noted above, the difficulties of containing conflict and enhancing the accumulation of capital have led to a more diverse process of circuit management involving a range of actors, agencies and regimes seeking to regulate aspects of the metamorphosis of capital.

Marx's theory of capitalist society rooted in the concepts of value, surplus value, capital and class remains the single most important contribution to developing a sophisticated radical analysis of the contemporary global economy. It should by now be clear that the open tradition rejects a 'sociological' understanding of 'class struggle' as either national or transnational and in particular rejects the view that class struggle equals trade union strategies (whether national or international). In the 'open' tradition, class struggle is an aspect of the class relation. The division into classes is an expression of the way in which exploitation is effected and to that extent there is an unceasing struggle between exploited and exploiting classes (de Ste. Croix, 1981, p. 66). This does not however mean that the open tradition is ahistorical or essentialist. Marx's infamous section in *Capital Volume 3* where he discusses the importance of the form in which unpaid surplus labour is 'pumped out', ends by noting that 'the same fundamental relations' can manifest infinite variations and gradations of aspect which can only be grasped by analysis of the empirically given circumstances (also see de Ste. Croix, 1981, p. 52). This, of course, has spawned many studies of struggle and the 'circulation of struggle' based not upon sociological or geographical characteristics but rather rooted in a clear articulation of the circuit of capital (for example, Cleaver, 1979).

By rescuing Marx's critique of political economy from the clutches of bourgeois social science, the CSE tradition has played a major role in furthering the aims of *Capital*. In an effort to 'update Marx' the neo-Gramscian critique unwittingly mystifies and reifies social relations in a manner reminiscent of the 'trinity formula' theorists who, as Marx (1981a, p. 969) noted, simply reproduced the everyday notions of the actual agents of production, giving them a certain comprehensible arrangement, and thereby obliterating the entire inner connection of the social relations of production.

Notes

1. See Bonefeld *et al.*, eds. (1992a and b). On autonomous Marxism see Witheford (1994), Cleaver (1979), and Negri (1984).
2. Also see Holloway (1995).

12
Class Formation, Resistance and the Transnational
Beyond Unthinking Materialism
Andreas Bieler and Adam David Morton

Open Marxism and neo-Gramscian perspectives clearly share a whole range of common historical materialist assumptions, concerns and objectives. Both reject the positivist separation of subject and object and the distinction between normative enquiry and empirical scientific research in the search for causal relationships. Rather, they understand themselves as a critical theory, which questions current world order and power relationships in an effort to contribute to a positive transformation of capitalism. Therefore, they both also reject any ahistoric notion separating the political and the economic, the state and market, the domestic and the international. Instead, they take the social relations of production as a starting-point of enquiry and acknowledge that as a result of capitalism being organized around private property and wage labour, these apparent dichotomies are simply different expressions, different forms, of the same configuration of social relations. For example, we would more than share Werner Bonefeld's sentiment that 'the understanding ... of the global relations of capital can not go forward through the rationalisation of the strategic calculations of particular transnational banks and multinational companies. It has to go forward through an examination of the relations of exploitation and that is through an understanding of the dependence of capital on labour' (this volume, Chapter 4, 45–68). Such commonalities make it possible to appreciate the historicity of capitalism, including also the possibility of change beyond the capitalist social relations of production (see Chapter 1).

Open Marxist and neo-Gramscian perspectives differ, however, in their understanding of the structural developments in the global economy since the early 1970s. Open Marxists simply regard the changes as an intensification of earlier developments with the basic contradiction between an integrated world market on the one hand, and a geopolitical split into independent nation-states on the other, unchanged (see, e.g., this volume, Chapter 11, 187–195). Moreover, Open Marxists have had difficulties in explaining the uneven development of the international states-system and the distinct emergence of capitalism (Lacher, 2002, 2005). This is evidenced in Bonefeld's equation of the emergence of the states-system and capitalist international relations of production (this volume, Chapter 4, 45–68). Elsewhere he goes on to argue that 'the global economy and the national state belonged together since the inception of capitalism, and the contradiction between the two is therefore not new' (this volume, Chapter 8, 133–152). There is a failure here to grant due regard to the origins of the inter-state system that lie in a prior period of absolutist sovereignty, which was crucial in subsequently determining the structure of capitalist social relations and the states-system (see Teschke, 2003). Neo-Gramscian perspectives, by contrast, think in terms of fundamental structural changes, expressed in the argumentation in this book by the most recent transnationalization of production and finance and the shift to neo-liberalism (although see Morton, 2005b on anterior developments). As a result of these changes in the social relations of production, it was argued that new, transnational social forces have emerged and class struggle is now taking place not only between capital and labour at the national level, but potentially also between national capital and labour and transnational capital and labour. It is this transnational form of class struggle which Open Marxists do not take into account. Class struggle, from their point of view, takes place in form only at the national level, but is played out at the international level through inter-state co-operation and conflict. From a neo-Gramscian point of view, however, this is another form of ahistoricism, where capitalism is capitalism is capitalism. To cite Bonefeld directly in this regard, 'whatever the specific historical form of capitalism, the law of value remains, as does the law of capital and its state' (this volume, Chapter 4, 45–68; see also Chapter 11, 187–195). The crucial structural differences, highlighted within a periodization of capitalism, are overlooked and this has significant consequences for the understanding of current developments. In Chapter 5 on European integration, for example, it was argued that Open Marxism understands EMU as a strategy of different national bourgeoisies/states co-operating in depoliticizing monetary policy at the European level in order to extend the exploitation of their various national working classes. A neo-Gramscian analysis, by contrast, understands EMU as a part of a transnational class conflict over the future model of capitalism, in which transnational capital has successfully pushed its project of 'embedded neoliberalism' moving the EU towards the Anglo-American model of capitalism.

The focus on transnational class formation by neo-Gramscian perspectives does not, however, imply that the international division into independent nation-states is considered to be increasingly a thing of the past. Neo-Gramscian perspectives do not think in terms of the withering away of the nation-state. Rather, what needs to be analysed are the different ways in which the neo-liberal interests of transnational social forces of capital are currently internalized, or not, into different national forms of state and the related national interests. Two principal ways of how this takes place can be identified. First, national forms of state can be restructured in a hegemonic way. Here, restructuring is pushed by, and based on, domestic social groups, forming a majority alliance around a hegemonic project that is capable of bringing these groups together into a coherent programme consisting of economic interests as well as cultural ideas, identities, moral values, etc. Austrian and Swedish accession to the EU in 1995 are good examples of this type of hegemonic transformation (Bieler, 2000; see also Chapter 5 in this volume). Neo-liberal restructuring, although in tune with developments at the level of world order, was brought about by national social groups, who perceived it as a necessary adjustment to global developments. Second, restructuring can take place through a strategy of passive revolution. Here, there is no dominant alliance of social forces at the national level behind transformation, meaning that restructuring becomes a predominantly elite-driven project, heavily reliant on external support for its implementation. Chapter 5 outlined how eastward enlargement of the EU was driven by Central and Eastern European state elites in close co-operation with officials of the IMF and subsequently EU representatives. In other words, neo-liberal restructuring was firmly anchored externally. Similarly, Chapter 7 highlighted how neo-liberal restructuring in Mexico was not driven by a hegemonic alliance of social forces at the national level. Rather, again in a strategy of passive revolution, neo-liberal ideas were imported from abroad via the education of elites in the United States as well as through a change in the Mexican social relations of production, relying increasingly on inward foreign direct investment as well as a development strategy of export-led growth since the late 1970s. At times, technocrats within specific political cliques (or *camarillas*), linked to transnational capitalism, zealously adopted neo-liberal interests and precepts in Mexico. As a result, some domestic social groups were co-opted into this strategy through selective measures of amelioration and co-optation such as projects like the National Solidarity Programme (PRONASOL) whilst participation in the North American Free Trade Agreement (NAFTA) provided the external anchor.

Of course, in the engagement between Open Marxist and neo-Gramscian perspectives, criticism is not one way. Initially, neo-Gramscian perspectives have been criticized by Open Marxism for an alleged overemphasis on the role of ideology, resulting in an empirical pluralism, which overlooks the explanatory primacy of the social relations of production (Burnham, 1991; see also Chapter 3 in this volume). As argued in Chapter 2 in this volume, however, neo-Gramscian perspectives do not simply regard ideas as an independent variable. Rather, ideas only gain relevance, when they are connected to social power and material interests. It is, therefore, the material structure of ideas, which is emphasized by neo-Gramscian perspectives. What counts is the way different ideas are related to specific constellations of the social relations of production (Bieler, 2001). Expecting a related charge of voluntarist politicism by Bonefeld, however, we were rather surprised that he accuses us of economic determinism, suggesting that 'social reality appears', in our argument, 'to be pre-structured by extra-mundane social and political structures, comprising a sort of meta-form of social reality which operates like a systemic framework within which empirically concrete forms of state develop as a consequence of interacting social forces' (Bonefeld, 2004a, p. 233; see also Chapter 10 in this volume). Clearly, our insistence on a focus on the various sites and forms of struggle involved in the mediating process of capital accumulation and state transformation in hard to justify as *both* voluntarist politicism *and* structurally determined materialism.

In response to Bonefeld's claim, our approach precisely poses the very question of the 'social constitution' of economic categories so desperately sought. After all, as Marx (1894a/1998, p. 801) put it, 'capital is not a thing, but rather a definite social production relation, belonging to a definite historical formation, which is manifested in a thing and lends this thing a specific social character.' The 'social constitution' of capital was forwarded in our original argument through the notion of *internalization*: how state apparatuses internalize the interests of capital through induced reproduction (Bieler and Morton, 2003, pp. 485–9). To put it differently, drawing from Marx, it is a process that begins with the *formal subsumption* of labour under capital whereby capital subsumes the labour process of a preceding mode of production as 'a *relation of compulsion* ... which does not rest on any personal relations of domination and dependence, but simply arises out of the difference in economic functions' (Marx, *c.* 1861–63/1994, p. 426, original emphasis). Subsequently, the process of the *real subsumption* of labour under capital reflects a more extensive fashioning of society by capital. Capitalist production proceeds historically from the formal subsumption of labour power, based on the simple exchange of labour power for wages, to real subsumption of labour in which the class relation embedded in this transaction is carried deep into the social organization of production (Marx, c.1861–63/ 1994, 424–442). To return to our original suggestion, this is a process involving the internalization of capital, the transformation of the labour process and its actual conditions, as well as an expression of a set of practices intrinsic to identity and interest formation. Internalization is thus one of the most potent expressions of a power relationship related to the structuring of identities and subjectivities.

Further, the 'human content of economic categories' is also compellingly illuminated by Antonio Gramsci in relation to the constitution of 'matter': 'for the philosophy of praxis ... the various physical (chemical, mechanical etc.) properties of matter which together constitute matter itself ... should be considered, but only to the extent that they become a productive "economic element". Matter as such therefore is not our subject but *how it is socially and historically organised for production*, and natural sciences should be seen correspondingly as essentially an historical category, a human relation' (Gramsci, 1971, p. 465, emphasis added). The clearest example is that of electricity:

> Electricity is historically active, not merely however as a natural force (e.g. as an electrical discharge which causes a fire) but as a productive element dominated by man [*sic*] and incorporated into the ensemble of material forces of production, an object of private property. As an abstract natural force electricity existed even before its reduction to a productive force, but it was not historically operative and was just a subject of hypothetical discourse in natural history (earlier still it was historical 'nothingness', since no one was interested in it or indeed knew anything about it). (Gramsci, 1971, pp. 466–7).

Nature therefore provides qualities of matter (electricity), which exist prior to our knowledge about them, but they only become significant when linked to the interests of social power and their conscious use as social productive relations. To summarize, we hold that our argument steers a careful course between idealist, pluralist empiricist explanations and economic determinist, materialist accounts. While in itself unfounded, Bonefeld's charge of unthinking materialism is a welcome reminder to remain alert in not straying from this course. We envisage a critical theory of the state that follows the above course whilst also, finally, cast within the shadow of Horkheimer's social function that has society as its object, as a dialectical critique of political economy, within the 'world of capital'. Along the way we therefore hope we have set 'an aggressive critique not only against the conscious defenders of the status quo but also against the distracting, conformist, or utopian tendencies within [one's] own household' (Horkheimer, 1937/1992, pp. 206–8, 216). Pushing this sense of critique, the remainder of this chapter will address a range of related theoretical, methodological and empirical issues.

Methodological challenges and empirical research

The way neo-Gramscian theoretical concepts are utilized for empirical research requires careful consideration. One method of proceeding with empirical research is to conduct analysis in relation to the three levels of activity outlined in Chapter 2: the social relations of production, forms of state and world order. Taking the first as a point of departure, research may start through an investigation of the production structure in order to identify social forces as the key collective actors. Globalization, in addition to a shift from Keynesianism to neo-liberalism, has been defined as the transnationalization of production and finance. A neo-Gramscian analysis, therefore, concludes that this change in the production structure has led to the emergence of new collective actors, that is transnational social forces of capital and labour. Additionally, rather than deducing particular positions of social forces from their location in the production process, neo-Gramscian perspectives try to find out through an empirical analysis which social class forces attempt to formulate a hegemonic project around which ideas. Gill (1995a) concludes that transnational capital within globalization is currently involved in formulating a project around the ideas of neo-liberal economics, since this furthers specific material interests best. Of course, such hegemonic projects also need to include other ideas in order to reach forces beyond transnational capital. Only then is the establishment of a historical bloc possible. As outlined in Chapter 5 of this volume, for example, transnational capital promoted a compromise of 'embedded neoliberalism' within the EU. It is predominantly based on neo-liberalism, but it also included mercantilist aspects to attract capital fractions, which concentrated on the European market and would prefer protection against global competition, as well as social aspects to attract trade unions and social democratic elements. Nevertheless, to be successful, hegemonic projects need to be concretized within a form of state, the second level of activity. Hence, one can investigate how these transnational forces of capital become internalized in a particular form of state or how they are resisted. Chapter 7 in this volume provides a very good example of an analysis outlining how transnational capital has become internalized within the Mexican form of state. Granting priority to the accumulation strategy of neo-liberalism, especially reflected in the era of *salinismo*, seriously eroded the historical basis of PRI hegemony in Mexico. Privileging the accumulation function of the state can undermine its legitimation function and weaken hegemony (Cox, 1982, p. 54). In this vein, the demise of Import Substitution Industrialization (ISI) and the rise of neo-liberalism were accompanied by the exhaustion of PRI hegemony. The analysis of neo-liberalism in Mexico traced these shifts in hegemony whilst highlighting how social class forces engendered common perspectives on the importance of fiscal discipline and market-oriented reforms between technocratic elites of a common social background; hence the expansion of transnational capital through the interiorization of interests between various fractions of classes within state–civil society relations.

Finally, one can investigate how neo-liberal hegemony, achieved within particular forms of state, such as the United Kingdom and the United States, is transferred to the world order sphere of activity. In general, this takes place through the expansion of a particular mode of social relations of production to other countries aided by international organizations. In concrete terms, in times of globalization, this refers to the increasing transnationalization and opening up of other countries' political economy, partly due to the investment of Transnational Corporations (TNCs) in developing countries, thereby transnationalizing these countries' production structures, and partly through the implementation of neo-liberal restructuring programmes by international organizations such as the International Monetary Fund (IMF) or World Bank, further opening up countries to foreign investment. Chapter 5 in this volume provides an example of how these processes of restructuring were implemented in Central and Eastern European countries in a strategy of passive revolution. In a different regional context, one has also witnessed in Chapter 7 how IMF austerity measures – involving reductions in state subsidies for foodstuffs and basic consumer items, increases in taxes on consumption, and tight wage controls targeted to control inflation – were adopted in Mexico. These are both classic conditions of passive revolution in which neo-liberalism is 'the reflection of international developments which transmit their ideological currents to the periphery' (Gramsci, 1971, p. 116). Again, the exact manner of how this outward expansion occurs in different forms of state and regional contexts is a matter of empirical investigation.

Alternatively, research may also start through an emphasis on the socio-cultural hegemonic struggle between ruler and ruled in state forms leading to various avenues along which domination and resistance can be analysed. Here, Gramsci's own criteria on the history of subaltern classes can be taken as a point of departure when analysing alternative historical and contemporary contexts (Gramsci, 1971, pp. 52–5).[1] The history of subaltern classes is intertwined with that of state–civil society relations and it is therefore important to try and unravel such contestations. One way of doing so is to identify the 'objective' formation of subaltern social classes by analysing developments and transformations within the social relations of production (Gramsci, 1971, p. 52). For example, historical and contemporary research would need to incorporate, as much as possible, a consideration of the mentalities and ideologies of subaltern classes, their active as well as passive affiliation to dominant social forms of political association, and thus their involvement in formations that might conserve dissent or maintain control (Gramsci, 1971, p. 52). Additionally, it can entail focusing on the formations which subaltern classes themselves produce (e.g. trade unions, workers' co-operatives, peasant associations, friendly societies, social movements) in order to press claims or assert their autonomy within the existing conditions of hegemony. Questions of historical and political consciousness expressed by subaltern classes can then be raised within this research strategy.

What this approach highlights is the process of class formation, whereby particular communities may experience new structures of exploitation and identify new points of antagonistic interest centred on issues of class struggle; even though forms of class-consciousness – involving a conscious identity of common interests – may not have immediately materialized (E.P. Thompson, 1978). This means that class identity emerges within and through historical processes of economic exploitation. As such this is an *emergentist* theory of class situated in particular historical contexts of struggle (Morton, 2006a). It is this emergentist theory of class that has been drawn upon in focusing on forms of resistance in the case of the *Ejército Zapatista de Liberación Nacional* (EZLN) in Mexico and how the capitalization of the land involved changing property relations and shifts from rank-based social ties and communal commitments of civil-religious hierarchies to cash derived from wage labour (Morton, 2002). It is therefore imperative to appreciate the common terrain occupied by the art of both domination and

resistance, or structure and agency, within the theatre of class formation. 'The history of subaltern social groups is necessarily fragmented
and episodic. ... Subaltern groups are always subject to the activity of ruling groups, even when they rebel and rise up' (Gramsci, 1971, pp. 54–5).
Issues of subjectivity, identity and difference can then be raised in ways
that do not bypass issues of materiality, inequality and exploitation
within a political economy approach. This focus on resistance to neo-
liberal restructuring, however, is frequently missing in contemporary
research. The final section of this chapter will therefore turn to this issue
in a little more detail.

Resistance to neo-liberal globalization and the European Social Forum

Optimistic analyses of the current changes in social movements speak
of an emerging transnational civil society at the global level, leading
almost automatically to a re-regulation of the negative implications of
a neoliberal market economy (for example, Held and McGrew, 2002,
pp. 135–6; Scholte, 2000, pp. 285, 291). This contrasts with neo-Gramscian
perspectives in several ways. First, neo-Gramscian perspectives assume
that forms of state remain important locations of exploitation and resistance. The idea that a transnational civil society would supersede the
international states-system is deemed, at present, unrealistic. Second, it is
argued that exploitation is rooted in the way production is organized
around wage labour. Simply re-regulating capitalism at the global level
will not overcome this problem. Third, even if there is something like
transnational civil society, many actors, which are a part of this society,
are actually driving forces behind neo-liberal restructuring, such as
transnational business groups, rather than opponents to the unfettered
market. Hence, the neo-Gramscian focus on the way the social relations
of production are organized in times of globalization. At issue here is an
extended notion of class struggle (see Chapter 2 in this volume), in
which social movements, which resist the extension of exploitation into
the sphere of social reproduction, are considered to be part of class
struggle as much as actors operating on behalf of the working class or
employers.

Such an extended notion of class struggle is in particular relevant to
an analysis of the European Social Forum (ESF), in which European
anti-neo-liberal groups meet in order to organize their strategies against
globalization. From 6 to 10 November 2002, European 'anti-globalization'
movements including trade unions, non-governmental organizations

and other social movements gathered in Florence, Italy for the first ESF. During 400 meetings around 32,000 to 40,000 delegates from all over Europe, plus 80 further countries, debated issues related to the three main themes of the Forum: 'Globalization and [neo-] liberalism', 'War and Peace', as well as 'Rights-Citizenship-Democracy'. The ESF culminated in one of the largest anti-war demonstrations ever on the afternoon of 9 November, when 500,000 protestors according to police estimates – almost 1 million according to the organizers – marched peacefully through the streets of Florence against the impending war on Iraq (Bieler and Morton, 2004). Clearly, there were differences between the various social movements, established trade unions and new unions. As for the latter, the very emergence of the new, radical trade unions was a result of the perceived accommodationist position of established trade unions vis-à-vis neo-liberal restructuring in Europe. In contrast with their established counterparts, new radical trade unions such as the French union Solidaires, Unitaires et Démocratique (SUD)-PTT regard themselves as rank and file unions, where strong emphasis is put on the opinions of members. While established trade unions continue to focus on 'social partnership' with employers and state representatives in order to assert the demands of their members, radical trade unions emphasize the importance of bottom-up organization with a focus on strikes, demonstrations and co-operation with other social movements to broaden the social basis of resistance. Moreover, tensions also exist between trade unions and social movements. While the latter are rather sceptical of trade unions' hierarchical internal organization and their willingness about confronting neo-liberal restructuring, the former question the representativeness and internal accountability of social movements. These differences, however, should not make us overlook the commonalities and resulting possible joint activities. Despite different structures and strategies, all movements present at the ESF identified neo-liberal globalization, in its economic, deregulatory form as well as militaristic version (as embodied in the war on Iraq) as the main target for resistance. Hence a convergence of opinions emerged around several areas for joint activities.

First, it was at the ESF that anti-war organizations agreed to hold European – and in the event worldwide – demonstrations against the impending war on Iraq on 15 February 2003. Second, neo-liberal restructuring of the public sector within the EU – pushed by the European Commission and the Lisbon European Council summit conclusions in 2000, and the General Agreement on Trade in Services (GATS) negotiations at the global level – was perceived as the main threats to peoples' livelihoods and the focal point for joint struggle. The consensus was that public services must not become a new realm for capital accumulation. As a result of the interaction at the ESF, demonstrations in Brussels were organized by Belgian unions and the Association for the Taxation of Financial Transactions for the Aid of Citizens (ATTAC), on 9 February 2003, to keep public services out of GATS followed by a day of national action, on 13 March 2003, linked to the same theme. Similar co-operation efforts were initiated and/or deepened in relation to the demand for a European minimum income, the combat of tax evasion, as well as the co-ordinated demands for the introduction of a Tobin Tax on currency speculations (Bieler and Morton, 2004, pp. 312–19). While the second ESF in Paris in November 2003 was a disappointment as far as the co-operation between social movements and trade unions was concerned, these links experienced renewed emphasis at the third ESF in London in October 2004. British trade unions were especially out in force for the first time. Moreover, resistance to neo-liberal restructuring in general and the privatization of public services in particular was still the main priority that brought together this wide range of different movements (Bieler and Morton, 2006b). Overall, the future of the ESF and the related resistances to neo-liberal restructuring (including earlier movements such as the EZLN) are open-ended. As Gramsci puts it in relation to some general features of social struggle:

> One may say that no real movement becomes aware of its global character at once, but only gradually through experience – in other words from the facts that nothing which exists is natural (in the non-habitual sense of the word), but rather exists because of the existence of certain conditions, whose disappearance cannot remain without consequences. (Gramsci, 1971, p. 158)

It is the task of theorists to render these developments critically and to give form to further lines of resistance against neo-liberal globalization and its associated processes of transnational class formation.

Note

1. This implies internalising Gramsci's method of thinking rather than reading Gramsci at face value. The contemporary use of Gramsci's concepts is not unproblematic but a clear method has been emphasised, which holds that ideas can be understood both within and beyond their original context, see Morton, 2003a.

Bibliography

Abercrombie, N., S. Hill and B.S. Turner (1980) *The Dominant Ideology Thesis* (London: Allen and Unwin).

Adorno, T. W. (1993) 'Zur logik der Sozialwissenschaften', in T. W. Adorno *et al.*, *Der Positivismusstreit in der Deutschen Soziologie* (Munich: DTV).

Adorno, T.W. (1971) 'Drei Studien zu Hegel', in *Gesammelte Schriften Vol. 5*, (Frankfurt: Suhrkamp).

Agnoli, J. (1996) *Subversive Theorie. 'Die Sache Selbst' und ihre Geschichte* (Freiburg: Ça ira).

——. (1997) *Faschismus ohne Revision* (Freiburg: Ça ira).

——. (2000) 'The Market, the State and the End of History', in W. Bonefeld and K. Psychopedis (eds) *The Politics of Change: Globalisation, Ideology and Critique* (London: Palgrave).

Agnoli, J. and E. Mandel (1980) *Offener Marxismus* (Frankfurt: Campus).

Althusser, L. (1969) *For Marx* (London: Allen Lane).

——. (1970) 'Marxism is not Historicism', in L. Althusser and E. Balibar, *Reading Capital* (London: Verso).

——. (1996) *For Marx* (London: Verso).

Altvater, E. (2002) 'The Growth Obsession', in L. Panitch and C. Leys (eds) *A World of Contradiction, Socialist Register 2002* (London: Merlin Press).

Anderson, P. (1980) *Considerations on Western Marxism* (London: Verso).

van Apeldoorn, B. (2001) 'The Struggle over European Order: Transnational Class Agency in the Making of 'Embedded Neo-Liberalism', in A. Bieler and A. David Morton (eds) *Social Forces in the Making of the New Europe: the Restructuring of European Social Relations in the Global Political Economy* (Houndmills: Palgrave).

——. (2002) *Transnational Capitalism and the Struggle over European Integration* (London: Routledge).

van Apeldoorn, B. and O. Holman (1994) 'Transnational Class Strategy and the Relaunching of European Integration: the Role of the European Round Table of Industrialists', paper presented at the 35th Annual Convention of the International Studies Association, Washington, DC (28 March–1 April).

van Apeldoorn, B., H. Overbeek and M. Ryner (2003) 'Theories of European Integration: A Critique', in A. W. Cafruny and M. Ryner (eds) *A Ruined Fortress? Neoliberal Hegemony and Transformation in Europe* (Lanham, MD: Rowman & Littlefield).

Armstrong, P., A. Glyn and J. Harrison (1984) *Capitalism since World War II* (London: Fontana).

Ashley, R.K. (1984) 'The Poverty of Neorealism', *International Organisation*, 38/2: 225–86.

——. (1989) 'Living on Border Lines: Man, Poststructuralism and War', in J. Der Derian and M. Shapiro (eds) *International/ Intertextual Relations: Postmodern Readings of World Politics* (Toronto: Lexington Books).

Auge, C. (2002) 'Argentina, Life after Bankruptcy', *Le Monde Diplomatique*, September. http://mondediplo.com/2002/09/13argentina, accessed 22 October 2005.

Augelli, E. and C. Murphy (1988) *America's Quest for Supremacy and the Third World: A Gramscian Analysis* (London: Pinter).

Backhaus, H. G. (1992) 'Between Philosophy and Science: Marxian Social Economy as Critical Theory', in W. Bonefeld, R. Gunn and K. Psychopedis (eds) *Open Marxism, Vol.1: Dialectics and History* (London: Pluto Press).

——. (1997) *Die Dialektik der Wertform* (Freiburg: Ça ira).

——. (2005) 'Some Aspects of Marx's Concept of Critique in the Context of his Economic-Philosophical Theory', in W. Bonefeld and K. Psychopedis (eds) *Human Dignity* (Aldershot: Ashgate).

Baker, A. (1999) '*Nébuleuse* and the "Internationalisation of the State" in the UK?', *Review of International Political Economy*, 6/1: 79–100.

Balanyá, B., A. Doherty, O. Hoedeman, and E. Wesselius (2000) *Europe Inc.: Regional and Global Restructuring and the Rise of Corporate Power* (London: Pluto Press).

Baldwin, D. A. (ed.) (1993) *Neorealism and Neoliberalism: The Contemporary Debate* (New York: Columbia University Press).

Bales, K. (2000) *Disposable People: New Slavery in the Global Economy* (San Francisco: University of California Press).

Barker, C. (1978/1991) 'A Note on the Theory of Capitalist States', *Capital & Class*, 4: 118–129 and in S. Clarke (ed.) *The State Debate* (London: Macmillan).

Beck, U. (1998) 'Die Seele der Demokratie. Wie wir Bürgerarbeit statt Arbeitslosigkeit finanzieren können', *Gewerkschaftliche Monatshefte*, 6/7: 330–4.

Bell, D. (1981) 'Models and Reality of Economic Discourse', in D. Bell and I. Kristol (eds) *The Crisis of Economic Theory* (New York: Basic Books).

Bellofiore, R. (1997) 'Lavori in Corso', *Common Sense*, 22: 43–60.

Benson, G. (1995) 'Safety Nets and Moral Hazards in Banking', in K. Sawamoto, Z. Nakajima, and H. Taguchi (eds) *Financial Stability in a Changing Environment* (London: Palgrave).

Berins C. R. (1992) *The Contradictory Alliance: State-Labour Relations and Regime Change in Mexico* (Berkeley: University of Berkeley Press).

Bieler, A. (2000) *Globalisation and Enlargement of the EU: Austrian and Swedish Social Forces in the Struggle over Membership* (London: Routledge).

——. (2001) 'Questioning Cognitivism and Constructivism in IR Theory: Reflections on the Material Structure of Ideas', *Politics*, 21/2: 93–100.

——. (2002) 'The Struggle over EU Enlargement: a Historical Materialist Analysis of European integration', *Journal of European Public Policy*, 9/4: 575–97.

——. (2003a) 'Labour, Neo-liberalism and the Conflict over Economic and Monetary Union: a Comparative Analysis of British and German Trade Unions', *German Politics*, 12/2: 24–44.

——. (2003b) 'Swedish Trade Unions and Economic and Monetary Union: the European Union Membership Debate Revisited?', *Cooperation and Conflict*, 38/4: 385–407.

——. (2005) 'European Integration and the Transnational Restructuring of Social Relations: the Emergence of Labour as a Regional Actor?', *Journal of Common Market Studies*, 43/3: 461–84.

——. (2006) *The Struggle for a Social Europe: Trade Unions and EMU in Times of Global Restructuring* (Manchester: Manchester University Press).

Bieler, A. and A.D. Morton (eds) (2001a) 'The Gordian Knot of Agency-Structure in International Relations: A Neo-Gramscian Perspective', *European Journal of International Relations*, 7/1: 5–35.

——. (eds) (2001b) *Social Forces in the Making of the New Europe: The Restructuring of European Social Relations in the Global Political Economy* (London: Palgrave).

——. (2003) 'Globalisation, the State and Class Struggle: A "Critical Economy" Engagement with Open Marxism', *British Journal of Politics and International Relations*, 5/4: 467–99.

——. (2004) ' "Another Europe is Possible"?: Labour and Social Movements at the European Social Forum', *Globalizations*, 1/2: 303–26.

——. (eds) (2006a) *Images of Gramsci: Connections and Contentions in Political Theory and International Relations* (London: Routledge).

——. (2006b) 'Canalising Resistance: Historical Continuities and Contrasts of "Alter-globalist" Movements at the European Social Forum', in A. Gamble, S. Ludlam, A. Taylor and S. Wood (eds) *Labour, the State, Social Movements and the Challenge of Neoliberal Globalisation* (Manchester: Manchester University Press).

Bieling, H.-J. and T. Schulten (2003) ' "Competitive Restructuring" and Industrial Relations within the European Union: Corporatist Involvement and Beyond', in A.W. Cafruny and M. Ryner (eds) *A Ruined Fortress? Neoliberal Hegemony and Transformation in Europe* (Lanham, MD: Rowman & Littlefield).

Bieling, H.-J. und J. Steinhilber (eds) (2000) *Die Konfiguration Europas: Dimensionen einer kritischen Integrationstheorie* (Münster: Westfälisches Dampfboot).

Bilgin, P. and A.D. Morton (2002) 'Historicising Representations of "Failed States": Beyond the Cold War Annexation of the Social Sciences?', *Third World Quarterly*, 23/1: 55–80.

Bloch, E. (1986) *The Principle of Hope* (Oxford: Basil Blackwell).

Block, F. (1977) *The Origins of International Economic Disorder* (California: University of California Press).

Bohle, D. (2000) 'EU-Integration und Osterweiterung: die Konturen einer neuen europäischen Unordnung', in H.-J. Bieling und J. Steinhilber (eds) *Die Konfiguration Europas: Dimensionen einer kritischen Integrationstheorie* (Münster: Westfälisches Dampfboot).

——. (2003) 'Neo-liberal Restructuring and Transnational Actors in the Deepening and Widening of the European Union', paper presented at the Global Tensions and their Challenges to Governance of the International Community Conference, sponsored by the International Studies Association and the Central and East European International Studies Association, Budapest (26–28 June).

Bohle, D. and D. Husz (2005) 'Whose Europe is It? Interest Group Action in Accession Negotiations: The Cases of Competition Policy and Labor Migration', *politique européenne*, 15: 85–112.

Bonefeld, W. (1987/1991) 'The Reformulation of State Theory', in W. Bonefeld and J. Holloway (eds) *Post-Fordism and Social Form: A Marxist Debate on the Post-Fordist State* (London: Macmillan).

——. (1992) 'Social Constitution and the Form of the Capitalist State', in W. Bonefeld, R. Gunn and K. Psychopedis (eds) *Open Marxism, Vol.1: Dialectics and History* (London: Pluto Press).

Bonefeld, W. (1993a) *The Recomposition of the British State During the 1980s* (Aldershot: Dartmouth).

——. (1993b) 'Crisis of Theory', *Capital & Class*, 50: 25–49.

——. (1994/2001) 'Aglietta in England: Bob Jessop's Contribution to the Regulation Approach', in B. Jessop (ed) *Regulation Theory and the Crisis of Capitalism*, 5 vols. Vol.2: European and American Perspectives on Regulation (Cheltenham: Edward Elgar).

——. (1995) 'Capital as Subject and the Existence of Labour', in W. Bonefeld, R. Gunn, J. Holloway and K. Psychopedis (eds) *Open Marxism, Vol. 3: Emancipating Marx* (London: Pluto Press).

——. (1996) 'Money, Equality and Exploitation', in W. Bonefeld and J. Holloway (eds) *Global Capital, National State and the Politics of Money* (London: Palgrave).

——. (1999) 'Notes on Competition, Capitalist Crisis, and Class', *Historical Materialism*, 5: 5–28.

——. (2000) 'Die Betroffenheit und die Vernunft der Kritik', in J. Bruhn, *et al.* (eds) *Kritik der Politik* (Freiburg: Ça ira).

——. (2001a) '*Kapital* and Its Subtitle', *Capital & Class*, 75: 53–64.

——. (2001b) 'Social Form, Critique and Human Dignity', *Zeitschrift für kritische Theorie*, 13: 97–113.

——. (2002a) 'European Integration: the Market, the Political and Class', *Capital & Class*, 77: 117–42.

——. (2002b) 'Capital, Labour and Primitive Accumulation. On Class and Constitution', in A.C. Dinerstein and M. Neary (eds), *The Labour Debate. An Investigation into the Theory and Reality of Capitalist Work* (Aldershot: Ashgate).

——. (2004a) ' "Critical Economy" and Social Constitution: A Reply to Bieler and Morton', *British Journal of Politics and International Relations*, 6/2: 231–40.

——. (2004b) 'Krise der Währungsunion', *Wildcat*, 68: 55–8.

——. (2005a) 'Europe, the Market and the Transformation of Democracy', *Journal of Contemporary European Studies*, 13/1: 93–106.

——. (2005b) 'Nationalism and Anti-Semitism in Anti-Globalisation Perspective', in W. Bonefeld, and K. Psychopedis (eds) *Human Dignity: Social Autonomy and the Critique of Capitalism* (Aldershot: Ashgate).

——. (ed.) (2001c) *The Politics of Europe: Monetary Union and Class* (Basingstoke: Palgrave).

——. The Capitalist State: Illusion and Critique', in W. Bonefeld (ed) (2003) *Revolutionary Writing: Common Sense Essays in Post-Political Politics* (New York: Autonomedia).

Bonefeld, W. and P. Burnham (1998) 'The Politics of Counter-Inflationary Credibility in Britain 1990–1994', *Review of Radical Political Economics*, 30/1: 30–52.

Bonefeld, W, A. Brown and P. Burnham (1995) *A Major Crisis? The Politics of Economic Policy in Britain in the 1990s* (Aldershot: Dartmouth).

——, R. Gunn and K. Psychopedis (eds) (1992a) *Open Marxism, Vol.1: Dialectics and History* (London: Pluto Press).

——. (eds) (1992b) *Open Marxism, Vol.2: Theory and Practice* (London: Pluto Press).

—— R. Gunn, J. Holloway and K. Psychopedis (eds) (1995) *Open Marxism, Volume 3: Emancipating Marx* (London: Pluto Press).

Bonefeld, W. and J. Holloway (eds) (1991) *Post-Fordism and Social Form: A Marxist State Debate* (London: Macmillan).

——. (eds) (1996) *Global Capital, National State and the Politics of Money* (London: Macmillan).

Bonefeld, W. and K. Psychopedis (eds) (2000) *The Politics of Change: Globalisation, Ideology and Critique* (London: Palgrave).

——. (eds) (2005) *Human Dignity: Social Autonomy and the Critique of Capitalism* (Aldershot: Ashgate).

Bonnet, A. (2002) 'The Command of Money-Capital and the Latin American Crises', in W. Bonefeld and S. Tischler (eds) *What is to be Done* (London: Ashgate).

Booth, K. (ed) (2005) *Critical Security and World Politics* (Boulder, CO: Lynne Rienner).

Bootle, R. (2003) *Money for Nothing* (London: Nicholas Brealey).

Boyer, R. and D. Drache (eds) (1996) *States against Markets* (London: Routledge).

von Braunmühl, C. (1978) 'On the Analysis of the Capitalist Nation State within the World Market Context', in J. Holloway and S. Picciotto (eds) *State and Capital* (London: Edward Arnold).

Brenner, R. (1977) 'The Origins of Capitalist Development: A Critique of Neo-Smithian Marxism', *New Left Review* I/104: 25–92.

——. (1998) 'The Economics of Global Turbulence', *New Left Review*, 229: 1–265.

——. (2002) *The Boom and the Bubble* (London: Verso).

Broad, R. and J. Cavanagh (1999) 'The Death of the Washington Consensus?', *World Policy Journal*, 16/3: 79–88.

Browne, H. (1994) *For Richer, For Poorer: Shaping US-Mexican Integration* (London: Latin America Bureau).

de Brunhoff, S. (1978) *The State, Capital and Economic Policy* (London: Pluto Press).

Buci-Glucksmann, C. (1979) 'State, Transition and Passive Revolution', in C. Mouffe (ed.) *Gramsci and Marxist Theory* (London: Routledge).

Burchill, S. and A. Linklater (2001) *Theories of International Relations* (London: Palgrave, 2nd edition).

Burnham, P. (1990) *The Political Economy of Postwar Reconstruction* (London: Macmillan).

——. (1991) 'Neo-Gramscian Hegemony and the International Order', *Capital & Class*, 45: 73–93.

——. (1994) 'Open Marxism and Vulgar International Political Economy', *Review of International Political Economy*, 1/2: 221–31.

——. (1995a) 'State and Market in International Political Economy: Towards a Marxian Alternative', *Studies in Marxism*, 2: 135–59.

——. (1996) 'Capital, Crisis and the International State System', in W. Bonefeld and J. Holloway (eds) *Global Capital, National State and the Politics of Money* (London: Palgrave).

——. (1997) 'Globalisation: States, Markets and Class Relations', *Historical Materialism: Research in Critical Marxist Theory*, 1: 150–60.

——. (1998) 'The Communist Manifesto as International Relations Theory', in M. Cowling (ed.) *The Communist Manifesto: New Interpretations* (Edinburgh: Edinburgh University Press).

——. (1999) 'The Politics of Economic Management in the 1990s', *New Political Economy*, 4/1: 37–54.

——. (2000) 'Globalisation, Depoliticisation and "Modern" Economic Management', in W. Bonefeld and K. Psychopedis (eds) *The Politics of Change: Globalisation, Ideology and Critique* (London: Palgrave).

Burnham, P. (2001) 'New Labour and the Politics of Depoliticisation', *British Journal of Politics and International Relations*, 3/2: 127–49.

Buttigieg, J.A. (1986) 'The Legacy of Antonio Gramsci', *Boundary 2*, 14/3: 1–17.

Caffentzis, G. (1995) 'The Fundamental Problem of the Debt Crisis for Social Reproduction in Africa', in M.R Dalla Costa and G.F. Dalla Costa (eds) *Paying the Price* (London: Zed Books).

Cafruny, A.W. and M. Ryner (eds) (2003) *A Ruined Fortress? Neoliberal Hegemony and Transformation in Europe* (Lanham, MD: Rowman & Littlefield).

Cairncross, A. (1985) *Years of Recovery: British Economic Policy, 1945–51* (London: Methuen).

Callinicos, A. (1992) 'Capitalism and the State System: A Reply to Nigel Harris', *International Socialism*, 54.

——. (2004) 'Marxism and the International', *British Journal of Politics and International Relations*, 6/3: 426–33.

Cammack, P. (1999) 'Interpreting ASEM: Interregionalism and the New Materialism', *Journal of the Asia Pacific Economy*, 4/1: 13–32.

Carchedi, G. (1997) 'The EMU, Monetary Crises, and the Single European Currency', *Capital & Class*, 63: 85–114.

——. (2001) *For Another Europe: A Class Analysis of European Economic Integration* (London: Verso).

Carchedi, B. and G. Carchedi (1999) 'Contradictions of European Integration', *Capital & Class*, 67: 119–53.

Carr, B. (1985) *Mexican Communism, 1968–1983: Eurocommunism in the Americas?* (San Diego, CA: Centre for U.S.–Mexican Studies).

——. (1991) 'Labour and the Political Left in Mexico', in K.J. Middlebrook (ed.) *Unions, Workers and the State in Mexico* (San Diego, CA: Centre for U.S.–Mexican Studies).

Carter, B. (1997) 'Restructuring State Employment', *Capital & Class*, 63: 65–84.

Cecchini, P., E. Jones and J. Lorentzen (2001) 'Europe and the Concept of Enlargement', *Survival*, 43/1: 155–65.

Centeno, M.A. (1994) *Democracy within Reason: Technocratic Revolution in Mexico* (Pennsylvania: Pennsylvania State University Press).

Centeno, M.A. and S. Maxfield (1992) 'The Marriage of Finance and Order: Changes in the Mexican Political Elite', *Journal of Latin American Studies*, 24/1: 57–85.

Cerny, P. (1990) *The Changing Architecture of Politics: Structure, Agency, and the Future of the State* (London: Sage).

——. (1993a) 'The Political Economy of International Finance', in P. Cerny (ed.) *Finance and World Politics: Markets, Regimes and States in the Post-Hegemonic Era* (Aldershot: Edward Elgar).

——. (1993b) 'The Deregulation and Re-regulation of Financial Markets in a More Open World', in P. Cerny (ed.) *Finance and World Politics: Markets, Regimes and States in the Post-Hegemonic Era* (Aldershot: Edward Elgar).

Charnock, G. (2006) 'Improving the Mechanisms of Global Governance? The Ideational Impact of the World Bank on National Reform Agendas in Mexico', *New Political Economy*, 11/1: Forthcoming.

Chase-Dunn, C. (1981) 'Inter-State System and Capitalist World Economy', *International Studies Quarterly*, 25/1.

Chossdovsky, M. (1997) *The Globalisation of Poverty* (London: Zed Books).

Clarke, S. (1977/1991) 'Marxism, Sociology and Poulantzas's Theory of the State', in S. Clarke (ed.) *The State Debate* (London: Macmillan).

——. (1977) 'Marxism, Sociology and Poulantzas' Theory of the State', *Capital & Class* 2: 1–31.

——. (1978) 'Capital, Fractions of Capital and the State: Neo-Marxist Analysis of the South African State', *Capital & Class*, 5: 32–77.

——. (1983) 'State, Class Struggle and the Reproduction of Capital', *Kapitalistate*, 10/11: 113–30.

——. (1987) 'Capitalist Crisis and the Rise of Monetarism', *Socialist Register 1987* (London: Merlin Press).

——. (1988) *Keynesianism, Monetarism and the Crisis of the State* (Aldershot: Edward Elgar).

——. (1989) 'M. Itoh's "Basic Understanding of Capitalism" ', *Capital & Class*, 37: 133–49.

——. (1990) 'The Limits of Pluralism: The Contradictions of Capital, Political Conflict and the State', paper presented at the International Conference 'After the Crisis', Amsterdam (April).

——. (1991a) *Marx, Marginalism and Modern Sociology* (London: Palgrave).

——. (ed.) (1991b) *The State Debate* (London: Palgrave).

——. (1992) 'The Global Accumulation of Capital and the Periodisation of the Capitalist State Form', in W. Bonefeld, R. Gunn and K. Psychopedis (eds) *Open Marxism, Vol.1: Dialectics and History* (London: Pluto Press). *Ru.*

——. (1994) *Marx's Theory of Crisis* (London: Palgrave).

——. (2001) 'Class Struggle and the Global Overaccumulation of Capital', in R. Albritton, M. Itoh, R. Westra and A. Zuege (eds) *Phases of Capitalist Development: Booms, Crises and Globalisations* (London: Palgrave).

Cleaver, H. (1979) *Reading Capital Politically* (Sussex: Harvester Press).

Clifton, J. (2000) *The Politics of Telecommunications in Mexico: Privatisation and State–Labour Relations, 1982–1995* (London: Macmillan).

Cockburn, A. and K. Silverstein (1995) 'War and Peso', *New Statesmen and Society*, 24 February 1995.

Cockcroft, J.D. (1983) *Mexico: Class Formation, Capital Accumulation and the State* (New York: Monthly Review Press).

——. (1998) *Mexico's Hope: An Encounter with Politics and History* (New York: Monthly Review Press).

Collier, D. (ed) (1979) *The New Authoritarianism in Latin America* (Princeton: Princeton University Press).

——. (1995) 'Trajectory of a Concept: "Corporatism" in the Study of Latin American Politics', in P.H. Smith (ed) *Latin American in Comparative Perspective: New Approaches to Methods and Analysis* (Boulder, CO: Westview Press).

Conley, H. Freeman, A., McCulloh, A. and Stewart, P. (2001) '*Capital & Class* Past and Present: Some Reflections on our First 25 years', *Capital & Class*, Issue 75: 1–13.

Cook, M.L. (1995) 'Mexican State–Labour Relations and the Political Implications of Free Trade', *Latin American Perspectives*, 22/1: 77–94.

Cook, M.L., K.J. Middlebrook and J.M. Horcasitas (1994) 'The Politics of Economic Restructuring in Mexico: Actors, Sequencing, and Coalition Change', in M.L. Cook, K.J. Middlebrook and J.M. Horcasitas (eds) *The Politics of Economic Restructuring: State-Society Relations and Regime Change in Mexico* (San Diego, CA: Centre for U.S.–Mexican Studies).

Cornelius, W.A. (1985) 'The Political Economy of Mexico Under de la Madrid: Austerity, Routinised Crisis and Nascent Recovery', *Mexican Studies/Estudios Mexicanos*, 1/1: 83–123.

——. (1996) *Mexican Politics in Transition: The Breakdown of a One-Party Dominant Regime* (San Diego, CA: Centre for U.S.–Mexican Studies).

Cornelius, W.A., A.L. Craig and J. Fox (1994) 'Mexico's National Solidarity Program: An Overview', in W.A. Cornelius, A.L. Craig and J. Fox (eds) *Transforming State-Society Relations in Mexico: The National Solidarity Strategy* (San Diego, CA: Centre for U.S.–Mexican Studies).

Coser, L. A. (1956) *The Functions of Social Conflict* (Glencoe: Free Press).

Cox, R.W. (1981) 'Social Forces, States and World Orders: Beyond International Relations', *Millennium: Journal of International Studies*, 10/2: 126–55.

——. (1982) 'Production and Hegemony: Toward a Political Economy of World Order', in H.K. Jacobson and D. Sidjanski (eds) *The Emerging International Economic Order: Dynamic Processes, Constraints and Opportunities* (London: Sage).

——. (1983) 'Gramsci, Hegemony and International Relations: An Essay in Method', *Millennium: Journal of International Studies*, 12/2: 162–75.

——. (1985/1996) 'Realism, Positivism, Historicism', in R.W. Cox and T.J. Sinclair (eds) *Approaches to World Order* (Cambridge: Cambridge University Press).

——. (1986) 'Social Forces, States and World Orders', in R. Keohane (ed) *Neo-Realism and its Critics* (New York: Columbia University Press).

——. (1987) *Production, Power and World Order: Social Forces in the Making of History* (New York: Columbia University Press).

——. (1989) 'Production, the State and Change in World Order', in E-O Czempiel and J.N. Rosenau (eds) *Global Changes and Theoretical Challenges: Approaches to World Politics for the 1990s* (Toronto: Lexington Books).

——. (1992/1996) 'Towards a Posthegemonic Conceptualisation of World Order: Reflections on the Relevancy of Ibn Khaldun', in R.W. Cox and T.J. Sinclair (eds) *Approaches to World Order* (Cambridge: Cambridge University Press).

——. (1992) 'Global *perestroika*', in R. Miliband and L. Panitch (eds) *The Socialist Register: New World Order?* (London: Merlin Press).

——. (1993) 'Structural Issues of Global Governance: implications for Europe', in S. Gill (ed) *Gramsci, Historical Materialism and International Relations* (Cambridge: Cambridge University Press).

——. (1993/1996) 'Production and Security', in R.W. Cox and T.J. Sinclair (eds) *Approaches to World Order* (Cambridge: Cambridge University Press).

——. (1994) 'The Forum: Hegemony and Social Change', *Mershon International Studies Review*, 38/2: 366–7.

——. (1995a) 'Critical Political Economy', in B. Hettne (ed) *International Political Economy: Understanding Global Disorder* (London: Zed Books).

——. (1995b) 'Civilisations: Encounters and Transformations', *Studies in Political Economy*, 27: 7–31.

——. (1997) 'Reconsiderations', in R.W. Cox (ed) *The New Realism: Perspectives on Multilateralism and World Order* (London: Macmillan).

——. (1999) 'Civil Society at the Turn of the Millennium: Prospects for an Alternative World Order', *Review of International Studies*, 25/1: 3–28.

——. (2000) 'The Way Ahead: Towards a New Ontology of World Order', in R.W. Jones (ed.) *Critical Theory and World Politics* (Boulder, CO: Lynne Rienner).

——. (2002) 'Reflections and Transitions' in R.W. Cox with M.G. Schecter (eds) *The Political Economy of a Plural World: Critical Reflections on Power, Morals and Civilisation* (London: Routledge).

Cox, R. W. with T. Sinclair (1996) *Approaches to World Order* (Cambridge: Cambridge University Press).

Craske, N. (1994) *Corporatism Revisited: Salinas and the Reform of the Popular Sector* (London: Institute of Latin American Studies).

Craske, N. and V. Bulmer-Thomas (eds) (1994) *Mexico and the North American Free Trade Agreement: Who Will Benefit?* (London: Macmillan).

Cristi, R. (1998) *Authoritarian Liberalism* (Cardiff: University of Wales Press).

de Ste. Croix, G.E.M. (1981) *The Class Struggle in the Ancient Greek World from the Archaic Age to the Arab Conquests* (London: Duckworth).

Cypher, J. (2001) 'Developing Disarticulation within the Mexican Economy', *Latin American Perspectives*, 28:3, 11–37.

Dalla Costa, M.R. (1995) 'Capitalism and Reproduction', in W. Bonefeld *et al.* (eds) *Open Marxism, Volume 3: Emancipating Marx* (London: Pluto Press).

——. (1998) 'The Native within Us', *Common Sense*, 23: 14–52.

——. (2003) 'Development and Reproduction', in W. Bonefeld (ed) *Revolutionary Writing: Common Sense Essays in Post-Political Politics* (New York: Autonomedia).

Davies, M. (1999) *International Political and Mass Communication in Chile: National Intellectuals and Transnational Hegemony* (London: Macmillan).

Davis, D.E. (1993) 'The Dialectic of Autonomy: State, Class and Economic Crisis in Mexico, 1958–1982', *Latin American Perspectives*, 20/3: 46–75.

——. (1995) 'Of Social Spaces, Citizenship and the Nature of Power in the World Economy', *Alternatives*, 20/1: 51–79.

Dimsdale, N. (1991) 'British Monetary Policy since 1945' in N. Crafts and N. Woodward (eds) *The British Economy Since 1945* (Oxford: Oxford University Press).

van Dormael, A. (1997) *The Power of Money* (London: Macmillan).

Drainville, A. (1994) 'International Political Economy in the Age of Open Marxism', *Review of International Political Economy*, 1/1: 105–32.

Dresser, D. (1991) *Neopopulist Solutions to Neoliberal Problems: Mexico's National Solidarity Program* (San Diego, CA: Centre for U.S.–Mexican Studies).

——. (1994) 'Bringing the Poor Back In: National Solidarity as a Strategy of Regime Legitimation', in W.A. Cornelius, A.L. Craig and J. Fox (eds) *Transforming State–Society Relations in Mexico: The National Solidarity Strategy* (San Diego, CA: Centre for U.S.-Mexican Studies).

——. (1996) 'Mexico: The Decline of Dominant-Party Rule', in J.I. Domínguez and A.F. Lowenthal (eds) *Constructing Democratic Governance: Mexico, Central America and the Caribbean in the 1990s* (Baltimore, MD: The Johns Hopkins University Press).

Economic Policy Institute (2002) 'Economic Snapshots', http://www.epinet.org/index.html, accessed 22 October 2005.

Fairbrother, P. (1994) *Politics and the State as Employer* (London: Mansell).

——. (1998) 'State Restructuring and Implications for Trade Unions: The Case of the United Kingdom', paper presented to the Labour Studies Conference, University of Warwick, March.

Fema, J.V. (1975) 'Hegemony and Consciousness in the Thought of Antonio Gramsci', *Political Studies*, 23/1: 29–48.

Fine, B and L. Harris (1986) *The Peculiarities of the British Economy* (London: Lawrence and Wishart).

Fine, B., C. Lapavitsas and J. Pincus (eds) (2001) *Development Policy in the Twenty-First Century: Beyond the Post-Washington Consensus* (London: Routledge).

Foster-Carter, A. (1978) 'The Modes of Production Controversy', *New Left Review*, I/107: 47–77.

Foweraker, J. (1993) *Popular Mobilisation in Mexico: The Teachers' Movement, 1977–87* (Cambridge: Cambridge University Press).

Fracchia, J. (2005) 'The Untimely Timeliness of Rosa Luxemburg', in W. Bonefeld and K. Psychopedis (eds) *Human Dignity* (Aldershot: Ashgate).

Friedman, B. M (1989) *Day of Reckoning* (New York: Vintage).

Fromm, E. (2001) *Fear of Freedom* (London: Routledge).

Gadamer, H. G. (1976) *Hegels Dialectics* (New Haven, CT: Yale University Press).

Gambino, F. (2003) 'A Critique of the Fordism of the Regulation School', in W. Bonefeld (ed) *Revolutionary Writing: Common Sense Essays in Post-Political Politics* (New York: Autonomedia).

Gamble, A. (2001) 'Neo-Liberalism', *Capital & Class*, 75: 127–34.

Gareau, F.H. (1993) 'A Gramscian Analysis of the Social Sciences', *International Social Science Journal*, 45/136: 301–10.

George, S. (1988) *A Fate Worse than Debt* (London: Penguin).

——. (1992) *The Debt Boomerang* (London: Pluto Press).

Germain, R.D. and M. Kenny (1998) 'Engaging Gramsci: International Relations Theory and the New Gramscians', *Review of International Studies*, 24/1: 3–21.

Giddens, A. (1981) *A Contemporary Critique of Historical Materialism* (London: Macmillan).

——. (1998) *The Third Way* (Cambridge: Polity).

Gill, S. (1986) 'Hegemony, Consensus and Trilateralism', *Review of International Studies*, 12: 205–21.

——. (1990) *American Hegemony and the Trilateral Commission* (Cambridge: Cambridge University Press).

——. (1991) 'Reflections on Global Order and Sociohistorical Time', *Alternatives*, 16/3: 275–314.

——. (1992) 'The Emerging World Order and European Change: The Political Economy of European Union', in R. Miliband and L. Panitch (eds) *The Socialist Register: New World Order?* (London: Merlin Press).

——. (1993) 'Epistemology, Ontology and the "Italian School" ', in S. Gill (ed) *Gramsci, Historical Materialism and International Relations* (Cambridge: Cambridge University Press).

——. (1994) 'Knowledge, Politics and Neo-Liberal Political Economy' in R. Stubbs and G. Underhill (eds) *Political Economy and the Changing Global Order* (London: Macmillan).

——. (1995a) 'Globalisation, Market Civilisation and Disciplinary Neoliberalism', *Millennium: Journal of International Studies*, 24/3: 399–423.

——. (1995b) 'The Global Panopticon? The Neoliberal State, Economic Life and Democratic Surveillance', *Alternatives*, 20/1: 1–49.

——. (1998) 'European Governance and New Constitutionalism: Economic and Monetary Union and Alternatives to Disciplinary Neoliberalism in Europe', *New Political Economy*, 3/1: 5–27.

——. (2000) 'Toward a Postmodern Prince? The Battle in Seattle as a Moment in the New Politics of Globalisation', *Millennium: Journal of International Studies*, 29/1: 131–40.

——. (2001) 'Constitutionalising Capital: EMU and Disciplinary Neoliberalism', in A. Bieler and A.D. Morton (eds) *Social Forces in the Making of the New Europe: The Restructuring of European Social Relations in the Global Political Economy* (London: Palgrave).

——. (2003) *Power and Resistance in the New World Order* (London: Palgrave).

Gill, S. and D. Law (1988) *The Global Political Economy: Perspectives, Problems and Policies* (London: Harvester and Wheatsheaf).

——. (1989) 'Global Hegemony and the Structural Power of Capital', *International Studies Quarterly*, 33/4: 475–99.

Gills, B.K. (1993) 'Hegemonic Transitions in the World System', in A. Gunder Frank and B.K. Gills (eds) *The World System: Five Hundred Years or Five Thousand?* (London: Routledge).

Gilpin, R. (1987) *The Political Economy of International Relations* (Princeton: Princeton University Press).

——. (2000) *The Challenge of Global Capitalism: The World Economy in the 21st Century* (Princeton: Princeton University Press).

Gledhill, J. (1996) 'The State, the Countryside ... and Capitalism', in R. Aitken, *et al.* (eds) *Dismantling the Mexican State?* (London: Macmillan).

Goldthorpe, J. (1978) 'The Current Inflation: Towards a Sociological Account', in F. Hirsch and J. Goldthorpe (eds) *The Political Economy of Inflation* (London: Martin Robertson).

Gordon, R. (1999) 'Has the New Economy Rendered the Productivity Slowdown Obsolete?', mimeo (14 June) http://faculty-web.at.nwu.edu/economics/gordon/334.htm.

Gower, J. (1999) 'EU policy to central and eastern Europe', in K. Henderson (ed) *Back to Europe: Central and Eastern Europe and the European Union* (London: UCL Press).

Grahl J. and P. Teague (1989) 'The Cost of Neo-liberal Europe', *New Left Review*, 174: 33–50.

——. (1990) *1992 – The Big Market* (London: Lawrence & Wishart).

Gramsci, A. (1971) *Selections from the Prison Notebooks*, ed. and trans. Q. Hoare and G. Nowell-Smith (London: Lawrence and Wishart).

——. (1977) *Selections from Political Writings, 1910–1920*, ed. Q. Hoare, trans. J. Matthews (London: Lawrence and Wishart).

——. (1978) *Selections from Political Writings, 1921–1926*, trans. Q. Hoare (London: Lawrence and Wishart).

——. (1985) *Selections from Cultural Writings*, ed. D. Forgacs and G. Nowell-Smith, trans. W. Boelhower. (London: Lawrence and Wishart).

——. (1992) *Prison Notebooks*, vol.1, ed. and intro. J. A. Buttigieg, trans. J. A. Buttigieg and A. Callari (New York: Columbia University Press).

——. (1994a) *Letters from Prison*, vol.1, ed. F. Rosengarten, trans. R. Rosenthal (New York: Columbia University Press).

Gramsci, A. (1994b) *Letters from Prison*, vol.2, ed. F. Rosengarten, trans. R. Rosenthal (New York: Columbia University Press).

——. (1994c) *Pre-Prison Writings*, ed. R. Bellamy, trans. V. Cox (Cambridge: Cambridge University Press).

——. (1995) *Further Selections from the Prison Notebooks*, ed. and trans. D. Boothman (London: Lawrence and Wishart).

——. (1996) *Prison Notebooks*, vol.2, ed. and trans. J. A. Buttigieg (New York: Columbia University Press).

Grant, W. (1993) *The Politics of Economic Policy* (London: Harvester).

Grieco, J. M. (1988) 'Anarchy and the Limits of Cooperation: A Realist Critique of the Newest Liberal Institutionalism', *International Organisation*, 42/3: 485–507.

Guerrieri, P. (1988) 'International Co-operation and the Role of Macroeconomic Regimes', in P. Guerrieri and P. Padoan (eds) *The Political Economy of International Co-operation* (London: Croom Helm).

Gunn, R. (1992) 'Against Historical Materialism: Marxism as First-Order Discourse', in W. Bonefeld, R. Gunn and K. Psychopedis (eds) *Open Marxism, Volume 2: Theory and Practice* (London: Pluto Press).

Halliday, F. (1989) 'Theorising the International', *Economy and Society*, 18/3.

Harman, C. (1993) 'Where is Capitalism Going?', *International Socialism*, 58: 3–57.

Harper, J. (1986) *America and the Reconstruction of Italy* (Cambridge: Cambridge University Press).

Hatton, T and K. Chrystal (1991) 'The Budget and Fiscal Policy', in N. Crafts and N. Woodward (eds) *The British Economy Since 1945* (Oxford: Oxford University Press).

Hay, C. (1994/2001) 'Werner in *Wunderland*, or Notes on a Marxism beyond Pessimism and False Optimism', in B. Jessop (ed) *Regulation Theory and the Crisis of Capitalism*, 5 vols. Vol.2: European and American Perspectives on Regulation (Aldershot: Edward Elgar).

——. (1999) 'Crisis and the Structural Transformation of the State: Interrogating the Process of Change', *British Journal of Politics and International Relations*, 1/3: 317–44.

Hegel, G.W.F. (1896) *Philosophy of Right* (London: George Bell and Sons).

Held, D. (1995) *Democracy and the Global Order* (Cambridge: Polity Press).

Held, D. and A. McGrew (2002) *Globalisation/Anti-Globalisation* (Cambridge: Polity Press).

Helleiner, E. (1994) *States and the Re-emergence of Global Finance* (Ithaca, NY: Cornell University Press).

Heredia, B. (1996) 'State-Business Relations in Contemporary Mexico', in M. Serrano and V. Bulmer-Thomas (eds) *Rebuilding the State: Mexico After Salinas* (London: Institute of Latin American Studies).

Hirsch, J. (1997) 'Globalisation of Capital, Nation-States and Democracy', *Studies in Political Economy*, 54: 39–58.

Hirst, P. and G. Thompson (1996) *Globalisation in Question* (Cambridge: Polity Press).

——. (1999) *Globalisation in Question: The International Economy and the Possibilities of Governance* (Cambridge: Polity Press).

Hobbes, T. (1996) *Leviathan* (Oxford: Oxford University Press).

Hobden, S. (1998) *International Relations and Historical Sociology: Breaking Down Boundaries* (London: Routledge).

Hobden, S. and J.M. Hobson (eds) (2002) *Historical Sociology of International Relations* (Cambridge: Cambridge University Press).

Hobden, S. and R. Wyn Jones (2001) 'Marxist Theories of International Relations', in J. Baylis and S. Smith (eds) *The Globalisation of World Politics: An Introduction to International Relations* (Oxford: Oxford University Press).

Hobsbawm, E. (1975) *The Age of Capital, 1848–1875* (London: Weidenfeld & Nicolson).

Hobson, J.M. (1997) *The Wealth of States: A Comparative Sociology of International Economic and Political Change* (Cambridge: Cambridge University Press).

——. (2000) *The State and International Relations* (Cambridge: Cambridge University Press).

Hodges, D. and R. Gandy (2002) *Mexico Under Siege: Popular Resistance to Presidential Despotism* (London: Zed Books).

Hoffmann, S. (1966) 'Obstinate or Obsolete? The Fate of the Nation State and the Case of Western Europe', *Daedalus*, 95/3: 862–915.

Holloway, J. (1988/1991) 'The Great Bear: Post-Fordism and Class Struggle. A Comment on Bonefeld and Jessop', in W. Bonefeld and J. Holloway (eds) *Post-Fordism and Social Form: A Marxist Debate on the Post-Fordist State* (London: Macmillan).

——. (1991a) 'Capital *is* Class Struggle (And Bears are not Cuddly)', in W. Bonefeld and J. Holloway (eds) *Post-Fordism and Social Form: A Marxist Debate on the Post-Fordist State* (London: Macmillan).

——. (1991b) 'In the Beginning was the Scream', *Common Sense*, 11: 69–77.

——. (1994) 'Global Capital and the National State', *Capital & Class*, 52: 23–49.

——. (1995) 'Global Capital and the National State', in W. Bonefeld and J. Holloway (eds) *Global Capital, National State and the Politics of Money* (London: Macmillan).

——. (1996) 'The Abyss Opens: The Rise and Fall of Keynesianism', in W. Bonefeld, and J. Holloway (eds) *Global Capital, National State and the Politics of Money* (London: Palgrave).

——. (2000) 'Zapata in Wallstreet', in W. Bonefeld and K. Psychopedis (eds) *The Politics of Change: Globalisation, Ideology and Critique* (London: Palgrave).

——. (2003) 'Capital Moves', in W. Bonefeld (ed) *Revolutionary Writing: Common Sense Essays in Post-Political Politics* (New York: Autonomedia).

Holloway, J. and S. Picciotto (1977/1991) 'Capital, Crisis and the State', *Capital & Class*, 2: 76–101 and in S. Clarke (ed) *The State Debate* (London: Macmillan).

——. (1977) 'Capital, Crisis and the State', *Capital & Class*, 2: 76–101.

——. (1978a) 'Towards a Materialist Theory of the State', in J. Holloway and S. Picciotto (eds) *State and Capital: A Marxist Debate* (London: Edward Arnold Publishers).

——. (eds) (1978b) *State and Capital: A Marxist Debate* (London: Edward Arnold Publishers).

Holman, O. (1992) 'Transnational Class Strategy and the New Europe', *International Journal of Political Economy*, 22/1: 3–22.

——. (1993) 'Internationalisation and Democratisation: Southern Europe, Latin America and the World Economic Crisis', in S. Gill (ed) *Gramsci, Historical*

Materialism and International Relations (Cambridge: Cambridge University Press).

——. (1996) *Integrating Southern Europe: EC Expansion and the Transnationalisation of Spain* (London: Routledge).

——. (1998) 'Integrating Eastern Europe: EU Expansion and the Double Transformation in Poland, the Czech Republic, and Hungary', *International Journal of Political Economy*, 28/2: 12–43.

——. (2001) 'The Enlargement of the European Union towards Central and Eastern Europe: the Role of Supranational and Transnational Actors', in A. Bieler and A.D. Morton (eds) *Social Forces in the Making of the New Europe: The Restructuring of European Social Relations in the Global Political Economy* (Houndmills: Palgrave).

Holman, O., H. Overbeek and M. Ryner (1998) 'Neoliberal Hegemony and European Restructuring', *International Journal of Political Economy*, 28/1–2: Special Issues.

Horkheimer, M. (1937/1992) 'Traditional and Critical Theory', in M. Horkheimer, *Critical Theory: Selected Essays* (New York: The Continuum Publishing Corporation).

——. (1985) *Zur Kritik der instrumentellen Vernunft* (Frankfurt: Fischer).

Howson, S. (1975) *Domestic Monetary Management* (Cambridge: Cambridge University Press).

ILO (2002) 'A Future without Child Labour', ILO Declaration on Fundamental Principles and Rights at Work, http://www.ilo.org, accessed 23 October 2005.

Itoh, M. (2000) *The Japanese Economy Reconsidered* (London: Palgrave).

Jay, P. (1994) 'The Economy 1990–1994', in D. Kavanagh and A. Seldon (eds) *The Major Effect* (Macmillan).

Jessop, B. (1985) *Nicos Poulantzas: Marxist Theory and Political Strategy* (London: Macmillan).

——. (1988/1991) 'Regulation Theory, Post-Fordism and the State: More than a Reply to Bonefeld', in W. Bonefeld and J. Holloway (eds) *Post-Fordism and Social Form: A Marxist Debate on the Post-Fordist State* (London: Macmillan).

——. (1990) *State Theory: Putting the Capitalist State in Its Place* (Oxford: Polity Press).

——. (1991) 'Polar Bears and Class Struggle: Much Less Than a Self-Criticism', in W. Bonefeld and J. Holloway (eds) *Post-Fordism and Social Form: A Marxist Debate on the Post-Fordist State* (London: Macmillan).

——. (1994) 'The Transition to Post-Fordism and the Schumpeterian Workfare State', in R. Burrows and B. Loader (eds) *Towards a Post-Fordist Welfare State?* (London: Routledge).

——. (2001) 'On the Spatial-Temporal Logics of Capital's Globalization and their Manifold Implications for State Power', Working Paper, published by the Department of Sociology, Lancaster University; http://www.comp.lanc.ac.uk/sociology/sco072jr.html, accessed 23 October 2005.

——. (2002) *The Future of the Capitalist State* (Cambridge: Polity Press).

Jojima, K. (1985) *Ökonomie und Physik* (Berlin: Duncker & Humblot).

Jones, E. (2002) *The Politics of Economic and Monetary Union* (Lanham, MD: Rowman & Littlefield).

Joseph, K. and J. Sumption (1979) *Equality* (London: John Murray).

Joslin, D. (1963) *A Century of Banking in Latin America* (Oxford: Oxford University Press).

Kalecki, M. (1971) *Selected Essays on the Dynamics of the Capitalist Economy 1933–1970* (Cambridge: Cambridge University Press).

Kant, I. (1974) *Grundlegung der Metaphysik der Sitten* (Stuttgard: Reclam).

Keech, W. (1992) 'Rules, Discretion and Accountability in Macroeconomic Policymaking', *Governance*, 5/3: 259–78.

Kempadoo, K. and J. Doezema (1998) *Global Sex Workers: Rights, Resistance and Redefinition* (London: Routledge).

Keohane, R.O. (1984) *After Hegemony: Cooperation and Discord in the World Political Economy* (Princeton: Princeton University Press).

——. (1989) *International Institutions and State Power* (Boulder, CO: Westview Press).

Keynes, J.M. (1979) *Collected Writings, Vol. 24* (Cambridge: Cambridge University Press).

Kydland, F. and E. Prescott (1977) 'Rules Rather than Discretion', *Journal of Political Economy*, 85/3: 473–91.

Kyle, D. and R. Koslowski (eds) (2001) *Global Human Smuggling* (Baltimore, MD: The John Hopkins University Press).

Lacher, H. (2002) 'Making Sense of the International System: The Promises and Pitfalls of Contemporary Marxist Theories of IR', in M. Rupert and H. Smith (eds) *Historical Materialism and Globalisation* (London: Routledge).

——. (2003) 'Putting the State in Its Place: The Critique of State-centrism and Its Limits', *Review of International Studies*, 29/4: 521–41.

——. (2005) 'International Transformation and the Persistence of Territoriality: Toward a New Political Geography of Capitalism', *Review of International Political Economy*, 12/1: 26–52.

Lebowitz, M. (1999) 'In Brenner, Everything is Reversed', *Historical Materialism*, 4: 109–29.

Lee, F.S. (2001) 'Conference of Socialist Economists and the Emergence of Heterodox Economics in Post-War Britain', *Capital & Class*, 75: 15–39.

Lee, K. (1995) 'A neo-Gramscian Approach to International Organisation: An Expanded Analysis of Current Reforms to UN Development Activities', in J. Macmillan and A. Linklater (eds) *Boundaries in Question: New Directions in International Relations* (London: Pinter).

Lenin, V.I. (1917) *The State and Revolution* (Moscow: Progress).

Lindstrom, N. and D. Piroska (2003) 'The Slovenian Way? The Politics of Europeanisation in Europe's Southeastern Periphery', paper presented at the conference 'Global Tensions and their Challenges to Governance of the International Community', sponsored by the International Studies Association and the Central and East European International Studies Association; Budapest (26–28 June).

Ling, L.H.M. (1996) 'Hegemony and the Internationalising State: A Post-colonial Analysis of China's Integration into Asian Corporatism', *Review of International Political Economy*, 3/1: 1–26.

Linklater, A. (1990a) *Men and Citizens in the Theory of International Relations* (London: Macmillan).

——. (1990b) *Beyond Realism and Marxism: Critical Theory and International Relations* (London: Macmillan).

Linklater, A. (1998) *The Transformation of Political Community: Ethical Foundations of the Post-Westphalian Era* (Cambridge: Polity Press).
——. (1999) 'Transforming Political Community: A Response to the Critics', *Review of International Studies*, 25/1: 165–75.
——. (2000) *International Relations: Critical Concepts in Political Science*, 5 vols. (London: Routledge).
List, F. (1904) *The National System of Political Economy* (New York: Longmans).
London Edinburgh Weekend Return Group (1979) *In and Against the State* (London: Pluto Press).
Luna, M. (1995) 'Entrepreneurial Interests and Political Action in Mexico: Facing the Demands of Economic Modernisation', in R. Roett (ed) *The Challenge of Institutional Reform in Mexico* (Boulder, CO: Lynne Rienner).
Madrick, J. (1995) *The End of Affluence* (London: Random House).
Madgoff, H., Foster, J.B., Mcchesney, R.W. and P. Sweezy (2002) 'The New Face of Capitalism: Slow Growth, Excess Capital, and the Mountain of Debt, *Monthly Review*, 53/11: 1–14.
Malloy, J.M. (ed) (1977) *Authoritarianism and Corporatism in Latin America* (Pittsburgh: University of Pittsburgh Press).
Mandel, E. (1975) *Late Capitalism* (London: New Left Books).
——. (1987) *Die Krise* (Hamburg: Konkret).
——. (1988) 'Der Börsenkrach. Dreizehn Fragen', in E. Mandel and W. Wolf (eds) *Börsenkrach und Wirtschaftskrise* (Frankfurt: IS Publikationen).
Mandel, E. and J. Agnoli (1980) *Offener Marxismus* (Frankfurt: Campus Verlag).
Marceau, G. (1997) 'NAFTA and WTO Dispute Settlement Rules', *Journal of World Trade*, 31/2: 25–81.
Marcuse, H. (1988) *Negations* (London: Free Association Press).
Marx, K. (1843a/1975) 'Contribution to the Critique of Hegel's Philosophy of Law', in K. Marx and F. Engels, *Collected Works, Volume 3* (London: Lawrence and Wishart).
——. (1843b/1975) 'Critique of Hegel's Doctrine of the State', in K. Marx, *Early Writings*, 2em dash. intro. L. Colletti, trans. R. Livingstone and G. Benton (Harmondsworth, Middlesex: Penguin Books).
——. (1843c/1975) 'On the Jewish Question', in K. Marx, *Early Writings*, intro. L. Colletti, trans. R. Livingstone and G. Benton (Harmondsworth, Middlesex: Penguin Books).
——. (1844a/1975) 'Critical Marginal Notes on the article by a Prussian', in K. Marx and F. Engels, *Collected Works, Volume 3* (London: Lawrence and Wishart).
——. (1844b/1975) 'Economic and Philosophical Manuscripts' in K. Marx and F. Engels, *Collected Works, Volume 3* (London: Lawrence and Wishart).
——. (1845–46/1975) 'The German Ideology', in K. Marx and F. Engels, *Collected Works, Volume 5* (London: Lawrence and Wishart).
——. (1857/1986) 'Bastiat and Carey', in K. Marx and F. Engels, *Collected Works, Volume 28* (London: Lawrence and Wishart).
——. (c.1861–63/1994) 'Results of the Direct Production Process', in K. Marx and F. Engels, *Collected Works, Volume 34* (London: Lawrence and Wishart).
——. (1867/1976) *Capital, Volume 1* (London: Pelican).
——. (1871/1986) 'The Civil War in France' in K. Marx and F. Engels, *Collected Works, Volume 22* (London: Lawrence and Wishart).

——. (1884a/1978) *Capital, Volume 2* (London: Pelican).

——. (1884b/1975) 'On the Jewish Question' in K. Marx and F. Engels, *Collected Works, Volume 3* (London: Lawrence and Wishart).

——. (1894a/1998) 'Capital, Volume 3', in K. Marx and F. Engels, *Collected Works, Volume 37* (London: Lawrence and Wishart).

——. (1894b/1981) Capital, *Volume 3* (London: Pelican).

——. (1963) *Theories of Surplus Value, Volume 1* (London: Lawrence & Wishart).

——. (1964) *The German Ideology* (Moscow: Progress Press).

——. (1966) *Capital, Volume 3* (London: Lawrence and Wishart).

——. (1968) 'Die revolutionäre Bewegung', in K. Marx and F. Engels, *Collected Works, Volume 6* (Berlin: Dietz).

——. (1969) *Theories of Surplus Value, Part 2* (London: Lawrence & Wishart).

——. (1972) *Theories of Surplus Value, Part 3* (London: Lawrence & Wishart).

——. (1973) *Grundrisse* (London: Penguin).

——. (1976a) *Capital, Volume 1* (Harmondsworth: Penguin).

——. (1976b) 'The Poverty of Philosophy', in K. Marx and F. Engels, *Collected Works, Volume 6* (London: Lawrence & Wishart).

——. (1977) 'Brief an P.W. Annenkow vom 28.12. 1846', in K. Marx and F. Engels, *Collected Works, Volume 4* (Berlin: Dietz).

——. (1978) *Capital, Volume 2* (Middlesex: Penguin).

——. (1981a) *Capital, Volume 3* (Middlesex: Penguin).

——. (1981b) *Zur Kritik der Politischen Ökonomie*, MEW 13 (Berlin: Dietz).

——. (1983) *Capital, Volume 1* (London: Lawrence & Wishart).

——. (1986) 'The Grundrisse', in K. Marx and F. Engels, *Collected Works, Volume 28* (London: Lawrence and Wishart).

——. (1987a) From the Preparatory Materials, Economic Works, 1857–61, in K. Marx and F. Engels, *Collected Works, Volume 29* (London: Lawrence & Wishart).

——. (1987b) *A Contribution to the Critique of Political Economy*, in K. Marx and F. Engels, *Collected Works, Volume 29* (London: Lawrence and Wishart).

Marx, K. and F. Engels (1848/1976) 'The Communist Manifesto', in K. Marx and F. Engels, *Collected Works, Volume 6* (London: Lawrence and Wishart).

——. (1970) *The German Ideology*, ed. C. Arthur (London: Lawrence & Wishart).

——. (1977) *Collected Works, Volume 9* (London: Lawrence and Wishart).

——. (1986) *Collected Works, Volume 28* (London: Lawrence and Wishart).

——. (1987) *Collected Works, Volume 29* (London: Lawrence and Wishart).

——. (1997) *The Communist Manifesto* (London: Pluto).

Marzani, C. (1957) *The Open Marxism of Antonio Gramsci* (New York: Cameron Associates).

Mattick, P. (1934), 'Zur Marxschen Akkumulations- und Zusammenbruchstheorie', *Rätekorrespondenz*, 4, reprinted in Korsch, K., P. Mattick and A. Pannekoek, *Zusammenbruchstheorie des Kapitalismus oder revolutionäres Subjekt* (Berlin: Kramer Verlag, 1973).

McIlroy, J. (1997) 'Still under Siege: British Trade Unions at the Turn of the Century', *Historical Studies in Industrial Relations*, 3: 93–122.

Meiksins Wood, E. (1981) 'The Separation of the Economic and the Political in Capitalism', *New Left Review*, 127: 66–95.

Middlebrook, K.J. (1993) 'Political Liberalisation in an Authoritarian Regime: The Case of Mexico', in G. O'Donnell, P. Schmitter and L. Whitehead (eds)

Transitions From Authoritarian Rule: Latin America (Baltimore, MD: The Johns Hopkins University Press).

——. (1995) *The Paradox of Revolution: Labour, the State and Authoritarianism in Mexico* (Baltimore, MD: The Johns Hopkins University Press).

Miliband, R. (1969) *The State in Capitalist Society* (London: Weidenfeld and Nicholson).

——. (1970) 'The Capitalist State: Reply to Poulantzas', *New Left Review*, I/59: 53–60.

——. (1973) 'Poulantzas and the Capitalist State', *New Left Review*, I/82: 83–92.

Milward, A. (1984) *The Reconstruction of Western Europe* (London: Methuen).

von Mises, L. (1949) *Human Action* (New Haven, CT: Yale University Press).

Monthly Review (2003) The Editors, 'What Recovery?', *Monthly Review*, 54/11: 1–13.

Moran, J. (1998) 'The Dynamics of Class Politics and National Economies in Globalisation: The Marginalisation of the Unacceptable', *Capital & Class*, 66: 53–83.

Moravcsik, A. (1998) *The Choice for Europe: Social Purpose and State Power from Messina to Maastricht* (London: UCL Press).

Morton, A.D. (2001) 'The Sociology of Theorising and Neo-Gramscian Perspectives: The Problems of "School" Formation in IPE', in A. Bieler and A.D. Morton (eds) *Social Forces in the Making of the New Europe: The Restructuring of European Social Relations in the Global Political Economy* (London: Palgrave).

——. (2002) ' "La Resurrección del Maíz": Globalisation, Resistance and the Zapatistas', *Millennium: Journal of International Studies*, 31/1: 27–54.

——. (2003a) 'Historicising Gramsci: Situating Ideas in and beyond Their Context', *Review of International Political Economy*, 10/1: 118–46.

——. (2003b) 'The Social Function of Carlos Fuentes: A Critical Intellectual or in the "Shadow of the State"?', *Bulletin of Latin American Research*, 22/1: 27–51.

——. (2005a) 'Change within Continuity: The Political Economy of Democratic Transition in Mexico', *New Political Economy*, 10/2: 181–202.

——. (2005b) 'The Age of Absolutism: Capitalism, the Modern States-System and International Relations', *Review of International Studies*, 31/3: 495–517.

——. (2006a) 'The Grimly Comic Riddle of Hegemony in IPE: Where is Class Struggle?', *Politics*, 25/4: 62–72.

——. (2006b) 'Globalisation, NAFTA and the Peasantry in Latin America: The Power of the Powerless', in J.M. Hobson and L. Seabrooke (eds) *Everyday International Political Economy: Non-elite Agency in the Transformations of the World Economy* (Cambridge: Cambridge University Press).

Moss, B.H. (2000) 'The European Community as Monetarist Construction: A Critique of Moravcsik', *Journal of European Area Studies*, 8/2: 247–65.

——. (2001) 'The EC's Free Market Agenda and the Myth of Social Europe', in W. Bonefeld (ed) *The Politics of Europe: Monetary Union and Class* (Basingstoke: Palgrave).

Murphy, C.N. (1994) *International Organisation and Industrial Change* (Cambridge: Polity Press).

Murphy, C. and R. Tooze (1991) (eds) *The New International Political Economy* (Boulder, CO: Lynne Rienner).

Naím, M. (2000) 'Fads and Fashions in Economic Reforms: Washington Consensus or Washington Confusion?', *Third World Quarterly*, 21/3: 505–28.

Negri, A. (1984) *Marx Beyond Marx* (Massachusetts: Bergen & Garvey Publishers).

——. (1992) 'Interpretation of the Class Situation Today', in W. Bonefeld *et al.* (eds) *Open Marxism Vol. II* (London: Pluto Press).

Negt, O. (2001) *Arbeit und menschliche Würde* (Göttingen: Steidl).

Nullis-Kapp, C. (2004) 'Organ Trafficking and Transplantation Pose New Challenges', in *Focus*, World Health Organization, 1 September 2004.

O'Brien, R. (1997) 'Subterranean Hegemonic Struggles: International Labour and the Three Faces of Industrial Relations', paper presented at the Annual BISA Conference, 15–17 December (Leeds).

——. (2000) 'Workers and World Order: The Tentative Transformation of the International Union Movement', *Review of International Studies*, 26/4: 533–55.

O'Donnell, G. (1973) *Modernisation and Bureaucratic-Authoritarianism: Studies in South American Politics* (University of California, Berkeley: Institute of International Studies).

——. (1978) 'Reflections on the Patterns of Change in the Bureaucratic-Authoritarian State', *Latin American Research Review*, 13/1: 3–38.

Ohmae, K. (1990) *The Borderless World* (New York: Fontana).

——. (1996) *The End of the Nation State: The Rise of Regional Economies* (New York: Free Press).

Overbeek, H. (1990) *Global Capitalism and National Decline: The Thatcher Decade in Historical Perspective* (London: Routledge).

——. (1994) 'The Forum: Hegemony and Social Change', *Mershon International Studies Review*, 38/2: 368–9.

——. (ed.) (1993) *Restructuring Hegemony in the Global Political Economy: The Rise of Transnational Neoliberalism in the 1980s* (London: Routledge).

Panitch, L. (1994) 'Globalisation and the State', in L. Panitch and R. Miliband (eds) *The Socialist Register 1994: Between Globalism and Nationalism* (London: Merlin Press).

——. (2000) 'The New Imperial State', *New Left Review*, I/2: 5–20.

Pansters, W. (1999) 'The Transition Under Fire: Rethinking Contemporary Mexican Politics', in K. Koonings and D. Krujit (eds) *Societies of Fear: The Legacy of Civil War and Terror in Latin America* (London: Zed Books).

Pashukanis, E. (1978) *Law and Marxism* (London: Pluto Press).

Peters, E.D. (2000) *Polarizing Mexico: The Impact of Liberalisation Strategy* (Boulder, CO: Lynne Rienner).

Petersmann, E. (1997) (ed) *International Trade Law and the GATT/WTO Dispute Settlement System* (London: Kluwer Law International).

Petras, J. (2003) *The New Development Politics* (Aldershot: Ashgate).

Petras, J. and H. Veltmeyer (2004) 'Aid and Adjustment', in H. Veltmeyer (ed) *Globalization and Antiglobalization* (Aldershot: Ashgate).

Phinnes, A. (2005) 'Trafficking of Women and Children for Sexual Exploitation in the Americas', World Health Organisation, http://www.who.com, accessed 23 October 2005.

Picciotto, S. (1988) 'The Control of Transnational Capital and the Democratisation of the International State', *Journal of Law and Society*, 15/1: 58–76.

——. (1990) 'The Internationalisation of the State', Conference on 'After the Crisis', University of Amsterdam, Amsterdam Netherlands (April).

Picciotto, S. (1991a) 'The Internationalisation of Capital and the International State System', in S. Clarke (ed) *The State Debate* (London: Macmillan).

——. (1991b) 'The Internationalisation of the State', *Capital & Class*, 43: 43–63.

Piester, K. (1997) 'Targeting the Poor: The Politics of Social Policy Reforms in Mexico', in D.A. Chalmers *et al.* (eds) *The New Politics of Inequality in Latin America: Rethinking Participation and Representation* (Oxford: Oxford University Press).

van der Pijl, K. (1984) *The Making of an Atlantic Ruling Class* (London: Verso).

——. (1989) 'Ruling Classes, Hegemony and the State System: Theoretical and Historical Considerations', *International Journal of Political Economy*, 19/3: 7–35.

——. (1993) 'Soviet Socialism and Passive Revolution', in S. Gill (ed) *Gramsci, Historical Materialism and International Relations* (Cambridge: Cambridge University Press).

——. (1998) *Transnational Classes and International Relations* (London: Routledge).

Pollert, A. (1999) *Transformation at Work in the New Market Economies of Central Eastern Europe* (London: SAGE).

Pollitt, C. (1990) *Managerialism and the Public Services* (Dartmouth: Blackwell).

Portelli, H. (1973) *Gramsci y el bloque histórico* (Mexico: Siglo XXI).

Poulantzas, N. (1968) 'Theorie und Geschichte', in W. Euchner and A. Schmidt (eds) *Kritik der Politischen Ökonomie* (Frankfurt: Europäische Verlagsanstalt).

——. (1969) 'The Problem of the Capitalist State', *New Left Review*, I/58: 67–78.

——. (1973) *Political Power and Social Classes*, trans. T. O'Hagan (London: New Left Books).

——. (1975) *Classes in Contemporary Capitalism*, trans. D. Fernbach (London: New Left Books).

——. (1976) 'The Capitalist State: A Reply to Miliband and Laclau', *New Left Review*, I/95: 63–83.

——. (1978) *State, Power, Socialism*, trans. P. Camiller (London: Verso).

Powell, K. (1996) 'Neoliberalism and Nationalism', in R. Aitken, *et al.* (eds) *Dismantling the Mexican State?* (London: Macmillan).

Procter, S. (1993) 'Floating Convertibility', *Contemporary Record*, 7/1: 24–43.

Proudhon, P.J. (1971) *Was ist Eigentum* (Vienna: Monte Verita).

Psychopedis, K. (1991) 'Crisis of Theory in the Contemporary Social Sciences', in W. Bonefeld and J. Holloway (eds) *Post-Fordism and Social Form: A Marxist Debate on the Post- Fordist State* (London: Macmillan).

——. (2000) 'New Social Thought: Questions of Theory and Critique', in W. Bonefeld and K. Psychopedis (eds) *The Politics of Change: Globalisation, Ideology and Critique* (London: Palgrave).

Radice, H. (1984) 'The National Economy: A Keynesian Myth?', *Capital & Class*, 22: 111–40.

——. (2000) 'Responses to Globalization: A Critique of Progressive Nationalism', *New Political Economy*, 5/1: 5–19.

Reich, R. (1991) *The Work of Nations* (New York: Vintage Press).

Reichelt, H. (2002) 'Die Marxsche Kritik Ökonomischer Kategorien', in I. Fetscher and A. Schmidt (eds) *Emanzipation als Versöhnung* (Frankfurt: Neue Kritik).

——. (2005) 'Social Reality as Appearance', in W. Bonefeld and K. Psychopedis (eds) *Human Dignity* (Aldershot: Ashgate).

Reyna, J.L. and R.S. Weinhart (eds) (1977) *Authoritarianism in Mexico* (Philadelphia: Institute for the Study of Human Issues).

Ricardo, D. (1995) *Principles of the Political Economy of Taxation* (Cambridge: Cambridge University Press).

Roberts, J.M. (2002) 'From Reflection to Refraction: Opening up Open Marxism', *Capital & Class*, 78: 87–116.

Robertson, W. (1890) *Works, Volume 2* (Edinburgh: Thomas Nelson).

Robinson, J. (1962) *Economic Philosophy* (London: C. A. Watts).

Robinson, W.I. (1996) *Promoting Polyarchy: Globalisation, US Intervention and Hegemony* (Cambridge: Cambridge University Press).

——. (2004) *A Theory of Global Capitalism: Production, Class, and State in a Transnational World* (Baltimore, MD: The John Hopkins Press).

Rosamond, B. (2002) 'Imagining the European Economy: "Competitiveness" and the Social Construction of "Europe" as an Economic Space', *New Political Economy*, 7/2: 157– 77.

Rosdolsky, R. (1977) *The Making of Marx's Capital, Volume 1* (London: Pluto Press).

Rosenberg, J. (1994) *The Empire of Civil Society* (London: Verso).

Ruggie, J.G. (1982) 'International Regimes, Transactions and Change: Embedded Liberalism in the Postwar Economic Order', *International Organisation*, 36/2: 379–415.

Ruigrok, W. and R. van Tulder (1995) *The Logic of International Restructuring* (London: Routledge).

Rukstad, M. (1989) *Macroeconomic Decision Making in the World Economy* (London: Dryen Press).

Rupert, M. (1995a) *Producing Hegemony: The Politics of Mass Production and American Global Power* (Cambridge: Cambridge University Press).

——. (1995b) '(Re)Politicising the Global Economy: Liberal Common Sense and Ideological Struggle in the US NAFTA Debate', *Review of International Political Economy*, 2/4: 658–92.

——. (2000) *Ideologies of Globalisation: Contending Visions of a New World Order* (London: Routledge).

Ryner, M.J. (2002) *Capitalist Restructuring, Globalisation and the Third Way: Lessons from the Swedish Model* (London: Routledge).

Ryner, M.J. and T. Schulten (2003) 'The Political Economy of Labour-market Restructuring and Trade Union Responses in the Social-democratic heartland', in H. Overbeek (ed.) *The Political Economy of European Employment: European Integration and the Transnationalisation of the (un)Employment Question* (London: Routledge).

Sachs, W. (1999) 'Introduction', in W. Sachs (ed.) *The Development Dictionary*, 7th edn (London: Zed Books).

Salinas de Gortari, C. (2002) *México: The Policy and Politics of Modernisation*, trans. P. Hearn and P. Rosas (Barcelona: Plaza & Janés Editores).

Sandholtz, W. (1993) 'Choosing Union', *International Organisation*, 47/1: 1–40.

Sassoon, A.S. (1987) *Gramsci's Politics*, 2nd edn (Minneapolis: University of Minnesota Press).

——. (2000) *Gramsci and Contemporary Politics: Beyond Pessimism of the Intellect* (London: Routledge).

——. (2001) 'Globalisation, Hegemony and Passive Revolution', *New Political Economy*, 6/1: 5–17.

Schmidt, A. (1974) Praxis, in *Gesellschaft: Beiträge Zur marxistischen Theorie* (Frankfurt: Suhrkamp).

Scholte, J.A. (2000) *Globalisation: A Critical Introduction* (London: Palgrave).

Schumpeter, J. (1965) *Geschichte der ökonomischen Analyse* (Göttingen: Vanderhoeck & Rubrecht).

——. (1992) *Capitalism, Socialism & Democracy* (London: Routledge).

Scott, J.C. (1998) *Seeing Like a State: How Certain Schemes to Improve the Human Condition Have Failed* (New Haven, CT: Yale University Press).

Scott-Smith, G. (2002) *The Politics of Apolitical Culture: The Congress for Cultural Freedom and the CIA and Post-War American Hegemony* (London: Routledge).

Seabrook, J. (2001) *Children of Other Worlds* (London: Pluto Press).

Sennett, R. (2000) *The Corrosion of Character* (New York: Norton).

Shaw, M. (2000) *Theory of the Global State: Globality as an Unfinished Revolution* (Cambridge: Cambridge University Press).

Shields, S. (2003) 'The Charge of the "Right Brigade": Transnational Social Forces and the Neoliberal Configuration of Poland's Transition', *New Political Economy*, 8/2: 225–44.

Sinclair, T. (1996) 'Beyond International Relations Theory: Robert W. Cox and Approaches to World Order', in R. Cox with T. Sinclair, *Approaches to World Order* (Cambridge: Cambridge University Press).

Sklair, L. (1993) *Assembling for Development: The Maquila Industry in Mexico and the United States*, Expanded edition (San Diego, CA: Centre for U.S.–Mexican Studies).

Smith, A. (1981) *The Wealth of Nations, Volume 2* (Indianapolis, IN: Liberty Fund).

Smith, D. (1992) *From Boom to Bust* (London: Penguin).

Smith, H. (1994) 'Marxism and International Relations Theory', in A.J.R. Groom and M. Light (eds) *Contemporary International Relations: A Guide to Theory* (London: Pinter Publishers).

——. (1998) 'Actually Existing Foreign Policy – or not? The EU in Latin and Centra America', in J. Peterson and H. Sjursen (eds) *A Common Foreign Policy for Europe?* (London: Routledge).

——. (2002) 'The Politics of "Regulated Liberalism": A Historical Materialist Approach to European Integration', in M. Rupert and H. Smith (eds) *Historical Materialism and Globalisation* (London: Routledge).

Smith, S. (1995) 'The Self-Images of a Discipline: A Genealogy of International Relations Theory', in K. Booth and S. Smith (eds) *International Relations Theory Today* (Cambridge: Polity Press).

——. (2000) 'The Discipline of International Relations: Still An American Social Science?', *British Journal of Politics and International Relations*, 2/3: 374–402.

Smith, S., K. Booth and M. Zalweski (eds) (1996) *International Theory: Positivism and Beyond* (Cambridge: Cambridge University Press).

Snidal, D. (1985) 'The Limits of Hegemonic Stability Theory', *International Organisation*, 39/4: 579–614.

Soederberg, S. (2001) 'From Neoliberalism to Social Liberalism: Situating the National Solidarity Program within Mexico's Passive Revolutions', *Latin American Perspectives*, 28/3: 102–23.

Solomon, T. (1979) 'The Marxist Theory of the State and the Problem of Fractions: Some Theoretical, and Methodological Remarks', *Capital & Class*, 7: 141–7.

Solomon, R. (1999) *Money on the Move* (Princeton: Princeton University Press).

Soros, G. (2003) 'Burst the Bubble of U.S. Supremacy', *The Miami Herald, International Edition*, 13 March 2003.

Stienstra, D. (1994) *Women's Movements and International Organisations* (London: Macmillan).

Strange, G. (1997) 'The British Labour Movement and Economic and Monetary Union in Europe', *Capital & Class*, 63: 13–24.

——. (2002) 'Globalisation, Regionalism and Labour Interests in the New IPE', *New Political Economy*, 7/3: 343–65.

Strange, S. (1987) 'The Persistent Myth of Lost Hegemony', *International Organisation*, 41/4: 55–74.

——. (1996) *The Retreat of the State: The Diffusion of Power in the World Economy* (Cambridge: Cambridge University Press).

——. (1997a) *Casino Capitalism* (Manchester: Manchester University Press).

——. (1997b) 'The Problem or the Solution? Capitalism and the State System', in S. Gill and J. Mittelman (eds) *Innovation and Transformation in International Studies* (Cambridge: Cambridge University Press).

——. (1998) *Mad Money* (Manchester: Manchester University Press).

——. (2004) 'The Declining Authority of the State', in F. Lechner and F. Bolil (eds) *The Globalisation Reader* (Oxford: Blackwell).

Teichman, J.A. (1996) 'Mexico: Economic Reform and Political Change', *Latin American Research Review*, 31/2: 252–62.

Teschke, B. (2003) *The Myth of 1648: Class, Geopolitics and the Making of Modern International Relations* (London: Verso).

——. (2005) 'Bourgeois Revolution, State Formation and the Absence of the International', *Historical Materialism*, 13/2: 3–26.

Thompson, E.P. (1968) *The Making of the English Working Class* (Harmondsworth: Penguin).

——. (1978) 'Eighteenth-Century English Society: Class Struggle Without Class?', *Social History*, 3/2: 133–65.

Thompson, H. (1994) *Joining the ERM: Core-Executive Decision Making in the UK, 1979–1990* (London: LSE, PhD Thesis).

——. (1995) 'Globalisation, Monetary Autonomy and Central Bank Independence', in J. Lovenduski and P. Stanyer (eds) *Contemporary Political Studies 3*, (Political Science Association).

Tischler, S. (2005) 'Time of Reification and Time of Insubordination', in W. Bonefeld and K. Pschopedis (eds) *Human Dignity* (Aldershot: Ashgate).

Tomlinson, G. (1981) 'Why there was never a Keynesian Revolution', *Economy and Society*, 10/1: 73–87.

Tranholm-Mikkelsen, J. (1991) 'Neo-functionalism: Obstinate or obsolete? A Reappraisal in the Light of the New Dynamism of the EC', *Millennium: Journal of International Studies*, 20/1: 1–22.

——. (1996) *The British Conservative Government and the European Exchange Rate Mechanism 1979–1994* (London: Pinter).

Ugalde, F.V. (1994) 'From Bank Nationalisation to State Reform: Business and the New Mexican Order', in M.L. Cook, K.J. Middlebrook and J.M. Horcasitas (eds) *The Politics of Economic Restructuring: State-Society Relations and Regime Change in Mexico* (San Diego, CA: Centre for U.S.–Mexican Studies).

Ugalde, F.V. (1996) 'The Private Sector and Political Regime Change in Mexico', in G. Otero (ed) *Neoliberalism Revisited: Economic Restructuring and Mexico's Political Future* (Boulder, CO: Westview Press).

UK Treasury (1965) *Treasury Historical Memoranda PRO T267/12, No. 8, July 1965: 'Policy to Control the Level of Demand 1953–58'* (London: Public Records Office).

——. (1976) *Treasury Historical Memoranda PRO T267/28 A Special Study of Government Incomes Policy* (London: Public Records Office).

——. (1998) *A Code for Fiscal Stability* (HMSO).

UN (2001) *World Investment Report 2001: Promoting Linkages* (New York/Geneva: United Nations).

UNCTAD (2002) *United Nations Conference on Trade and Development, Escaping Poverty* (New York: United Nations Publication).

Underhill, G.R.D. (1994) 'Conceptualising the Changing Global Order', in R. Stubbs and G. Underhill (eds) *Political Economy and the Changing Global Order* (London: Macmillan).

——. (1997) 'The Making of the European Financial Area: Global Market Integration and the EU Single Market for Financial Services', in G.R.D. Underhill (ed) *The New World Order in International Finance* (Basingstoke: Palgrave).

UNDP (2000) *United Nations Development Programme, Human Development Report* (Oxford: Oxford University Press).

Urquidi, V.L. (1994) 'The Outlook for Mexican Economic Development in the 1990s', in M.L. Cook, K.J. Middlebrook and J.M. Horcasitas (eds) *The Politics of Economic Restructuring: State–Society Relations and Regime Change in Mexico* (San Diego, CA: Centre for U.S.–Mexican Studies).

Veltmeyer, H. (ed) (2004) *Globalization and Antiglobalization* (Aldershot: Ashgate).

Vulliamy, E. (2002) 'US in Denial as Poverty Rises', *The Observer*, 3 November 2002.

Wacquant, L. (2000) *Elend hinter Gittern* (Konstanz: Universitätsverlag Konstanz).

Wallerstein, I. (1984) *The Politics of the World-Economy* (Cambridge: Cambridge University Press).

Walter, A. (1993) *World Power and World Money* (London: Harvester Wheatsheaf).

Waltz, K.N. (1979) *Theory of International Politics* (Reading, MA: Addison-Wesley).

Weber, M. (1948) 'The Social Psychology of the World Religions', in H. Gerth and C.Mills (eds) *From Marx to Weber* (London: Routledge & Kegan Paul).

——. (1989) 'Science as Vocation', in P. Lassman *et al.* (eds) *Max Weber's 'Science as Vocation'* (London: Routledge).

Weeks, J. (1981) *Capital and Exploitation* (London: Edward Arnold).

Weiss, L. (1998) *The Myth of the Powerless State: Governing the Economy in a Global Era* (Cambridge: Polity Press).

Wendt, A. (1999) *Social Theory of International Politics* (Cambridge: Cambridge University Press).

Whitehead, L. (1980) 'Mexico From Bust to Boom: A Political Evaluation of the 1976–1979 Stabilisation Program', *World Development*, 8/11: 843–64.

——. (1989) 'Political Change and Economic Stabilisation: The "Economic Solidarity Pact" ', in W.A. Cornelius, J. Gentleman and P.H. Smith (eds) *Mexico's Alternative Political Futures* (San Diego, CA: Centre for U.S.–Mexican Studies).

Whitworth, S. (1994) *Feminism and International Relations: Towards a Political Economy of Gender in Interstate and Non-Governmental Institutions* (London: Macmillan).

WHO (2005) 'World Health Organization, 'Debt', Globalization, Trade and Health: Glossary', http://www.who.com, accessed 22 October 2005.

Wilding, A. (1995) 'The Complicity of Posthistory', in W. Bonefeld, R. Gunn, J. Holloway and K. Psychopedis (eds) *Open Marxism, Volume 3: Emancipating Marx* (London: Pluto Press).

Williams, D. (1968) 'The Evolution of the Sterling Area System', in C. Whittlesey (ed.) *Essays in Money and Banking* (Oxford: Clarendon).

Witheford, N. (1994) 'Autonomist Marxism and the Information Society', *Capital & Class*, 52: 85–125.

Wolf, M. (1997) 'Far from Powerless', *Financial Times*, 13 May 1997, p. 20.

Wolf, M. (2001) 'The Need for a New Imperialism', *Financial Times*, 10 October 2001.

——. (2004) 'We Need More Globalisation', *Financial Times*, 10 May 2004.

Wolff, R. D. (2002) 'The US Economic Crisis', *Rethinking Marxism*, 4/1: 118–131.

Wood, E.M. (1995) *Democracy against Capitalism: Renewing Historical Materialism* (Cambridge: Cambridge University Press).

——. (2002) *The Origin of Capitalism* (London: Verso).

World Bank (2000) *World Development Report 2000/01: Attacking Poverty* (Oxford: Oxford University Press).

Wrong, D. (1961) 'the Over Socialised Concept of Man in Modern Sociology', *American Sociological Review*, 26/2: 183–93.

WTO, Annual Reports (Geneva).

Wyn Jones, R. (1999) *Security, Strategy and Critical Theory* (Boulder, CO: Lynne Rienner).

——. (ed.) (2000) *Critical Theory and World Politics* (Boulder, CO: Lynne Rienner).

Index